THE
DRUIDIC
ART
OF
DIVINATION

THE
DRUIDIC
ART
OF
DIVINATION

Understanding the Past and Seeing into the Future

JON G. HUGHES

Destiny Books
Rochester, Vermont

Destiny Books
One Park Street
Rochester, Vermont 05767
www.DestinyBooks.com

Destiny Books is a division of Inner Traditions International

Cataloging-in-Publication Data for this title is available from the Library of Congress

ISBN 978-1-64411-024-9 (print)
ISBN 978-1-64411-025-6 (ebook)

Printed and bound in the United States by P. A. Hutchison Company

10 9 8 7 6 5 4 3 2 1

Text design by Virginia Scott Bowman and layout by Debbie Glogover
This book was typeset in Garamond Premier Pro with Farm House Rough,
Hermann, Stone Sans, Gill Sans, and Bell used as display typefaces

To send correspondence to the author of this book, mail a first-class letter to the
author c/o Inner Traditions • Bear & Company, One Park Street, Rochester, VT
05767, and we will forward the communication, or contact the author directly at
jonhughes@eircom.net.

To my loving and hugely supportive wife, Yve,
without whom I could not have written this book.

I would also like to thank my colleagues in Wales,
who have expressed their preference for remaining
anonymous, but whose help and advice has
proved invaluable.

Finally, my love and affection to
Sophie and Ben
Oliver, Cornelius, and Tabitha

Contents

ONE

THE THEORY OF
PRE—CELTIC DIVINATION

TWO

THE PRAXIS

THREE

CRAFTING

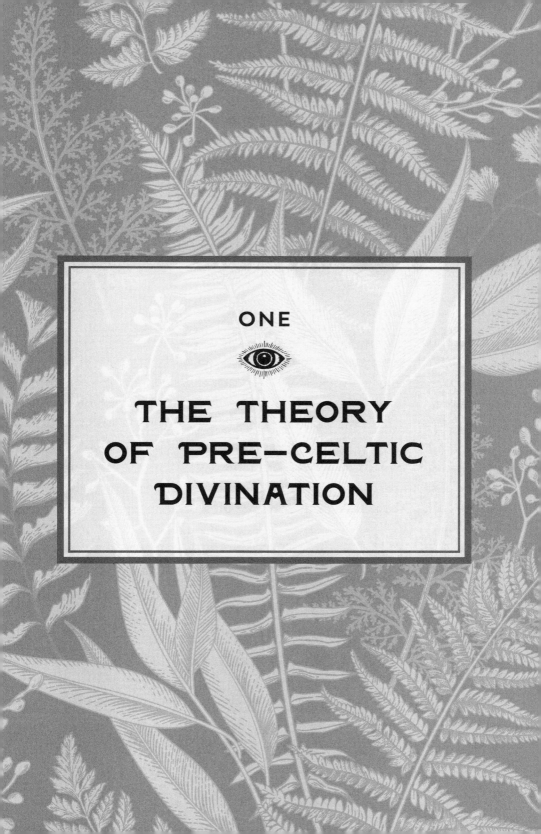

ONE

THE THEORY OF PRE-CELTIC DIVINATION

Keepers of the Knowledge

Ever since the dawn of human history, mankind has had a fascination with divination. It has played a part in the making and ruin of chieftains and kings, and at the same time it has offered comfort and guidance to lowly people in their everyday toil and struggle for existence.

In the world of the Celtic Pagans of Wales, Ireland, Scotland, and northern France—the four main areas of Celtic domination—the science and art of divination lay within the trusted hands of the Druids, one of the three learned classes of Celtic society, and for thousands of years before the arrival of the Celtic culture, chieftains and tribal kings sought the advice of Druids to help determine their destiny.

But in addition to these lofty Druids who served the royal courts, there were more commonplace Druids—those who lived and worked within the tribal communities. Their tasks were much humbler, but no less important. They served the peasant communities who sought their advice on everyday matters, matters that though humdrum and mundane may well have meant life or death to individuals, families, or even entire communities.

It would be a mistake to think of these ancient societies as being well organized and structured, or as a cohesive "nation" in the same way as we think of today's highly structured nations, with governments and organized social structures.

Beginning as a hunter-gatherer culture, the first evidence we can see of any form of social cohesion would have been small family groups working together as hunters. As they progressed to an agrarian society, these family groups developed into tribes who farmed crops and tended small herds as an interdependent group. Even though these tribes may have been larger in number than the earlier extended family groups, they were by no means a coherent nation, but rather isolated groups of people with little contact or communication between each other. Most tribes would have a chieftain at their head; some would even be referred to as a king, and in a very few cases, a number of tribes would come together under a high king, or King of Kings. These alliances were usually a defensive strategy at a time when strength in numbers was a very important tactic in defending homes, crops, and cattle from aggressive neighboring tribes, or in launching attacks to gain territory and assets.

Living so close to nature and totally dependent on her gifts, the people of these tribal communities were desperate for advice on when to sow crops, when to begin their harvest, when to store their grain, when their cattle were due to give birth, and a myriad of other concerns about the simple matters that governed their daily lives. The predictions of their tribal Druid gave them hope and guidance. When things went wrong and nature dealt them an unexpected blow, it was their Druid who was expected to tell them what had happened, how they had offended nature, and what they needed to do to put things right or prevent such things from happening again. History tells us that it was the role of the tribal Druid to instruct the tribe as to when their festivals were due and predict auspicious dates for marriages, births, battles, and other major events.

Accounts vary as to the methods used by these ancient Druids, but one thing is common to all the historical accounts: the tribal Druid, through whatever means, was expected to provide crucial information of past events, interpret the present, and foretell the future, in order that the recipients of this information could use it in some form of decision-making process. This process could involve the destiny of a nation or simply the best time to gather hazelnuts; the skill of the Druid-seer was expected to provide direction to chieftains and peasants alike.

Today, divination, in its various forms, plays a very different role in our society. Astrology, tarot, and crystal gazing have taken over from the older Pagan methods, and few people understand or follow the arcane rites that served the pre-Celtic Pagans so well and for so long.

Having been a practicing Druid in the pre-Celtic Pagan tradition for some forty years now, I have had many, many occasions to call upon the Druidic divination techniques that I was taught as a young man in the 1960s. Divination was, and still is, an essential element of Druidic practice, one that requires a good degree of training and insight. More importantly, it requires a large amount of conviction and practice so that the practitioner may transcend the mundane and explore the hidden world of the Druidic cosmos.

The Druidic mantic arts are many; some of the more ancient practices, primarily the socially unacceptable ones, have been abandoned, but a collection of very specific techniques remain and continue to be passed on through the restricted oral tradition of the Druids. This book explores the techniques that have survived and explains the cosmos of the pre-Celtic Pagans within which they functioned.

Much of what you will find as you read through the following chapters is seen here in print for the first time and has been taken from the oral tradition that defines the belief system that has governed my life since I was a child.

Some of what you will read will contradict the popular mythical accounts of pre-Roman society in what may now be considered as the Celtic homelands. Similarly, some will challenge many of the assertions made by various neo-Druidic individuals and groups who have formulated their own interpretation of the ancient belief systems, based on a combination of Romano-Christian influenced accounts, romanticized fiction, and the elevation of mythical characters to Celtic deities.

I was brought up in a Pagan household and taught in the Welsh tradition of pre-Celtic Paganism. Purely by chance of birth, I belong to a family lineage of Druids going back at least five generations, and I understand from my parents and grandparents that I have been taught an unbroken and uninterrupted tradition that extends far back into the history of my homeland. I point this out not in an attempt to ascribe to my writing any special credibility, but to demonstrate that the Druidic tradition is still maintained, though not very visibly, in many of the Celtic nations and that it plays a part in everyday life within the communities of simple, unassuming Celtic folk.

The tradition that I write about is the tradition maintained in the tribal area of Wales in which I was born and grew up. Forty years of practicing and teaching this tradition has taught me, among many other things, that the tradition I know so well is not the only Druidic tradition, nor do I suggest that it is better or holds sovereignty over any other Druidic tradition. It is merely the one that I know and follow. My experience has also taught me that most of the Celtic Druidic traditions have a great deal more in common than they have differences, particularly if you compare the rural community traditions, as opposed to the neo-Druidic national and global orders. While it is true that the history of the many interconnected pre-Celtic and Celtic tribes throughout northern Europe spawned a diverse collection of folklore and mythical legends, it is also true to say that much of the core of the spiritual belief systems of these tribes show a great deal in common, as does the history of their ritual and divination methods.

In researching the diversity of the methods contained in this book, I have discovered that the Welsh tradition I was brought up in not only shares many of its techniques with the other northern European Druidic traditions, but also that they have a great deal in common with many of the other metaphysical traditions from around the world. Whether these traditions come from a single source, were shared though cultural exchange, or grew independently is impossible to determine, although the latter seems the most likely. One thing is apparent, though: the widespread use of divination in its many forms illustrates that it serves a fundamental human need—our desire to know what the future holds for us and our common belief that the source of this information is not to be found in the mundane physical world, but somewhere outside it.

THE ROLE OF PRE-CELTIC DIVINATION

When you go to sleep tonight, it will be in the firm knowledge that in the morning the sun will rise and the new day will begin. In fact, we are so confident of the sun rising that I doubt if any one of us even gives a thought to the alternative.

Science gives us an understanding of why the sun rises in the morning and sets each night. It gives us a model of our earth spinning on its tilted axis, with the sun appearing above the eastern horizon each morning and disappearing below the western horizon each night.

We know that the moon orbits the earth and that the earth, along with the other planets, orbits the sun at the center of our solar system. Knowing all this allows us to predict the passing of the days, months, and years with perfect accuracy. Why? Because we understand how this function of the universe works. We know that it's a consistent, repetitive cycle, and we *know* the sun will rise in the morning.

Imagine if we lived in an age where this sort of knowledge and understanding was beyond even the greatest imagination. Why should the sun reappear in the morning? Why does it stay light longer on some days than on others? Why is it colder sometimes, and will the warm days ever return?

Each of these questions, and more, had a crucial impact on the everyday lives of the tribal groups living in the British Isles for millennia before the arrival of the Celtic influence.

Without an awareness of the workings of the solar system—and with no real understanding of the seasons, the life cycles of the plants they gathered, or the animals they hunted—anyone who was able to predict a good time to plant crops, and just how long it would be before they could be harvested, was of great value to the community.

It was these types of simple but vital predictions that first established the Druidic role in pre-Celtic society. The oral tradition of Welsh Paganism records these predictive processes in a series of stories that explain why and how the role of Druid evolved and how divination became a major function of Druidic lore.

The tradition tells us how divination became an essential part of everyday life and lay at the core of tribal culture. From the most modest task to major collaborative plans, nothing was undertaken without some aspect of divination being employed.

This was an age when people lived in an intimate relationship with nature, much closer than we have ever had since. Mankind was a *part of* nature, on an equal standing with the other animals, the plants, the wind, and the water in rivers and streams. Everything in nature was equal.

There is a story in the tradition that tells of how the harmony of nature was abandoned when Man first proclaimed himself separate and above nature, setting out on a path to control it and harness it to his advantage.

Druids renounce this division and consider themselves to be an integral part of nature, seeking equality with the rest of nature and an understanding of it as a whole. Without this motivation, effective divination will never be achieved. All of the techniques of divination within the tradition, both historic and present-day, depend entirely on a symbiotic relationship between the diviner and nature. Nature provides all of the tools and energies that offer an insight into the future, and the Druid takes nothing from nature that cannot be returned.

Divination played an imperative role in pre-Celtic Pagan society at every level. Its practices and techniques have been preserved in an oral tradition, containing stories and instructions that make it available to us today in the same form. The things that have changed immeasurably and irretrievably over time are our relationship with nature, our cynical view of anything considered nonscientific, and our inability to easily step beyond the mundane in search of the esoteric.

All the same, the oral tradition is important to our understanding of the historic elements of pre-Celtic divination, why and how it works, and how it may be applied in today's context. All that follows is drawn from and subject to the specific oral tradition that I grew up in.

THE ORAL TRADITION OF THE PRE-CELTIC DRUIDS

Virtually every account relating the history of the Druids and Druidic lore has some mention of what is most commonly referred to as the oral tradition, a tradition that has kept the lore of the Druids shrouded in mystery for thousands of years. Unlike the majority of ancient belief systems, neither the Pagan socioreligious beliefs of the pre-Celtic population nor the lore of its priestly caste, the Druids, were written in any form whatsoever.

The Druids, the keepers of this arcane knowledge, chose to maintain it through an oral tradition, passed on from generation to generation, usually within an extended family and very often from father to son or mother to daughter.

As a Druid, I have had the privilege of learning this ancient lore from a succession of tutors, beginning with my grandfather and developing through five other teachers before I was considered experienced enough to pass through my final initiation as a Druid. At a number of stages of my training I was required to undertake vows of secrecy that relate to specific practices and arcane lore, and I did this with a full understanding of the reasons for secrecy and the consequences that could result if these vows were broken.

Contrary to popular belief, and to the great disappointment of many of the people who have asked me about these vows, the reason for this secrecy is not as mysterious as it may first appear. Quite simply, the reason some aspects of Druidic lore are made the subject of these vows is that, like most traditions of arcane metaphysical lore, some practices are considered physically, mentally, or spiritually dangerous, and it is essential that these areas of knowledge are only made available to those with sufficient skills and knowledge to use them wisely. It makes good sense then to make these areas of knowledge available to initiates as they reach the prerequisite levels of training and not before. Similarly, it also makes good sense not to make these areas of potentially dangerous knowledge available to anyone outside the tradition, for the same reasons.

As a Druid, I have had to think long and hard about what I can justifiably include in my writing without, first, contradicting my vows of secrecy and, second, endangering my potential reader's physical, mental, or spiritual well-being. I believe that I have strived to achieve this delicate balance both in my writing and lecturing, and I am constantly aware of the need for caution in many of the areas in which I work.

In exercising care and consideration in the ways I write and lecture, I ensure the maintenance of my vows, as I would never allow myself to reveal any form of practice to any individual that I felt unready to receive it. After all, that is the purpose of the vows of secrecy in the first place.

I mention all of this to put the reader's mind at rest and to ensure you that as you progress through this book, moving from one section to another, if you fully understand all the practices that it contains, you will run no risk of damage to yourself or others that you may involve in your exploration of the Druidic science and art of divination.

But what of the oral tradition mentioned throughout the history of the Druids? Is this a secret tradition available only to the initiated? Am I breaking a fundamental law of secrecy by recounting *any* of what I have learned in this and any other of my writings?

To answer these and many other questions that I have been asked about the oral tradition, it is important that we first define exactly what we understand as the oral tradition and then consider how long it can last as such in today's technology-based world.

Both of these points have been debated at length, not only by the initiates of the Druidic tradition itself, but also by members of other arcane groups and orders.

This, then, is how the debate goes:

When we talk of the oral tradition, are we using the term to define a body of knowledge that, in the past and up to the present day, has been maintained through word of mouth, and has therefore, by definition, been accessed by few, purely because of circumstance and reluctance to embrace advancing skills from early writing to today's technologies? Or are we talking of a body of knowledge that is considered *so sacred* that it can *only* be transmitted orally and cannot be committed to writing without defiling it? There is, of course, a third argument that suggests that the sacred Druidic lore was kept secret to the Druids themselves as a sociopolitical means of ensuring the continued status and elite privileges of the Druidic class.

Early classical accounts of the Druids and their traditions fail to give us any clear indication of which argument may be the strongest, as may be seen from the following quote taken from Julius Caesar's writings on his early encounters with the Druids.

> Nor do they deem it lawful to commit those things (relating to their lore) to writing; though generally, in other cases and in their public and private accounts, they use Greek letters. They appear to have established this custom for two reasons: because they would not have their tenets published; and because they would not have those who learn them, by trusting to letters, neglect the exercise of memory. (Caesar, *De Bello Gallico,* book 6, chapter 14; quoted in M. H. Gaidoz, "The Religion of the Gauls," *The Celtic Magazine* vol. 12 [1887], 399)

In fact, Julius Caesar gives us a fourth suggestion: committing their lore to memory, rather than writing it into lengthy tomes, helps maintain the Druids' metal agility.

The teachings about the oral tradition tell us that it is itself a tradition of teaching, a methodology or pedagogy if you prefer. This is borne out in practice, where all traditional Druidic teacher/learner relationships are one-to-one and the teaching style is what could now be called contextual learning, using a form of parable that relates to the individual learner's life experiences and interests. So, the term "oral tradition" refers to a teaching methodology, not a body of knowledge that is too sacred to set into words.

Unfortunately (or fortunately, depending on your point of view) this methodology, by definition, restricts access to the body of knowledge to those people who may come into personal contact with the learning system (i.e., you must be personally taught by, and in the presence of, a Druidic teacher).

So, the oral tradition itself tells us that the body of knowledge is not "too sacred" to be written down. It does, however, also tell us that there is a need for it to be taught and learned via a specific method that relates it to the learners' life experiences and enhances their memory. This, then, is core of the oral tradition: the need for *oral transmission as a methodology of teaching.*

The next question is how valid is this tenet in today's society? Does the need for personal contact and memory enhancement still have the same significance as it once did? And can contextual learning apply as the type of "distance learning pedagogy" that may be experienced by reading books or undertaking a training program on the internet, without the direct contact with a teacher that the traditional methods demand?

Then there's the big question: Should this body of knowledge, one that could benefit so many, remain shackled by a training methodology that may no longer be relevant?

My personal opinion? I believe that the whole body of knowledge that we have been calling the oral tradition should be made available in a responsible way to anyone and everyone that seeks it, through whatever means possible, as long as they do not compromise, corrupt, distort, or impinge on what we believe to be the truth. This does not make the knowledge that is revealed any the less valuable, as long as the knowledge itself is not defiled or abused. As a personal receptacle of this knowledge, I feel both an obligation and desire to give people access to what, through circumstance of birth, has been made available to me.

As far as the contextual learning pedagogy is concerned, I think that the benefits of learning through parable related to an individual's experience is outweighed by the opportunity to make the body of knowledge available to a much larger and wider-reaching audience. For better or worse, individuals in today's society are much more sophisticated than those for whom the oral tradition was devised, and most people's ability to absorb and understand abstract concepts of spiritual and metaphysical ideals and practices is far more developed than that of the people of the pre-Celtic era.

It is for individuals to decide whether or not they think that the ancient memory enhancement element of the training is still relevant. Having experienced this aspect in my own training, all I can say is that I found it laborious and tedious, and I personally found it a serious distraction from the more important and relevant aspects of the actual lore itself. If you feel that memory enhancement is an important factor, there are numerous modern-day courses and programs that provide more than adequate opportunities to improve and expand your memory, without adding the extra burden to your insight into Druidic lore.

Finally, on the topic of the oral tradition versus a detailed written account, there is a consideration that many chose to ignore, even though it is extremely relevant and mind-numbingly obvious.

The earliest written form of the Irish language (known to linguists as "Primitive Irish") is known only from small fragments inscribed on standing stones in the Ogham* alphabet. The earliest of these inscriptions probably date from the third or fourth century CE. These Ogham inscriptions are found primarily in the south of Ireland, Wales, and Cornwall, where it is believed to have been brought by settlers from Ireland to sub-Roman Britain.

---

*Ogham is an early medieval alphabet used primarily to write the Old Irish language on standing stones.

From what we can tell, these inscriptions represent the names of people who may have been prominent members of the communities, chieftains, or tribal leaders and appear to be some form of memorial text.

Although Julius Caesar refers to the Druids using Greek letters in their everyday texts, it is commonly believed that the first written texts in Ireland and Wales were introduced following the Roman conquest, some four thousand years after the practices of the oral tradition are said to have begun.

So, could it simply be that the oral tradition depended on learning by rote because no form of written language existed until millennia after the practices first began?

Whatever the reason may be, the fact is that there is no written body of knowledge recording the practices of Druidic lore, and this, for some people, is a problem.

Irrespective of the fact that most, if not all, of our ancient religious and historical texts existed for millennia as oral traditions prior to being written down in one form or another and that, even then, most refer to an era of vague recollection prior to the beginning of the recorded text. It seems important to the majority of people that they can find comfort in the authenticity of what they consider to be contemporary accounts and records of the events that define their religious beliefs, even though the facts may contradict their assumptions.

It is customary in writing a book of this nature to add to its credibility by referring to the sources of the material used and citing the origins of the facts and quotations presented in order that the reader may know the provenance of the information and may also follow up and expand on the material given by referring to the original source. In this particular instance, the majority of the source material comes from a particular oral tradition that endures in the valleys of southeast Wales. This is the tradition that I was taught and that forms my worldview. It is one tradition among many, and although I have discovered that it shares some of its beliefs and lore with others, it is, in my experience, a unique tradition containing a holistic range of practices and beliefs. Among these practices is the art and science of divination.

A CAUTIONARY NOTE

Like many other metaphysical disciplines, divination engages the body, mind, and spirit—in other words, the whole of one's being. Any practice that involves every part of one's conscious and physical existence exposes the person or people involved to the risk of emotional, psychological, and spiritual damage if the disciplines are not approached in the correct way.

If you progress through this book in a step-by-step manner, ensuring a full understanding of each stage before progressing to the next, then there is little chance of upsetting your well-being. You may expose yourself to difficulties if you jump from one section to another with no sense of progression or sequential development.

Some of the meditative disassociation techniques used need to be approached with respect, as they attempt to induce an alternative state of mind. This is an experience that can cause anxiety, distress, or even panic when first encountered, and some induced phenomena like false awakening can be especially disconcerting if one is not aware of what is happening.

You will find that each technique used is explained in full detail before any practical experimentation is suggested so that the learner will be fully aware of what to expect from the exercise. Please take the time to read through each section and, if necessary, read it again until you feel you have a thorough understanding of what is to be done and what the expected experience or outcome is intended to be.

This progressive learning technique is a fundamental part of the oral tradition, as is the repetition of information until it is fully committed to memory. In the past, the Druid teacher ensured that the student or learner had memorized information by using individual testing techniques, but of course this can only be done in a face-to-face situation. So, being conscious of the differences between the relationship of the teacher and learner in a face-to-face situation and that of the student learning from a book without supervision, I have laid out the contents of this book in a progressive learning manner, while having to trust in the reader's ability and motivation to read through and fully understand each section as it appears before engaging in the practical experimentation and techniques described.

SOME DEFINITIONS AND CLARIFICATION

The oral tradition discussed above originated in a language that has evolved over many thousands of years. As we will see later, it predated the arrival of both the Celtic languages and the evolution of primitive Irish and Welsh into the languages of modern Irish and Welsh that we know today.

Even though I am a lifelong Welsh speaker, many of the words I have encountered are unknown to me, and if I had not had the benefit of Druidic teachers who were able to explain the meaning of these words in a contextual situation, I would not have been able to understand the true meaning of much that I was told.

It is my intention to avoid the use of **Welsh** or **Irish** (Primitive, Old, or Modern) wherever possible throughout the following text, as in my opinion this will only lead to confusion. (However, I shall introduce the reader to the occasional Welsh or Irish word where it is particularly relevant to the text.) The use of what can only be considered as minority languages to add credibility to arcane practices only invites multivalent interpretation and what students of philosophy would call pseudo-profundity*—using unfamiliar words to increase the gravitas of a statement.

Having said that, some regular words and expressions in the

---

*I have always enjoyed the irony of the word *pseudo-profundity,* as most of the times I have seen it used, it has itself been used as a pseudo-profundity.

tradition have a particular meaning that may not be the same as that understood in everyday speech, so to clarify this usage I have compiled below a very brief glossary of words that have a specific meaning within the tradition that may differ from their commonly accepted meaning.

The tradition: In the context of this book, *the tradition* refers to a corpus of knowledge relating to the pre-Celtic Pagan worldview that has been kept alive in detail by a custom of oral teaching and learning, particularly in the region of the valleys of southeastern Wales.

Druid: We shall see later that the word *Druid* evolved from an older word used following the arrival in Wales and Ireland of the Celtic influence and culture. It is commonly accepted that Druids were the priestly caste of Celtic society and enjoyed particular rights and privileges within the Celtic social structure. It is, however, evident that prior to the arrival of the Celtic influence (and the word "Druid"), there was a priestly presence in Pagan Ireland and Wales for thousands of years. We shall see that these "priests" were considered the elite of their society—the builders of complex burial chambers, stone circles, and standing stones and the holders of the ancient lore that became the body of the oral tradition referred to throughout this book. Even though these Pagan priests had a name (one that unfortunately I cannot divulge here), I will continue to call them Druids. Despite the fact that this is an obvious misnomer, the word *Druid* has attracted an understanding in the context of the ancient belief system of Ireland and Wales, and I can see no harm in using it as a nominal title for the pre-Celtic Pagan priestly caste.

Divination: Although the word *divination* is formally defined as foreseeing the future through consultation with the gods, it is used in a much broader sense in popular speech. Even so, it still has a more formal feel than expressions like *fortune-telling* and *clairvoyance,* and it is often associated with more structured religious practices. As we need a name for the practices that we are about to explore and I am unable to use the name used in Druidic lore,* the word *divination* is as good as any. I will, however, underscore the fact that none of the practices of Druidic divination involve consulting any gods or depend on divine inspiration. The reasons for this will become very obvious as we progress.

Mantic: Of, relating to, or having the power of divination; prophetic.

Mantic art or techniques: When I was a young man learning the various skills of divination, it was not unusual to hear my teachers using the term *mantic art* or *mantic techniques* when referring to the art and techniques of divination. The term was used because it avoided using the word *divination* with its association with consulting the gods for information of future events. This, as we shall see, contradicts the tenets of Druidic Lore. The word *mantic* seems to have disappeared from common speech, but here I use it as a synonym for *divination,* maybe in the hope that it may return to popularity, as it has a much closer meaning to the ancient Druidic term than *divination* has.

---

*As readers of my previous books will know, the "naming" of things and activities is a very formal practice and is associated with appropriate oaths of secrecy. Some of the reasons for this are outlined in the oral tradition section above. The principle reason supporting this, however, is the belief that knowing the true name of something gives one power and control over it.

1

The Cultural Context of Pre-Celtic Divination

THE DRUID IN PRE-CELTIC SOCIETY

To understand the ways that Druidic divination works in a modern world, it is necessary to appreciate not only the fundamental worldview on which it is based, but also the cultural context in which it was originally used. In this way, it is possible to see just how appropriate it can be in today's culture.

We should then begin this section by considering what we actually know about Druids and their lore. For the moment, we will look outside the body of knowledge contained in the oral tradition discussed above and look instead at the accounts of the classic historians of the ancient world.

During my lifetime, I have read hundreds of books, articles, and papers on the subject of Druids and their activities—literally millions of words—and I am sure that there are many more accounts that I have yet to read. Some are based on academic research, others are pure fantasy; where can we find an accurate account of the Druids that we can depend on? Maybe from the people in history who may have had contact with the ancient Druids, who would have had firsthand experience and witnessed their rituals and ceremonies? What can we gather from the writings of the ancient Greeks, Romans, and early Christians who lived alongside the Druids in their heyday?

Well, it may surprise many readers to learn that if we took all of the accounts written by the historians of the time and the people who may have had direct contact with the ancient Druids, they would total less than two thousand words! To put this into proportion, by the time you read this you will have read over five thousand words of this book. Everything else is mere speculation. Bear this in mind when you are looking at all of the books about Druids on the shelves and listed online or when you hear references to historical accounts, as opposed to oral traditions.

All of the thousands of books and millions of words written about the Druids are based on these two thousand words. So how accurate and reliable are these precious few accounts?

It seems they differ depending on who actually wrote them, given that writers from different cultures describe their observations in the context of their own experiences. The Greeks describe them as philosophers, orators, and debaters, just as their learned classes were. The Romans ascribe to them the powers of prophesy and foretelling the future by reading the entrails of murdered criminals, just as their own soothsayers did. They also describe them as fierce warriors, leading their tribes into battle with bloodcurdling cries, once again applying the attributes of their own cultural traits to the Druids they observed.

In commenting on aspects of worship, both the Greeks and the Romans assign the names of the gods in their own pantheons to the forces and spirits the ancient Druids used and focused on. They drew parallels with their Gods of thunder, lightning, sea, and war, among many others.

The final and most relevant comment on all of the known writings of these ancient historians is that they were writing about the Celtic Druids, who were a product of the arrival of the Celtic influence that began around 350 BCE, just three hundred years before the arrival of the Romans in the British Isles. These are very different from the pre-Celtic Druids who were the creators and practitioners of the tradition we are exploring in this book. These pre-Celtic Druids lived in Ireland and Wales around 4500 BCE, more than four thousand years prior to the arrival of the Celtic influence, in an era we now call the Neolithic Age. These ancient Druids left their legacy in an oral tradition and, later, by adorning our landscape with a large array of monumental stoneworks. So now is a good time to acquaint ourselves with the early history of these islands and the emergence of the priestly class of the Druids. To do this, we have to look back some ten thousand years to a time when the coastal regions of Ireland and Wales were being repopulated following the last major ice age.

The early history of the populations of Wales and Ireland and the emergence of the Druids can be explored in two separate but complementary accounts. The first are the stories of their origins contained in the oral tradition, and we shall look at this in detail later when we look at the rudiments of the Druidic worldview. The second is described by the archaeological evidence laid out below. I have woven into this history some indication of how the original Druids evolved along with the population. This is not to suggest that the archaeological evidence gives any indication at all of the Druids' development; it does not. Neither am I engaging in speculation based on the famous two thousand words of the ancient historians. I have simply taken points in time that coincide with the archaeological records and the lore contained in the oral tradition so that when we look at this in more detail later, it will be easier to relate events in the lore to the timescale laid down by the archaeological evidence.

So, to begin this short history, we must go back some ten thousand years to a time when the environment was harsh and simple survival was a daily struggle. As the freezing ice of the last major ice age (circa 16,000 BCE) began to retreat from the British Isles, the region slowly began to be repopulated by small groups of hunter-gatherers who, unsurprisingly, settled mainly in the coastal areas. This repopulation began around 8000 BCE in the Mesolithic Age, a period that ran from 8000 to 4500 BCE. These early settlers were seafaring people, who arrived following coastal routes from the northwestern areas of mainland Europe and depended on the sea for much of their livelihood. Living mainly on seafood, their diet changed as they migrated inland, where they hunted birds and wild boar and gathered nuts, edible plants, and berries. They hunted with spears, arrows, and harpoons tipped with small flint blades (microliths) and lived in small family groups, using rude shelters made by stretching animal skins over light wooden frames. It is thought that during the Mesolithic Age the population of Ireland was never more than a few thousand, with a similar sized population occupying the coastal regions of Wales. There is no archaeological evidence to suggest that these tribes developed any form of overall ruling structure or religious/ceremonial activities, but were most likely separate, seminomadic family groups preoccupied with survival in a still-harsh environment.

By the end of the Mesolithic Age (circa 4500 BCE), there began a long, slow process of change that saw the introduction of farming, agriculture, and animal husbandry. This is thought to have resulted from overseas trade and contact with agricultural communities in continental Europe. It resulted in the establishment of small settlements of a more permanent nature, with groups and extended families coming together to share the tasks of tending the crops and animals.

In northern Europe, 4500 BCE saw the transition from the Mesolithic Age (the Middle Stone Age) to the Neolithic Age (the New Stone Age), a period that was to run until about 2500 BCE. Slowly, agriculture began to establish itself in the British Isles with the arrival of goats, sheep, and cereal crops from neighboring continental Europe. It is interesting to note here that the oldest known Neolithic field system in the world is found in county Mayo, Ireland, and at the same time numerous settlements began to appear all over the region. Also around this time, we see the first evidence of pottery, which seems to have appeared with the advent of agriculture and the more settled lifestyle.

Figure 1.1. A representation of a typical settlement of the period at the Museum of Welsh Life in Saint Fagans, near Cardiff in south Wales.

As agriculture continued to become more and more established, for the first time there was enough food available to feed the family members without the constant need to hunt and gather wild food and game. Evidence also suggests that there may have even been a surplus of food in some communities, enabling the residents to trade their surplus crops for other commodities. The burgeoning agricultural society also freed up time for people to turn their attention to other aspects of life, like crafts, art, and religion. It was during this time that we see the emergence of the priestly class we are calling the pre-Celtic Druids.

With their basic needs for food and security met, certain members of the family tribe now had the time and motivation to turn their thoughts to matters of what Abraham Maslow* called self-actualization—

---

*In his 1943 paper "A Theory of Human Motivation" Maslow proposed his widely accepted theory of a hierarchy of needs. Maslow spent time with the Blackfoot nation of Native Americans, learning and adapting much of this theory from them.

the processes of creativity, morality, religion, and awareness of the environment and cosmos.

The need for a new understanding of nature and the ability to predict natural phenomena—like the seasons, the weather, and the life cycles of plants and animals—were just a few of the essential requirements for the well-being of the small, close-knit communities.

The individuals who put their minds to the close observation of nature and committed to memory the cycles of weather, growth, planting, and harvesting and the movement of sun and moon became the Druids. Their understanding of nature afforded them the ability to "foretell the future" by predicting the seasons, the rising and setting of the sun (and moon), and the influence these and other events had on their lives.

As these skills developed, we see the appearance of some of the most visible and lasting evidence of the period: the monumental megalithic tombs, standing stones, and stone circles that define the era.

At the time, these sites represented the center of religious and ceremonial life, and their scale and accuracy illustrate the great importance the tribal groups placed on them. Many sites are surrounded by evidence of dwellings and settlements, which suggests that populations were drawn to the sites because they felt the need to be close to their spiritual energy.*

There are more than 1,200 of these Neolithic monuments known to us today, with 234 surviving stone circles in Ireland alone. Of these, 103 are located in the counties of Cork and Kerry, the region in which I am fortunate enough to live. Recent carbon-14 dating technology suggests that most were built between four thousand and five thousand years ago, placing them firmly in the Neolithic period between 3000 and 2000 BCE.

Most of these stone circles share a specific alignment—defined as the siting along the line between a single axial (recumbent) stone and the space between the two tall portal stones. Some 70 percent of the Cork and Kerry circles share an alignment to the same calendrical dates

---

*This is a relatively recent discovery that contradicts the earlier theory that the circles were built within existing settlements. In other words, it now seems that the stone circles arrived before the settlements and not the other way around.

Figure 1.2. The Seven Sisters stone circle near Killarney, county Kerry, Ireland. One of the 234 surviving stone circles in Kerry and its neighboring county, Cork.

or times in the Greater Lunar cycle. We now know that these standing circles represent the first early astronomical observatories and provided their technicians, the ancient Druids, with one of the very first predictive devices used to foretell future natural phenomena.

It is estimated that at the height of the Neolithic era the population of Ireland and Wales grew to a peak of around 150,000, reducing significantly at the end of the era with evidence of an economic collapse around 2500 BCE.

The early part of the Bronze Age, between 2500 and 2000 BCE, could more accurately be called the Copper Age (or Chalcolithic Age), as this was a time when copper dominated as the most commonly used metal. It was not until after 2000 BCE that tin, imported from the Cornish coast, was alloyed with native copper to create bronze, a harder and more durable metal.

One of the earliest and most prolific copper mines of the age was located on the Ross Peninsula, on the lakes of Killarney in south Kerry,

Ireland. It has been established that work at the Ross mines began around 2400 BCE, and by the time the first excavations are believed to have stopped some six hundred years later at around 1800 BCE, it is estimated that 370 tons of copper had been excavated and smelted into bronze.

Although archaeological excavations of the region have found an array of bronze jewelry, weapons, vessels, and other artifacts, it is estimated that less than 0.2 percent of the mined copper has been evidenced as being used by the local community, meaning that a flourishing export market accounted for more than 99 percent of the mine's production. A similar story may be told of the copper mines at Y Gogarth (The Great Orme) in Llandudno in north Wales and the historic tin mines in Cornwall and southwestern England.

It is this trade with the UK mainland and northwestern mainland Europe that was to dominate the development of Ireland and Wales for the next two thousand years until the arrival of the Romans.

The Bronze Age (2500 to 700 BCE) was a golden age for the Druids, as their Pagan belief system spread to encompass the whole of the region, and their knowledge of the natural world grew. They became an important resource for the tribal communities and their leaders. As the family groups grew into larger tribes of settled communities and allegiances were negotiated to protect their herds and crops from raiders, advice was sought from the Druid as to propitious dates for ceremonies, marriages, and other important events. The Druids' counsel was sought for negotiations, and, as their reputation grew, they became an increasingly valued asset to the tribal group.

As their importance increased, so did their power. Originally conducting their ceremonies in wooded groves (of which there were, and still are, an abundance), they were now powerful enough to instigate the building of an increasing number of stone monuments as the focus of their activities.

During this period, it is thought that the population stabilized at around 150,000, even though there is some evidence of climate deterioration and deforestation.

By the end of the Bronze Age, around 700 BCE, the well-established trade routes between Ireland, the UK mainland, and northwestern Europe made it possible for the new "wonder metal," iron, to arrive on the islands from Europe. Harder than bronze, iron was the ideal metal for weaponry and other utilitarian uses. It began a new era in the history of the region, the Iron Age; it was during this age, around three hundred years after it began, that we see the single most important event in Druidic history since its establishment, an event that would change the history of Druidic law forever and impose a massive influence on how we perceive Druids to this very day. I refer, of course, to the arrival of the Celtic influence and culture.

THE ARRIVAL OF THE CELTIC INFLUENCE

In 1946 Thomas Francis O'Rahilly* published his extremely influential work *Early Irish History and Mythology* (Dublin: Dublin Institute for Advanced Studies), in which he proposed a model of Irish prehistory based on his study of language, mythology, and pseudo-history.

In his famous model, he distinguishes four separate waves of Celtic invaders:

- The Cruithne or Priteni (c. 700–500 BCE)
- The Builg or Érainn (c. 500 BCE)
- The Laigin, the Domnainn, and the Gálioin (c. 300 BCE)
- The Goidels or Gael (c. 100 BCE)

His theory proposes a series of aggressive invasions by Celtic tribes from the northwestern shores of Europe. These warlike invaders were apparently responsible for two major changes in Ireland (and, by inference, Wales). The first was the importation of their culture and

---

*Born in Listowel, north Kerry, Ireland, Thomas Francis O'Rahilly (Irish: Tomás Proinsias Ó Rathaile; 1883–1953) was an Irish scholar of the Celtic languages, specializing in the fields of historical linguistics and Irish dialects. He was a member of the Royal Irish Academy and died in Dublin in 1953.

language. Their cultural influence affected nearly all aspects of the lives of the indigenous population—religion, art, music, food, and much, much more—and we shall look in detail at some of these later. Their influence on the languages of the population is complex and beyond the purview of this exploration. The other major effect of these suggested invasions is that by interbreeding with the indigenous peoples, they propagated the popular "Celtic race" that to this day binds the peoples of Ireland, Wales, Scotland, the Isle of Man, Cornwall, and northern France in a common bond of ethnic identity—that of the Celt.

Intriguingly, recent developments have overturned O'Rahilly's proposition and much of what was believed about the Celtic invasion of Ireland and the British Isles. It appears that the truth (and I always use that word with great reluctance and reservations) may be much more complex and subtle.

In December of 1993, John Collis,* professor of archaeology at the University of Sheffield (UK), presented a paper entitled "Celtic Fantasy" at the Celts in Europe conference in Cardiff, Wales. Controversial at the time, a version of the same paper was published four month later (March 1994) in the prestigious *British Archaeological News*.

In his paper Collis proposes that, "There were no cross-European Celtic people. There was no broad-based Celtic art, society, or religion. And there were never any Celts in Britain!" He goes on to suggest that, "No ancient author ever referred to the inhabitants of Britain—the Britanni—as Celts. It was not until the sixteenth century that the term was applied to Britain, and then it was used mainly to denote a group of languages spoken in Western Britain and Brittany (N. France)."

Collis's assertions were certainly considered extreme at the time, but more recent DNA evidence goes a long way to support his thesis.

---

*John Collis, born in 1944 in Winchester, England, is a British prehistorian. He studied in Prague and Tübingen and was awarded his Ph.D. at Cambridge, where he studied from 1963–1970. He joined the Archaeology Department in Sheffield in 1972 and was made professor in 1990. He has acted as head of department and became emeritus professor there in October 2004. His speciality is the European Iron Age.

An article published in the August 1997 edition of the *Journal of Human Genetics* (100, no. 2: 189–94) following an extensive DNA sampling/analysis program, gives a telling insight into the DNA signature of the current population of Ireland:

> The analysis of phenylketonuria (PKU) DNA mutations in Ireland shows that most major episodes of immigration have left a record in the modern gene pool. The mutation 165T can be traced to the Palaeolithic people of Western Europe who, in the Mesolithic period, first colonized Ireland. R408W (on haplotype 1) in contrast, the most common Irish PKU mutation, may have been prevalent in the Neolithic farmers who settled in Ireland after 4500 BC. *No mutation was identified that could represent European Celtic populations,* supporting the view that *the adoption of Celtic culture and language in Ireland did not involve major migration from the continent. . . . Our results show that the culture and language of a population can be independent of its genetic heritage."* (emphasis added)

This last sentence is undoubtedly the most telling of all.

It makes perfect sense that if the DNA signature of the current Irish population (who would, I am sure, all claim to be of Celtic origin and belong to the family of Celtic nations) shows no mutations representing the European Celts—despite language, cultural practices, and artifacts similar to those found in northwestern Europe—then the cultural influences of the Celtic tribes must have arrived through a process of cultural exchange and not wholesale invasion, occupation, and interbreeding, as was previously suggested. The debate has, in recent years, been categorized as migrationism verses diffusionism, two distinct approaches explaining the spread of culture and innovation. The debate has been more simply described as "pots not people" as, since the development of archaeogenetics in the early 2000s, a convincing argument has come down on the side of pots.

It appears that what we can now call the Celtic influence arrived slowly through interaction with European mainland groups, most likely resulting from the extensive trading activities we know took place on a regular basis.

The arrival of the Celtic influence prompted a huge change in the social, artistic, and religious activities of the existing populations of the region. The artistic influence may be seen in the many "Celtic" artifacts recovered over the past two centuries and in the well-known Celtic knotwork art and illustrative style. Jewelry, drinking vessels, weapons, and many other items have been recovered that display the particular style that has become known as Celtic. Even though there is little evidence to suggest that a common pan-European artistic style ever existed that may be categorized as Celtic, we have readily given the style of decoration and artwork visible on these artifacts a Celtic branding.

Similar influences may be seen in the evidence of clothing, food, and other aspects of everyday life following this period of change. The greatest of all was the introduction of iron. Whether we accept that iron be considered as part of the Celtic influence, or whether its arrival was a separate but coincidental phenomenon, the idea of the Celtic influence and the arrival of iron are synonymous to most historians.

The religious impact appears, on the face of it, to have been a slow and unimpressive takeover of the existing beliefs. For the greater part, it consisted of a renaming of much that was already established and the adoption of a small number of ceremonies and eventful dates that fitted neatly into the existing calendar of activities.

Some of the forces of nature recognized by the pre-Celtic population were given names by the new religion, and many of the heroes of the old tales of the region were elevated to the status of gods and given the names of the deities of Europe and Scandinavia.

The existing keepers of the nature lore were given a new name too, "Druid," and introduced to the philosophy of the new culture, some of which they accepted and some of which they rejected. This change, however, was the last and greatest influence on the lore of the Druid that we are exploring, and we shall read more about it as we progress.

The Iron Age, also known as the Age of the Celts, continued until the invasion of the Romans, their early attempt to eliminate the Druids, and the eventual arrival of Christianity that, for all intents and purposes, saw the suppression of the Druids and our Pagan belief system, a position from which we were never to fully recover.

The first extensive Roman campaigns in Britain were made by the armies of Julius Caesar in 55 and 54 BCE, but the first significant campaign of conquest did not begin until 43 BCE, in the reign of the emperor Claudius. As the Romans arrived at the borders of Wales, they encountered substantial resistance from the indigenous tribes who used the dense forests and mountains to wage a war of resistance.

The Druids were soon identified as a powerful force, and their long-standing Pagan belief system was a common force helping to bind the otherwise disparate Welsh tribes together.

The island of Anglesey was seen as having a particularly important role in the conquest of Wales. It was, at the time, the focal point of this common religion that bound the tribes together and of the Druids, who occupied the island, presenting the potential threat of a unified resistance against the imposition of the Pax Romana.

Finally in 61 CE Suetonius Paulinus,* Roman governor of Britain, invaded Anglesey, massacred the Druids, and burned their sacred groves. Unconvinced of their victory and aware of the reputation of the Druids' magic, the Romans remained conscious that the Druids posed a continuing threat. In an effort to subdue them, the Romans constructed the fortress of Segontium, present-day Caernarfon, to suppress the Druids' activities and contain them on the island.

The Druid massacre was a key event leading to Boudica's uprising, because Paulinus attacking Anglesey left the rest of the country open to attack, and as a result the history of Great Britain was changed.

The Romans occupied Britain for around 450 years, and very soon

---

*Gaius Suetonius Paulinus (first century CE) was a Roman general, best known as the commander who defeated the rebellion of Boudica.

following their initial campaigns the divine emperor Claudius decreed that throughout the entire Roman Empire, including Britain and Gaul, Druids were to be outlawed and executed on sight.

This action alone showed the fear that the Roman Empire had for the Druids. Renowned for their tolerance and acceptance of the religious practices of their subjects, the Romans had never before, or since, declared a priestly class outlawed.

The last of the occupying Roman forces left Britain around 410 CE, which began the sub-Roman period (the fifth through sixth centuries), but the legacy of the Roman Empire was felt for centuries, and neither the Druids nor their Pagan belief system ever regained their social significance.

Despite the efforts of the Romans, and others since, the Druidic lore survived. Much of the nature lore found its way into the rural folklore that survives to the present day, while a large amount of the herbal lore established itself in the cloisters and herbariums of the burgeoning Christian monasteries and was passed on to the apothecaries of the Middle Ages, who pioneered much of today's medicine and chemistry. Some of the magical lore was passed to the wisewomen and green men that carried it through the Dark Ages that followed, but the main corpus of Druidic knowledge, however, was retained within the oral tradition that we are exploring.

Following the Roman departure, nothing, and I repeat, nothing, has occurred to change or modify the Druidic lore. In short, the events of the subsequent seventeen hundred years to date have resulted in two outcomes. The first is the continuation of the oral tradition, which embodies the lore and belief system that originated in the early Neolithic period around six thousand years ago. The second is the emergence of a highly romanticized version of the Druidic character and a collection of what can at best be described as "Druid-friendly societies," which have facilitated the growth of a range of orders and guilds based on a mix of contemporary religious beliefs and the extrapolation and re-extrapolation of the famous two thousand words we discussed earlier.

This brief history is important to us as it paints a picture of the development of the peoples from whom the Druidic tradition emerged and reinforces the history contained within the oral tradition. The Pagan belief system, the ways of the Druid, and the lore that arose in the Neolithic Age continued without change until the arrival of the Celtic influence and underwent their final changes as a result of the Roman invasion.

Since then, the lore and tradition have remained unchanged and as such have survived the rigors of time, religious persecution, and romanticized exploitation.

And what has been the purpose of this brief voyage into the history of pre-Celtic society? It has been to demonstrate that there was a developed and sophisticated belief system existing for thousands of years before the Celtic influence arrived in Ireland, Wales, and the rest of what has come to be known as the Celtic homelands. The beliefs and practices that follow are drawn from a tradition that evolved during this pre-Celtic period and are much older and deeper than the Celtic-influenced belief system that arrived much later. The survival of this older, more fundamental worldview is due to the continuance of the Druidic oral tradition.

It has to be said that the Celtic influence had a major impact on all aspects of life, from the individual to the community, and many of the practices that follow were replaced or amended to encompass the new order.

Throughout all of this, the main character of our exploration has also survived intact, the class of learned men and women who were later given the name of Druid; and now we must look at what characterizes the Druid and his or her beliefs.

THE TRI-EMINENCE OF THE DRUID

We could begin this section by listing all of the comments and descriptions of the ancient Druids contained within the arcane historical accounts, primarily the accounts of the contemporary historians who may have actually encountered the Druids during their lifetime, the famous two thousand words, or maybe by looking at all of the subsequent accounts that have emerged from these two thousand words and the creative imagination of the writers.

Alternatively, we could begin with the etymology of the word *Druid* and follow the history of the language(s) and societies from which it arose.

Fortunately, both these routes have been well-trodden, and a plethora of books and articles exist that may be explored outside of this account.

Instead, we shall look at what is contained within the oral tradition, and at this stage we shall confine ourselves to what attributes make up the Druid and how these attributes align with the aspects of the natural world that the Druid works with. We shall leave the rudiments of the belief system until a later section.

The first notion of the Druid to be dispelled is that of the white-robed, golden-sickle-carrying ceremonial priest. The second is the relatively new contention that a student Druid progresses through the stages of Ovate and Bard before becoming a full-fledged Druid. Both of these notions are, as we shall see, misguided at best and misleading to anyone wishing to understand the world of the Druid.

We shall begin at what some may consider the end by asking, "When does a Druid become a Druid?"

In reply to this, we can refer to the many accounts of the rigors of learning Druidic lore, involving years of study and committing vast amounts of knowledge to memory. Some quote twenty or more years of preparation before the Druid is initiated, but what does the living oral tradition tell us? And at this point I will remind the reader that I refer only to the oral tradition that I have been taught and have grown up with. There are others, some of which agree with what follows, others of which have their own notion of teaching and initiation. I should also point out that, as the title of this book suggests, we are considering the aspects of the Druid in the pre-Celtic context, as this is the period when the Druid excelled in divination, so much so that only a small number of elements of the practice were subject to the later influence of Celtic culture. These elements may be considered as irrelevant to our exploration, which focuses entirely on the older tradition.

I have mentioned in the sections above two of the principles of progression toward being a Druid. The first is the idea of oaths of secrecy taken at specific points of learning; the second is the tenet of "naming." Other than these two secretive bindings, there is no actual initiation of the student Druid, as there is the universal belief that no one is actually in the position to declare a student qualified or conduct an initiation. Learning is described as the student sharing knowledge with the teacher on an equal status, with the student learning from the teacher and the teacher learning from the student/teaching process.

In short, students are considered to be Druids once they are accepted as such by the community they serve. Teachers introduce their students to the community when, and only when, they consider their pupils' knowledge to be whole. On most occasions, there follows a period where the community perceives the student as immature and consults mainly through or including the teacher, then inevitably, sooner or later, the community begins to consult the student as a Druid. This is when the Druid becomes a Druid. It is the decision of the community, not the teacher; and most importantly of all, students know when they are able to call themselves Druids. Typically, students are the last people to realize their competence and recognize their own status.

If we now take ourselves to the other end of the learning process, we can ask, "What makes someone want to become a Druid, and what personal attributes should one have to begin the rigorous training?"

In response to the first part of this question, I can say that I have encountered so many people with so many differing motivations that I find it difficult to define exactly what makes someone want to become a Druid.

If I ask this question of anyone, I have found that the most promising response is "I don't really know" or "I just do." It is my experience that the students who reply in this way are expressing an inner feeling that they may not be able to put into words, a feeling that is both instinctive and heartfelt and one that often results in the most committed and motivated students.

On the other hand, I have received responses that clearly indicate a deep thought process and serious soul searching. Often these replies reveal an unconscious connection to one of the three distinct methodologies of the Druid, also known as the tri-eminence of the Druid.

Of course, there are many, many other responses, and it is only by a mix of experience and intuition that one is able to determine which replies suggest a student will progress to become a Druid.

In reply to the part of the question that asks, "What personal attributes should a potential student possess?" we need to look first at the three natures of the Druid before we can align personal attributes to the requirements of each.

I have yet to encounter a single written account of Druidic lore or practice that identifies the three natures or eminences of the Druid, even though these three natures are paramount in defining the practices of the individual Druid. I have no idea why this is the case, as they are such a fundamental part of Druidic practice. I am happy to rectify this situation and explain the tri-eminence of the Druid as follows.

As most student Druids enter the early stages of their learning, it becomes apparent to the teacher that the student will adopt one of the three eminences of the Druid. All three are of equal status, all work within the same belief system, but each employs a different methodology in applying his or her skills.

The names of the three natures are translated as Craft Druid (or possibly Tool-user Druid), Elemental Druid, and Intuitive Druid. The titles describe the skills, methods, and attributes of the Druid and how she or he exercises these attributes within the tradition.

The Craft Druid applies his or her skills through the use of craft implements such as wands, stones, woods, herbs, and other items to be found on the recumbent working stone.* They are the wand makers, the skrying-mirror grinders, the stave carvers, and other craftsmen. As they are responsible for their crafting, they are also the great experts in their use.

The Elemental Druid is at one with the elements and works intimately with the forces of nature—water, air, earth, and fire. They do their divination using the forces of nature, such as rain (water), wind (air), and the other elements.

The Intuitive Druid is rare. We typically see no more than one Intuitive Druid in a generation. These are the individuals who are born with intuition that gives them insight into the relationship of mankind and the cosmos. In the early tradition, these were the Druids that revealed the lore and defined the practices that we are exploring here. They continue to bring to light new understandings and clarify complex issues. They are the Druidic philosophers, the resolvers of disputed issues, and the researchers and teachers that maintain and enrich the tradition over the years.

It is essential to remember that all three natures are considered equal; there is no hierarchy, and none are mutually exclusive. Craft Druids may call upon the elements in their rituals, Elemental Druids may use rude wands in their workings just as the Intuitive Druid may employ the wand in practice. Druids are trained in all three methodologies before finding their natural place in one of the three natures, just as medical doctors are trained in all aspects of medicine before they specialize in one field of practice.

History tells us that the Craft Druid has been the greatest in number and the Intuitive Druid is the rarest, with typically one or less per generation.

Throughout the history of the tradition, it has been a common practice for groups of three Druids to come together to form a

---

*The working stone is the Druidic equivalent of an altar. A recumbent stone is a long, flat stone similar to those in a stone circle, only lying on its side so that it may be used as a working stone.

binding. This binding is signified by a stele or token, usually made from clay. The clay token, in the form of a disc, is scribed into three sections before it is fired. A single section will eventually be given to each individual Druid and is inscribed with that Druid's unique mark (or "touch"). Once fired, the disc is ceremoniously broken into three pieces along the scribed lines, and each of the three Druids is given the piece bearing that Druid's own touch. This is how a binding is created. When the three Druids subsequently meet, they establish their binding by reassembling the disc, joining together the unique fractures that form the "combination code" of their binding. The strongest and most significant bindings in the tradition have been composed of one Druid from each nature, giving each equal status as all bindings do.

So, to return to the question of what attributes are required to become a Druid, you will see that different attributes may best suit any one of the three natures of Druid and will be identified during the early stages of the Druid's training.

The training and practice of every Druid is based on an arcane, but still vital, worldview. As we shall see, this worldview is a comprehensive belief system, embracing moral and ethical codes as well as the fundamental core values of a still apposite Pagan belief structure.

These core values are surrounded by what we can call generic wisdoms—traditions based on observation, experience, experimentation, and intuition. We can see that these wisdoms represent areas of tradition like ethics, nature, and magic. Although they are represented in figure 1.3 (on page 38) as being separated by strict border lines, in reality they often blur one into the other. It will not be difficult to imagine that, for example, it would be impossible to engage in weather lore without involving nature energies and elemental forces, but it seems to be in our nature to categorize things in a stricter way than we really should. It should also be borne in mind that each of these wisdoms has equal status. Although they are laid out in a particular way in the illustration below, this does not mean that they bear a strict relationship

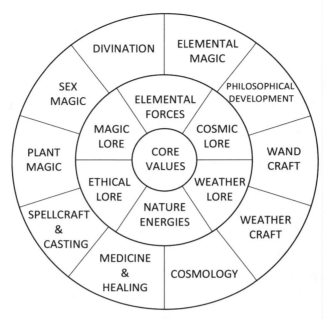

Figure 1.3. The core values of the Pagan belief system
maintained by the Druidic tradition.

to each other or that they are placed next to each other to suggest any specific relationship between adjoining sections.

In turn, these generic wisdoms are surrounded by the specific practices that allow the Druid to interpret them into everyday life. It is these specific practices and skills that form the interface between the tradition and the world at large—the Druid and the community.

Fortunately, it will not be necessary to explore all the aspects of Druidic lore to understand and practice pre-Celtic Druidic divination, but an understanding of the fundamental worldview is essential. This being the case, we should now begin our voyage of discovery into the rudiments of pre-Celtic Druidic divination by exploring the core values on which everything is built.

2

The Rudiments of the Pre-Celtic Druidic Worldview

We have seen that it would be difficult, if not impossible, to understand and eventually become involved in any of the crafts and skills of Druidic lore, including divination, without first gaining an understanding of the fundamental beliefs that underpin the knowledge and practices we intend to engage with.

Before embarking on writing this book, I spent the best part of a year consulting with two brother Druids of the same tradition as myself, meeting regularly to discuss exactly how the tradition could best be revealed in the context of the written word and what should not be disclosed for fear of misinterpretation. As a group we were amazed that even when we combined our experience, research, reading, and contacts, none of us had ever read a concise written account of the fundamental beliefs of Druidic lore. At various times, each of us had encountered tales of invented Druidic gods, fictitious myths, and distorted stories of arcane fables. Some of these were products of inventive imaginations, some claim to be the result of conversations with wood sprites and water nymphs, others were disguised as academic theory and research. Even though many of these accounts are written with the very best of intentions, none revealed what we had been taught as Druidic lore and tradition.

The eventual outcome of our deliberations was that it is for individuals to believe whatever they choose, and if the existing accounts convince a person, then all well and good, but it was time that the tradition that we each knew and were brought up with should be, to some extent, revealed. So, we set about debating just what should be included in this account.

We unanimously agreed that the single most important topic to be included was the core beliefs that have been so conspicuously absent from any previous publication, so we began exchanging the tales, parables, poems, and penillion* that we each held in our memories. This was an intriguing and entertaining experience, with each of us discovering new renderings of the version of the tradition we had remembered from our youth.

We finally decided to combine all that we had exchanged and render it into more direct language and, where possible, try to relate it to modern-day philosophical outlooks, to make it as relevant as possible to today's culture and the prospective reader.

What follows is the result of that combined process. We estimate that approximately 350 various poems, tales, parables, and penillion have contributed to the outcome. Each account has been evaluated, synthesized, and finally distilled into this account.

I have attempted to place each subject into a topic group so that the reader may approach them as different subject areas; however, like all aspects of nature, they are really all interrelated with no strict borders, each overlapping and intermingling with the other. Neither does this topic grouping suggest any hierarchy or infer that one topic holds prior-

---

*Penillion is the Welsh art or practice of speaking poetry in harmonious counterpoint to a traditional melody played on the harp. This was one of the skills of the Welsh bards that differentiated them from the Druids of the other regions of Great Britain. Penillion is still a thriving art and may be heard regularly at any *eisteddfod,* a Welsh festival of culture and the arts.

ity over another. Again, in nature, all things have equal status, and all are held in a natural balance.

ON CREATION

In 2007 Gallup undertook a poll with the title "Evolution, Creationism, Intelligent Design,"* an ambitious task to say the least. One of the most significant results indicated that 39 percent of the Americans polled believed that God (the Christian God) DEFINITELY created human beings in their present form within the last ten thousand years; a further 27 percent said that this was PROBABLY the case. This means that 66 percent (exactly two-thirds) believe that the Christian God definitely or probably created human beings within the last ten thousand years. A very significant majority!

Fifty-three precent of respondents in the same poll believed that God (again the Christian God) created man in his own image and by the methods exactly as described in the Bible.

Whatever your opinion may be regarding these results, they go some way toward illustrating our fascination in knowing how we originated, how long we have been here, and how long the planet that we inhabit has been in existence, as well as just who created it all in the first place.

This is by no means a new phenomenon. In fact, as far back as the seventeenth century, at least 128 different dates for the creation were calculated, the youngest being 3761 BCE and the oldest being 6904 BCE. Some of the most renowned individuals who calculated these various dates of creation include the Venerable Bede, who calculated the date as 5199 CE; Martin Luther, who gave the date as 4000 BCE; and the astronomer Johannes Kepler, who gave the date of the creation as 3992 BCE.

---

*2007 Gallup poll reference 21814. Available at https://news.gallup.com/poll/21814 /evolution-creationism-intelligent-design.aspx.

The precision of these individual dates is quite remarkable, but the most remarkable of them all was the date calculated by Archbishop James Usher,* the Irish-born archbishop of Armagh, who in his life's work *The Annals of the World,* first published in 1650, declares in the most quoted paragraph of the book that the world was created on:

Saturday, 22nd October, 4004 BCE,
at Six-o-clock in the afternoon.

The date, calculated in the most meticulous way, became the accepted date for the creation of the world for the next 250 years, and Christian Bibles printed as late as the early 1900s still had the date 4000 BCE inscribed in the margin alongside the beginning of Genesis, with subsequent dates inscribed for all the major events of the Old and New Testaments calculated from this starting point.

Most, if not all, of these dates have been calculated by taking an event at a known fixed date in history and calculating the generations back to Adam. This is, of course, not without its problems, and the apparent ages of some of the individuals included in the generation chain may stretch the imagination a little.

In reflection of the subject of divination, it is interesting to note that this same saintly James Usher, archbishop of Armagh, if he had happened to live in an earlier period, would most probably have been among those whose wide learning gained for themselves the title of magician or diviner, but he was, without discrimination, credited with prophetical powers. Most of his prophecies may be discovered in a small pamphlet of just eight pages, entitled "Strange and Remarkable Prophecies and Predictions of the Holy, Learned, and Excellent James Usher, &c. . . . Written by the Person Who Heard It from This Excellent

---

*James Usher was born in Dublin, Ireland, in January 1580. He entered Trinity College, Dublin, in 1593 at the remarkable age of thirteen. He was ordained as a priest at the tender age of twenty-one and was elevated to the archbishop of Armagh at forty-four. He took twenty years to write *The Annals of the World,* which was first published in Latin in 1650 and contained over two thousand pages.

Person's Own Mouth," published around 1656. Within this little pamphlet he is said to have foretold the 1641 rebellion in a sermon preached in Dublin in 1601.

> And of this Sermon the Bishop reserved the Notes, and put a note thereof in the Margent of his Bible, and for twenty years before he still lived in the expectation of the fulfilling thereof, and the nearer the time was the more confident he was that it was nearer accomplishment, though there was no visible appearance of any such thing.

Interestingly, he also foretold his own coming poverty and loss of property, which he actually experienced many years before his death.

The Reverend William Turner in his *Compleat History of the Most Remarkable Providences* (1697) recorded that: "A lady who was dead, appeared to him in his sleep, and invited him to sup with her the next night. He accepted the invitation, and died the following afternoon, 21st March 1656."

It is a remarkable fact that, despite the attitude of the church at the time, the archbishop was not persecuted in any way for his unorthodox practices and was never criticized or disciplined for his divination activities.

Having said all that, and to return to the main topic of this section, it is true that most of the world's religions have their own version of the origins of the universe, the world, and mankind. It is surprising just how similar many of them are, particularly as many of these civilizations would have had no contact whatsoever.

But what of the origin myth of the inhabitants of pre-Celtic Britain and Ireland? How did these ancient Pagans explain the coming into being of the universe, our world, and the arrival of mankind?

The Cosmogonic Myth

I have deliberately used the word *cosmogonic* here instead of *creation*. It describes the origins of the world and mankind in a neutral fashion as opposed to creation, which implies a creator. This latter, as we shall see later, is wholly inappropriate.

It may, or may not, surprise the reader to discover that our Pagan ancestors had no particular preoccupation with the way in which the universe came into being. Our small research group managed to recall three stories within the oral tradition describing how the universe appeared, but these refer to a chaotic cosmos that had no beginning, continues through the present, and has no end—a temporal and spatial continuum that just "is." It has been there forever.

For all intents and purposes, the universe of the Druidic lore we are exploring begins not when the cosmos came into being, but when ancient mankind first recognized the world around them and began our ongoing relationship within it.

The definitive story relating to this is one of the first to be introduced to students and one to which they will return to time and time again throughout their training. The relevant opening section begins

And when the time was right, and the mists had cleared, we came down from the high mountain and out of the dark forests into the unspoiled light to begin the endless journey of mankind within nature.*

In its original form, this brief account may be appreciated on a number of levels. The simplest interpretation is the obvious literal meaning. On other levels, the "mist" may be considered as humans' ignorance of their surroundings, and the "unspoiled light" is their growing intelligence and their understanding of the world around them and its gifts. This simple, short statement has been the source of endless hours of debate and meditation for students and teachers alike, and I continue to be amazed at the endless interpretations that have been offered over my years of teaching.

---

*This is the best translation the three of us could arrive at, though we all had to admit that it lacks both the poetic nature and profundity of the original Old Welsh.

Three other words from the quotation are of particular importance: "mankind within nature." This refers to mankind's intimate relationship with nature, a relationship that has a profound significance for mankind's progress and deserves a more detailed explanation.

The idea of mankind being an integral part of nature is a core belief in Druidic lore. We frequently hear discussion of mankind's relationship with nature and the impact that our actions are having on the environment and the natural balance of our world, but the fundamental problem here is the expression "mankind's relationship *with* nature." This suggests that mankind and nature are two different things. We are the only entities in our world (as far as we know) that have the arrogance to consider ourselves "outside" nature. Not only that, we also consider ourselves as being above or superior to nature. This is humanity at its most arrogant and self-opinionated. It is this idea of otherness or detachment from nature, which seems to have been the product of most developing civilizations, that leads to the greatest misunderstanding of Druidic lore.

The idea that mankind stands outside of nature, as an observer and *occasional* participant, is anathema to Druidic lore. No one, for example, would talk of a tree's relationship with nature or a butterfly's relationship with nature; the tree and the butterfly are considered part of nature. More than that, they *are* nature, and so is mankind. The folly of believing otherwise is there to be seen every day, yet we still have the conceit to proclaim ourselves as beyond what is seen to be the cruelty and savagery of nature and still seek to develop our feeble and inconsequential influence over nature's forces. It is the role of the Druid to ensure the oneness of mankind and nature and to try to understand at least some of nature's ways.

The other important message we can take from the quotation above is that Druidic lore has no creation myth and does not concern itself with how the cosmos came into being or if there was a prime mover, but rather considers the beginning of "our time" as when mankind first perceived the world and began its interaction with nature. Mankind's emergence from ignorance and recognition of our surroundings is the alpha point of Druidic lore and the first moment in the history of the tradition.

The Cosmos

Here, we should again remind ourselves that we are exploring the lore of the pre-Celtic Pagans of the isles of Britain and Ireland, the same peoples who erected the many megalithic monuments that still attest to their skills and insight. We must be cognizant of the cosmological theories that are associated with some of the stone circles and tombs they built at such effort and with such skill and accuracy.

There are many varied theories relating to the alignment of the various features of the stone circles and tombs, the reasons they were built the way they were, and the purposes they serve. Some of these theories are more fanciful than others. The more rational theories take note of the alignment of portal stones and recumbent stones to cosmological events at specific times of the year. Some alignments correspond to spring and autumn equinox and some to winter and summer solstice, all of which are indeed very important events in the Pagan and agricultural annual cycles. The consistency of the alignments suggests that they were not just random coincidence but were highly engineered to achieve their goal, a task that must have taken generations of observation and a sophisticated understanding of the annual cycle. As we are exploring methods of predicting future events, we cannot ignore the fact that these monumental "calendars" seem able to predict the imminent arrival of cosmic alignments and, more mundanely, the coming and passing of the seasons in a very practical way. It is not unreasonable to assume that much of the Druids' esteem may have been derived from their ability to foretell the coming of the spring or to forewarn of the imminent arrival of winter by using these cosmic clocks. Being able to predict the coming of such an awe-inspiring event as an eclipse must have given the average folk the impression of the Druid as being a magician or a wizard with an intimate relationship with nature. We are certainly led to believe that it gave the Druids the ear of chieftains and high kings of the time.

There is little doubt that the priestly/learned class of these early civilizations were closely involved in the planning, building, and regular use of these stone circles and tombs, and we cannot understate the important role these megalithic constructions played in the life of the community. Indeed, recent research has pointed to these megaliths as being not only the main focal point of the community, but the main founding point in the establishment of many of the tribal villages during this period of history.

Originally it was thought that once a small tribe, usually an extended family group, came together and began to abandon their nomadic hunter-gatherer lifestyle for a more settled agricultural and farming existence, sowing crops and raising herds of animals, they used the time they freed up from their hunting trips to develop belief systems that resulted in the building of the stone circles and tombs we see today. But recent research now leads us to believe that the circles and stones were built in auspicious locations *before* the communities were established, and once these extremely important sites were built, they attracted a population to settle around them.

Apart from the ever-increasing scientific evidence amassing in favor of this theory, it also goes some way to explaining why these early settlements were not always established in the most favorable locations for crop farming and animal husbandry. It also explains why many of the stone circles in particular are aligned to external features in the surrounding landscape, making use of mountain peaks and valleys to extend their projections instead of being placed amongst fertile pastureland or adjacent to water supplies.

This growing theory of the circle or tomb being built first and the population arriving after illustrates just how important our ancestors considered the edifices to be, so important that they would change their location and settle in a community just to be close to one of these features and be within the protection and guidance of the Druids, who were the only people with the knowledge to understand their function.

Druids, then and now, understand that by carefully observing our cosmos, we can predict when certain celestial features align and different seasons begin and end. This in turn tells us when it is the right time to plant crops, harvest and store food for the winter, see herds breeding and giving birth to new generations of livestock, build winter shelters, and so many other activities that have defined everyone's livelihood, both then and now.

These cosmic clocks and calendars were as important then as computers are today, and a similar form of dependence existed then as it does now, with everyone forming their lives around access to the technology of the day.

The tradition tells us that the cosmos is in a constant state of chaotic flux, and any appearance of order is a temporary phenomenon, with the cosmos soon reverting back to its natural chaotic state. This is the lesser-known reason for the early fascination with measuring the annual cycle and the alignment of celestial bodies. In addition to measuring the passing of the year, it also monitored the decay of the cosmic order and the inevitable return to chaos.

The idea of the cosmos being in a constant state of chaotic flux is fundamental to Druidic lore and pervades every aspect of the lore, from ethics and morals to the facilitation of rituals. We shall encounter this concept again and again as we progress through the following chapters, and it plays a central role in the practice of divination.

We shall see how the tradition explains our existence within a chaotic cosmos in detail later in this section.

The Passing of Time

Closely linked to the notion of observing the cosmos and the construction of stone circles and tombs is the pre-Celtic Pagan's concept of the passing of time.

The concept of time has been a major philosophical focus since mankind began its search to understand the universe we live in.

If you subscribe to the big bang theory, time began when the singularity containing our universe exploded and began its expansion. In this case, we can say that time is the measurement of the expansion of the universe. When did it actually begin? Well, as yet we have no definitive date. When and where it will finish? Again, the jury is still out. From the point of view of the Druid, time is a much more mundane and localized phenomenon.

We have become accustomed to measuring time by how long it takes us to orbit our sun, the time it takes our planet to rotate on its axis, and how long it takes our moon to orbit the earth.

In the days of the pre-Celtic Pagan, the passing of the years was measured by the position of the rising or setting sun in our sky in relation to fixed points on the horizon or in relation to the sun's alignment with standing and recumbent stones that were carefully positioned in the natural landscape by the learned Druids. The months were measured by the moon's phases, fattening and thinning as the month progressed. The days were measured by the rising and setting of the sun, knowing that the days lengthened and shortened as the seasons progressed.

A combination of these celestial movements and observations allowed the identification of the four most important days in the Druidic calendar: the two solstices and the two equinoxes. The two solstices are the longest and shortest days of the year, and the equinoxes are the two days of the year when night and day are of equal length. These were the times to mark the changing of the seasons and celebrate surviving the long hard winter, the planting of crops and birth of livestock, the fullness of the annual harvest. They also signified when to begin storing food for the coming winter.

The importance of these yearly rituals was observed by the early Christians, who tagged on their major festivals to the existing Pagan calendar. They fixed their major festival celebrating the birth of Christ to the winter solstice and the date of the crucifixion to the spring equinox (still a "movable feast" associated with the full moon of Pagan lore). Other Pagan features were also assimilated into the Christian festivals, such as the Christmas tree, the holly and the ivy, wreaths, and Yule logs. All were Pagan symbols of the evergreen gifts of nature that carry us through the winter with the anticipation of the abundant summer to come. The Easter egg now so familiar with the Easter celebration was originally a Pagan symbol of fertility and the fecundity of the burgeoning spring; the name of the Christian celebration itself, Easter, was the adaption of the Nordic Pagan goddess of fertility, Ester.

As well as these important quarter days, there is a similar importance placed on the midpoints of each quarter in the Pagan calendar. These days are also marked with celebration and feasting as significant points in the passing of the year.

In this way, the Pagan year is divided into understandable sections, each with its own relevance to the individual and the community, and each signifying a change in the work and life pattern of the pre-Celtic Pagan. It is not difficult to see how important a role the Druid played in being able to identify and even predict these unfolding seasons and the prestige the Druid must have enjoyed as a result.

It is also important at this point to consider the significance of the passing of time on the main subject of our exploration, divination. After all, the objective of divination is foretelling the future, predicting future events, even cheating time itself. We'll see in detail how we are able to do this later. For now, we will just look briefly at how the concept of the passing of time relates to pre-Celtic divination.

For a long time now, we have been encouraged to believe the ancient Celts used a wheel as a way of understanding the passing of time. We even have a popular modern image of the Celtic Wheel of Time, for which there is no provenance, divided into sections representing each of the quarter-years and with the cross-quarters subdividing each quarter. The year progresses around the rim of the wheel, moving from section to section as it goes. There are, however, two major difficulties with this representation. The first is that there is absolutely no historical evidence that this system was ever used by whom we now seem happy to call "the Celts," let alone the Druids of the pre-Celtic Pagans. Furthermore, it does not appear in any of the oral traditions that are commonly accepted. It is therefore difficult to suggest that this is a valid depiction, and this being the case, it may be inappropriate to use it as a foundation for divination.

The second difficulty is that the fixed wheel suggests that each successive year unfolds in exactly the same way. If your life is anything like mine, nothing can be further from the truth. While we can accept that the celestial year progresses through a predictable sequence, where the celestial bodies may be accurately placed at (slowly moving) fixed points, life on earth does not accurately repeat itself each year as a fixed wheel suggests. On any one day, in successive years, we may experience vast differences in weather, health, events, and so many other factors. It is not possible to represent such a random existence by using a fixed-wheel model. However, here we have a remarkable coincidence. There is a cartwheel involved in the principal story in the oral tradition relating to the passage of time.

In one of the paragraphs above, I mentioned the fact that there is no categorical evidence of the use of the Celtic Wheel of Time that we can use to substantiate its validity. I must, however, temper this comment by saying that the events we are exploring are prehistoric, by which I mean that they happened at a time and in a place where there were no contemporary means of recording the information. Similarly, there are no written accounts of the oral tradition that forms the basis of this exploration, so why should one version be believed and the other dismissed? The only reason I can give is that the one that I am going to relate makes more practical sense, whereas the fixed-wheel model is elaborated with titles and text that we know originated during the Romantic Period, where everything "Druidic" became extremely popular and embellished with Greek and Roman mythology, along with the use of modern Welsh and Irish language that would not have been around during the time of the early Druids. It is eventually for readers to determine which they consider to be most appropriate.

The parable my tutor shared with me is the story of a young man

in the early days of his Druidic training, when first gaining an understanding of the predictability of the celestial bodies and the alignments
of the rising and setting of the sun and moon. In awe at the magnitude
of the vast knowledge required to interpret the meaning of the celestial
bodies, he was also perplexed by what he considered to be an unresolv-
able contradiction. If the celestial bodies move in such a predictable way
that we can use their location to foretell the changing of the seasons,
how is it that we cannot use them to foretell the other daily events
in our lives? If the summer begins on the same day every year, with
the rising of the sun in exactly the same alignment, then why isn't the
weather the same on that day every year? And why is it that the same
events don't repeat themselves on the same day each year? Last year the
river froze on midwinter's day; this year it's running free. How can the
predictability of the planets be contradicted by the unpredictability of
daily events? Unable to resolve this dilemma, the student approached
his tutor for advice.

In those early days, the tracks were rugged, muddy, and littered
with stones, while the carts were crude with wooden wheels in need of
regular repair. When the student explained his dilemma to his tutor,
the learned Druid upturned a nearby wheelbarrow and began carving deep notches into the rim of its single wooden wheel. He continued until he had carved eight equally spaced grooves in the rim of the
wheel. Bidding his student to sit close to him, he began slowly rotating
the wooden wheel. As he did, he positioned a finger at a fixed point
near the rim of the wheel and explained to the young man:

"Each of these grooves represents an auspicious day in the cycle
of the year. Midsummer's day, the half quarter, the autumn equinox.
As the wheel rotates, each groove passes my finger in the same fixed
sequence, one after another, with an equal distance between each one
and at the same interval every time. Think of this as the cycle of the
celestial bodies. Each year, if viewed from the same location, the planets appear in a fixed sequence, one after another, at a fixed interval in
time. The sun rises at a fixed point, sometimes marked by a stone circle

alignment, sometimes by an alignment on the horizon, but always at the same time and in the same position. Similarly, it sets in the same way. Like our slowly spinning wheel, the celestial bodies rotate in a fixed, predictable manner."

The young student understood the fixed nature of the cosmos, but still remained confused by the contradiction of the random nature of everyday events. The tutor restored the wheelbarrow to its usual upright state and instructed the student to follow him to the edge of the rough track, studded with stones and deep muddy ruts.

"Would you agree that our rough, uneven track, with its ups and downs, bumps and grooves, could be seen as an illustration of how the world seems to present us with wholly unpredictable ups and downs, unseen obstacles, and unexpected occasional opportunities?"

The student agreed. He could see how the uneven track, strewn with muddy potholes and haphazardly littered with random-sized stones and rocks could represent the unpredictable world we live in. The tutor continued with his discourse.

"So, if the notches on the rim of the wheelbarrow's wheel represent the fixed system of the cosmos, and the uneven surface of the track embodies the randomness of everyday existence, what's missing from our example?"

The student thought hard. His eventual conclusion: "It must be us, mankind."

"Exactly. Let's see what happens when we introduce mankind, in the form of the simple worker, into the equation."

The Druid pushed the wheelbarrow along the rugged track and came to a halt around ten yards along. Walking halfway back along the track, he crouched down and called for his student to join him. Pointing to the furrow the wheel had made in the rough track, the Druid began his explanation.

"Here in this single furrow we see how mankind merges his existence with the cosmos and the chaos of the world. In forming the furrow, the wheel imprints each of the grooves we carved in it as it moves forward. Each equally spaced and each taking the same time to appear, always in the same rigid sequence, representing the fixed, predictable progression of the cosmos. At the same time, as the furrow is formed, the wheel navigates the uneven, random surface of the track, overcoming all the obstacles it encounters, big and small, ups and downs, surmounting every eventuality in its course, just as we do every day of our lives. So we can see that the true course of mankind may be seen, not in the rigid, repetitive order of the cosmos or the chaotic, uneven journey of worldly existence, but in the combined furrow each of us creates as we live our lives. Neither the fixed regimen of the wooden wheel nor the uneven surface of the track can represent a true depiction of our existence. Only the combined influence of the wheel, the track, and our efforts in making the furrow can truly represent our past, present, and future. Look to the furrow to understand the holistic nature of our being."

This parable is typical of the large number of similar stories that make up a significant part of the oral tradition as a whole, and like many others, it teaches us a number of things on a number of different levels.

In the broad sense, it reveals the importance of the one-to-one, intimate relationship of teacher and learner, the significance of the face-to-face learning process cherished by the Druidic community. It also illustrates the value of what we now describe as experiential learning—learning by discovery and demonstration. In particular, it demonstrates how the tutor uses everyday common objects and familiar events to explain complicated metaphysical concepts in a simple, easily understood way, like contextual learning. This has been the way of the Druid tutor for millennia, from a time long before the Celtic influence arrived on our shores.

On another level, it explains just how we, mankind, are the catalyst that combines the rigid system of the cosmos and the random events of our unpredictable existence in the mundane world. We, and not fate, forge our own unique furrow and make our own progress through the passage of time.

We shall encounter more parables as we progress through the chapters of this book. I hope they will present the reader with opportunity for reflection and provide inspiration for meditation. Over the years, I have found it useful to return to these valuable insights on a regular basis, and on each occasion, I have inevitably discovered a new revelation.

ON NATURE

Although humans are part of nature, human activity is often understood as a separate category from other natural phenomena.

The quotation I have included above is the second paragraph of Wikipedia's lengthy definition of "nature." Though to me it is a direct contradiction of all that I have been taught and believe, it is nevertheless part of a general description accepted by many of our fellow human beings. Every day, we witness the disastrous results of mankind's arrogance and ignorance of the true ways of nature. As we decimate forests, pollute our seas, consume our precious and irreplaceable natural resources, and continue to poison our atmosphere at an alarming rate, we seem to be working against nature and not within it. It is not a question of technological development, neither is it a defect in human intellect; it is a direct misunderstanding of our relationship within nature. Long before we began our scientific progress, long before the Industrial Revolution, eons before we began to develop thermonuclear devices, we had a very different relationship with nature. As I mentioned in the opening sections, when humanity began its development we considered ourselves nothing more than another aspect of a holistic nature that embraced all living entities.

Compare the quotation below from the Greek philosopher Socrates, some 420 years before the Common Era: "This world is indeed a living being, endowed with a soul and intelligence . . . a single visible living entity, containing all other living entities, which by their nature are all related."*

One may wonder how far we have developed intellectually as a race of beings in the last 2,500 years?

We will, however, see just how closely the early pre-Celtic Pagan Druidic lore agrees with this totally unconnected Socratic philosophy later. For now, we will simply concern ourselves with the concept of nature as a single, all-embracing entity, containing all living things in a delicate, equal balance.

Druidic lore provides that there is a cosmic force that permeates all living things, similar to Plato's anima mundi, or world soul.

The only significant difference is that Druidic lore extends this all-pervading force beyond the confines of the world to the entire cosmos. In particular, it tells us that it is also the force that drives and controls the entire cosmos, linking us to the celestial bodies and the energy that governs them. This belief is fundamental in understanding the functionality of the megalithic stone circles and tomb chambers that decorate our landscape in the hundreds, but this is a subject for another day.

ON GOD(S)

There are no gods! The forces and energies of nature control all that "is," and it is for us to acknowledge them as the supreme elements of our existence.

This very stark and bold statement is again taken from a parable maintained in the oral tradition. It is unambiguous in the extreme and leaves no room for misinterpretation.

If there were (and still are) no gods in the Druidic belief system, then we need to explain how many of the classical accounts refer to

---

*Taken from Plato's *Philebus* and also *Timaeus,* where he argues for the idea of a world soul or anima mundi.

ancient Druids worshiping a varied pantheon of gods, apparently easily aligned to the gods of other cultures.

The Druidic belief system does not, and never has, worshiped any gods whatsoever. We only venerate the elemental forces of nature, their origins, and their products. In witnessing the ancient veneration rituals, many of the uninvited raiders and occupying invaders misinterpreted these activities as acts of worship to the gods representing and controlling these same elemental forces in their own religions.

Unlike these other ancient religions, the ancient Pagan Druids had never subjected the natural forces they knew so well to the same process of personification.* Instead, they chose to interact in their own exclusive way directly with the forces that controlled their very existence. Neither the Vikings, the Pagan Romans, nor the later Christians understood this direct interaction with the elements. Instead, they in turn chose to identify the elemental forces with the humanistic god forms they had created for themselves, thinking that they were only translating the Druidic "god" names to their own language and aligning their beliefs with those of the Druids. They completely missed the fundamental differences in their attempts at religious syncretism. Fortunately for us remaining Druids, they did not succeed in their misguided efforts to blend religions, and our belief system remains unaffected; we still engage directly with nature without having to invent humanlike representations to worship.

A Teleological Argument?

If we are to accept that, as we stated at the beginning of this section, 53 percent of respondents polled believed that the Christian God created humans in his own image and by the methods exactly as described in the Bible, then it is important for us to address the teleological argument, also known as the argument for intelligent design. Stated simply,

---

*Personification is the attribution of human form and characteristics to abstract natural forces, like the seasons or the weather.

the argument goes that God, as an intelligent creator, must exist, as there is observable evidence of deliberate design in the natural universe. After all, our thesis is that there is NO God, so if there is no God, then who or what created us, how did it happen, and why do we look the way we do?

The tradition tells us that nature created and sustains us. The elemental forces of nature crafted us in the same way they crafted everything else in the natural world. This answer may not be as naïve and trite as it first sounds. It of course depends on how you define nature. Without going into pages of detailed explanation (as this is not the main topic of our exploration), I will suggest a few brief salient comments distilled from another of the parables within the tradition.

The Druidic worldview is not far removed from the Darwinian theory of evolution, stating that we were originally crafted in a simpler, less sophisticated form than we find ourselves in today and that we developed as we progressed through the ages and began to interact with our surroundings. This idea of evolving is repeated throughout the teachings of the tradition. There is no need for a creator god in this explanation, just a simple life-form created by nature that progressively developed into sentient human form and became the intelligent being that we are today. We were not created in the blink of an eye in the exact form of the creator, but became who and what we are because of the necessities of the natural world and our need to live as part of it—a natural process of physical and mental evolution.

The Apotheosis of Forces

When considering how outsiders may have viewed the ancient Druids' form of ritual, we should also consider the fact that Druids then and now also revere their predecessors as learned teachers, particularly their Intuitive Druid ancestors. This may well have been seen as apotheosis by onlookers who failed to understand the true meaning of what they were witnessing. For the sake of clarity here I should explain that in this analogy, apotheosis refers to the idea that an individual has been raised to godlike stature and becomes a subject of worship as a god in his or her own right. But in the case of the ancient Druids, it is more the case that the very forces that they acknowledged as being the vital elements of existence were subjected to ritual veneration and that ancient ancestors are only venerated for their knowledge, achievements, and the insights they revealed to their descendants.

It is critically important, however, to understand the absence of a creator god in the context of this work as, although we have adopted the term *divination*, we are not in any way consulting a divine being to foresee the future as the word suggests. We will be working with very visible natural forces and not conferring with imaginary divine entities.

ON HUMANITY

Another equally important aspect of the core values of Druidic lore is how we view humanity, what being human means, and what values we apply when interacting with other human beings. This was, and still is, the basis of our society—dictating our behavior, morals, and ethics—and it also forms the basic rules by which we live and behave.

The Composition of Life—The Ternary Self

Each of us is composed of three building blocks. The Old Welsh word for this translates best as *ternary*—a single thing made up of three equally significant parts; each depending on the other in symbiosis and neither one able to exist without the presence of the other two.

The most obvious and most visible of these three components is our physical form, our material self. To some, our physical self represents our presence in the world, to others it is the receptacle that holds our spiritual being. In Druidic lore, our physical form is an inseparable part of the ternary self. It's what we look like, it's how we move, and it can be other peoples' first impression of who we are.

The other two components are more esoteric in their nature.

The first of these is the all-pervading world force—the elemental energy that fuels all animate entities. This energy has been variously described as the world soul, anima mundi, *unus mundus,* and many other titles. The Welsh best translates as "communal energy"—the force that belongs to us all and drives all living things, including ourselves.

The remaining force is the most personal and individual of all. It's a tiny but unique portion of this communal force that we each hold as a personal energy. This energy fuels our personality—our unique self that identifies us as an individual among the many.

These three components combined make us who and what we are; they're what make me ME and what make you YOU.

The Beginning of Life—The Life Force

I imagine we all know the process of the creation of our material self: conception, gestation, and birth. It's yet another three-step process that appears so often in the natural world. Each of us is imbued with the communal energy, the anima mundi, even before we are conceived. As this energy is present in all living things, it is present in both of our parents; it's in our father's sperm and our mother's egg. These two things come together at the moment of conception and are nurtured in our mother's womb, immersed in the communal energy of her body.

At the moment of birth, precisely at the moment of our very first breath, we breathe in our greatest gift from nature: our own unique life force or our personal energy. This is the moment we become the distinct creation, our self.

The Passing of Life

During our lives each of the three components change. The changes in our material, physical self are the easiest to perceive. Our material bodies grow through childhood to maturity, changing as they develop. As we grow old, our material bodies deteriorate until eventually they cease to function and we die. It's a slightly cynical but accurate synopsis. At the moment of death, the world spirit, our communal energy, ceases to exist, as it is only present in living entities. But what of our personal energy, the force that nature gave us at the very moment of our birth? Is this extinguished at death? Does this force that we have fashioned and developed throughout our lives just evaporate?

Herein we find another of the great misconceptions of Pagan Druidic lore. According to the sparse historical accounts, we Druids believe in reincarnation. Apparently, we die only to be born again in the same form as the same "self." It is not difficult to understand how this misunderstanding occurred; hopefully the next paragraph will explain.

The tradition tells us that during our lifetime our personal force dwells within us. It forms us, and we form it. When we are imbued with our individual personal force at our first breath of life, it is already influenced by every other living entity that preceded our birth. Once again, this is best explained by a parable from the teachings of the tradition.

We imagine a Druidic teacher and his neophyte pupil walking along the shoreline of an infinitely long beach. The young pupil eats berries as he walks barefoot at the edge of the ocean. Already content with his understanding of his material self, he searches for an insight into the two other components of his being. His tutor begins his explanation:

"In searching for knowledge of the communal energy, let me ask you, "Do you feel the warm wind against your face?" The young student nods. "Do you hear the sound of the waves, smell the salty air, and see the power of the ocean as the waves crash on the sand?" Again, the student nods his agreement. "Well, these are just some of the forces that fuel and nurture all living things, along with the elements. This same force is within you and drives you in the same way as the waves at your feet and the wind in your hair. Do you feel this energy within you, just as you feel the wind and the water?"

"Yes," replied the student. "I understand how this force drives us and how it is extinguished when we die, just like the flame of a candle dies when there is no longer any material for it to burn. But what I don't understand is how our personal energy doesn't die or become extinguished in the same way?"

The Druid gives his student a wooden beaker and asks him to fill it with sea water from the ocean beside him. The student does as he is asked and holds the beaker out before his tutor who continues to explain.

"This is your personal energy, taken from the infinite reservoir of the ocean. It already has its own qualities when you received it; it is wet, salty, and cold. It has a weight and an odor. It has sustained life, fish, seaweeds, and other unknown species of the deep. It is yours to possess during your lifetime, and you may do with it as you choose, but bear in mind that whatever you do will affect it and that it will remember your actions and decisions and hold you to account for them. Now, take three of your dark berries and squeeze the juice from them into the beaker."

Again, the young student follows his tutor's instructions and squeezes the berry juice into the seawater in the beaker. As he does so, the water turns dark red.

"You see how your actions have changed the color of the seawater in the same way that they influence your personal energy, changing it forever. You can never change the seawater back to its original color, and you can never undo the influence your actions have in forming your personal energy. Now pour your beaker of water back into the sea, from where you took it in the first place."

For the final time, the student adhered to his tutor's instructions. He poured the dark red water back into the ocean. As he did so, the berry-colored water stained the ocean momentarily before being diluted and dispersed into the vast waters of the ocean.

"When we die, this is how our personal energy is returned to the world soul, the communal energy. We are imbued with our own small portion of the greater energy for our lifetime, and then it returns to the whole. It is not extinguished but reunited. But with this gift comes responsibility. You saw how your berry-colored water stained the ocean and was absorbed by its vastness? This is exactly how your personal energy influences the much greater energy, by influencing it when it is reunited with its original source. No matter how small and insignificant this influence may be, it is still there. And just as the next person who fills a beaker with seawater from the ocean will take with him some small part of the water colored by your actions, no matter how little it may be, so will the next newborn, taking its first breath, be imbued with its small part of the world soul as its own unique personal energy, colored and influenced by your life actions. No matter how diluted the influence of your actions may be in the vastness of the world soul, it is still there, shaping every future generation, until the end of time. Every action you take and every decision you make influences every other individual, forever. Understand the importance of this responsibility, and you will live a full and useful life."

The idea of this ternary being is comparable to the Cartesian dualist model of the mind-body relationship, where the mind (for mind, read personal energy) is considered an independent nonmaterial entity temporarily inhabiting a material body. It is also comparable to Gilbert Ryle's "Ghost in the Machine" concept—when the machine dies, the ghost leaves the machine—even though Ryle argues against the dualist proposition.

Behavior, Morals, and Ethics

The tradition tells us that we have no god(s). This in turn means that we have no judgmental being to reward us with everlasting life in heaven at the end of a "good" life or punish us with eternal damnation in hell if we transgress. We have no divine being to hand down to us a code of behavior, dictate a moral code, or determine our ethical standards. There's no divine intervention, no one to pray to at times of difficulty, no one to offer forgiveness for our sins, and no one to offer us absolution so that we may live forever in heavenly bliss. Instead, we are told that all of this is left to us, with individuals forming their own life code and free to live a life with only themselves to determine what is right and what is wrong. But, as we shall see, with this freedom comes great responsibility.

As we have no gods to dictate how we live our lives, how then do we establish our life code and personality? Are we born with a set of instinctive rules of good and bad that allow us to live our lives and interact with the society in which we live? The simple answer is no, we are not.

We are told by the tradition that we are born with our minds in a totally free and empty state, unprogrammed and containing no pre-established rules or standards, in what has been called a state of tabula rasa, meaning blank slate. Therefore, all knowledge comes from experience or perception. From the very moment of birth, we begin to learn our life code and establish our own standards of behavior, moral integrity, and ethical values. All of these aspects of our self are a result of nurture and not nature.

Nearly all of us live within a society that, for good or bad, subjects us to a certain set of rules that determine our mutual behavior in order for the society to survive. Some might suggest that these rules are god-given, even though each religion interprets them differently. For all the Abrahamic faiths, for example, the Ten Commandments form the basics of their moral code. Literally carved in stone, these few simple laws were expanded to suit the various priorities of the individual belief systems as they evolved. This, of course, cannot apply to Druidic lore as we have no god to hand us down such a set of rules. Others suggest that we are born with an inherent sense of what is right and wrong, a set of universal values that determine how we behave. Again, within Druidic lore this cannot be the case, as each of us is born in a state of tabula rasa, without any preprogrammed values. Therefore, there is no universal human nature, so all the aspects of our personality, social behavior, understanding, and knowledge must be learned. But, as we shall see, this does not mean that each of us needs to discover all these things for ourselves. We needn't reinvent the wheel for each new generation. The rules become established, and they are passed on. To illustrate this, let's look at one of the most significant rules within our society: you must not kill another human being.

It is not difficult to imagine a time early in our evolution when we first began to gather together in groups and establish our first small societies. Usually extended families would have stayed together for protection and to combine their efforts in hunting and gathering. No longer alone, the individuals in the group would have enjoyed not having to be constantly on guard, looking out for the invasive dangers around them, by being able to share this protective role with others in their small group. They were now able to turn their attention to other things. But this could only happen if they were confident in the other members of the group's ability to stand guard, secure in the knowledge that they were safe within their own protected society. But what if they were under constant threat of being harmed or even murdered by the other members of their group? We are told by the tradition that the members of these small tribes came together and agreed that they would not, under any circumstances, harm each other. If anyone was to do so, then the other members of the tribe would punish them accordingly. This may well have been their first rule, the first law, making individuals accountable for their actions and imposing punishment where due.

We go on to learn that other rules were agreed on: no one would take another person's possessions, no one would take another person's family members, and so it went on as needs demanded. Eventually a set of rules evolved, a Ten Commandments of the pre-Celtic Pagan world that went on to form the basis of such systems as the Brehon Law of early Ireland.

This evolving system of law was passed on from generation to generation, developing as time progressed and becoming more complex as these small groups grew into larger and larger tribal societies. The rules survived and continued to develop simply because they worked. They made it possible for people to coexist. Passed from one tribe to another, they laid down ground rules and a code of behavior that allowed tribes to live alongside each other, settle disputes, and avoid conflict. They eventually became common laws, agreed to by neighboring chieftains, and subsequently entered the domain of the Druid. It is important to remember that the ethical and moral code of Druidic lore applies equally to mankind's relationship within nature as it does to each person's relationship to other people.

As there was no god to dictate what was right and wrong, our ancestors evolved a natural code of conduct based on their observation of nature and the practicalities of everyday coexistence.

The dualistic concept of good and bad, right and wrong, and light and dark is discussed at length throughout the teachings of the tradition, so it is only right that we look at how Druidic lore embraces the notion of the conflict of good and bad in nature.

As we have seen, we are not brought into this world with any sense of what is good or bad. We each have to build our own unique understanding from what we observe, what we experience, and what we are taught, synthesizing all of this learning into our own individual set of values. This in turn means that every individual possesses an absolute right of self-determination, together with the responsibility that accompanies it. We have no gods or devil to blame when bad things happen, no ultimate being to offer us a meaning to our lives, and no universal goal for salvation or enlightenment. There is also no supreme being tempting us with a promise of eternal life after death in an elusive paradise beyond the clouds. We do, however, have the teachings of the tradition to help and guide us in our life journey.

The dualistic model of good and bad, although not innate, is more or less universal to all worldviews, though it is expressed in a myriad of different ways. The overarching question is "Who decides what is good and what is bad?" In Druidic lore, the answer in threefold.

First, as individuals, we each arrive at our own sense of what is good and what is bad through the process described above. This is an intrinsic element of our individual worldview. It is part of what makes each of us who we are.

Second, we do not live in isolation; we each live within a society that has its own interpretation of good and bad. Different societies have different values. Some are set by consensus, others may be imposed by secular or religious dictatorship. Hopefully we each have the freedom to choose which society we live in, and an important factor in that decision is consideration of the rules that govern that society. In simple terms, individuals should consider how the values of the society they live in compare with their own personal set of values. If they are compatible then there is accord, if they are not then maybe the individual should relocate or, alternatively, seek to change the values of the society by reasonable means. This imperative applies as equally to modern societies as it did to the ancient tribal groups we looked at earlier, bearing in mind that an individual's sense of good and bad, as fundamentally important as it is, is only one aspect of what shapes the society in which we live.

Third, in nature there is no such thing as bad; there is only good. No actions in nature are a result of a prior consideration of what is good or bad. This is one of the primary proofs of the lack of a predetermined universal concept of good and bad. In nature, things just "are." People have said to me that natural fires, floods, hurricanes, and volcanic eruptions, each of which may result in the death of thousands of innocent individuals, are examples of nature being bad, but although the results of these natural disasters are of course bad for the people involved, they are not the result of nature making a conscious decision to be bad. They are, for the greater part (if we ignore the consequences of our abuse of nature as a whole), random events with no intentional cause. In nature, the opposite of good is not bad, it's random chaos. The only bad things that happen in nature are due to our own irresponsible interference.

The tradition goes on to tell us that all morals and ethics are subjective. Each is a value judgment made from the perspective of the individual, within a specific set of circumstances and at a certain time. This is not so contentious at both extremes of the good-bad continuum but means that each individual is free to decide where to position each action along the infinite shades of gray that extend from absolute bad to absolute good.

Because we live in a world that is ultimately controlled by nature, despite our futile efforts to subject it to our will, we can assume that the normal state of being is inherently good. Therefore, we cannot be bad without making a conscious effort to be so. It is not possible to be accidentally bad; it has to be a deliberate intention. There are no such things as involuntary acts of evil.

In the medieval manuscript the *Malleus Maleficarum* ("The Witch's Hammer"), there is an interesting quotation from Aristotle. The manuscript, written as the handbook of the Catholic witchfinders, outlines the characteristics that help to identify a witch and goes on to outline the many "authorized" forms of torturing and killing of the poor suspected witch. Within the manuscript, there is a debate on the definition of good and evil, and to quote from the learned script on the subject of involuntary evil deeds: "Aristotle 3 *Ethics*. A wicked act, [he says] is a voluntary act, and he proves it by saying that no one acts unjustly unless he wants, of his own will and accord."

For our part, there is a simple demonstration used to illustrate this proposition.

Imagine if we take a piece of plain white paper, place it on a table, and position a small ring (like a wedding ring, for example) near the center of the paper. It would help if the ring were secured in its position with a little blue tack or something similar to stop it from moving. Now, using a pencil, write "bad" inside the ring. Place the pencil tip anywhere on the paper and begin to draw a continuous, random line on the paper without lifting the pencil; the line represents the progress of our everyday lives. We can draw our line in any direction—straight, curved, in circles, however we like—but, as we cannot lift the pencil tip from the paper, if we bump up against the outer side of the ring we have to go around it or set off in another direction. We can continue indefinitely, drawing our path in whatever random direction we choose, but if we want to go inside the ring we have to make the conscious decision to lift the pencil tip and place it in the "bad" area. The purpose of the exercise, as you may have deduced, is to demonstrate that the white paper represents the inherent state of good within nature, the pencil line represents our life path when we live within nature, the ring is the boundary between good and bad, and the area inside the ring represents the bad actions in our lives. The demonstration illustrates the concept that we live naturally in a state of good and have to make a conscious decision and action in order to be bad. The glaring question that remains is "Who decides the diameter of the ring, and how high its wall is?" We each decide these things for ourselves using the conditions set out above.

We shall see later that a sense of good and bad is essential to the practice of divination, at least in the Druidic tradition, and by embracing the criteria outlined above when we contemplate the insights we gain, we can interpret them within our own moral and ethical code.

ON DIVINATION AND FORESIGHT

We will look at the various aspects of Druidic divination in the next part, but it is worthwhile to explore one of the most quoted methods attributed to Druidic lore in recent history.

Inevitably, whenever I mention the idea of divination as practiced in the ancient societies that lived in the lands we now call Ireland, Wales, Scotland, Cornwall, northern France, and the Basque region on the borders of France and Spain, people first talk of the Celts, maybe not realizing that the history of divination goes back to long before the Celtic influence arrived in these regions. Secondly, they mention the Ogham runes of the Druids, one of the methods of divination most people seem to know and still use today. This being the case, I think it important for this exploration that we take a little time to look at the Ogham alphabet system, as it is not included in any of the methodologies outlined in the praxis section later in this book.

Before we consider how Ogham is used for divination, we should look at Ogham itself.

There are many varied accounts of the origin and history of Ogham, a system described as an early medieval alphabet used to write the Primitive Irish language. Originating around 100 to 400 CE, it consists of a series of markings, usually carved in groups of horizontal and diagonal grooves on two sides of one edge of small and medium-sized stone megaliths. There are some four hundred surviving examples, the bulk of which are in the southern region of the Irish province of Munster (where I happen to live), with the largest number outside Ireland in Pembrokeshire, Wales (close to the area where I was born). Examples may be found in their original locations and in the national museums of both Ireland and Wales. The vast majority consist of inscriptions of personal names, assumed to be the names of local chieftains and other important individuals. Some may mark graves, while others may be purely commemorative.

Figure 2.1. An ancient Ogham stone at the Gap of Dunloe, Killarney, county Kerry, Ireland.

In considering how and why they were invented, there are many and varied sources, each claiming greater credence than the other and each claiming to be the authentic and original authority. For the sake of clarity, I have chosen to refer to the seminal account compiled and edited by George Calder and published in November 1916.

Calder's *Auraicept na n-Éces* (The Scholars' Primer) is considered the most authoritative account of the origins and meaning of the Ogham alphabets (yes, there is more than one alphabet). It is a compilation of three ancient manuscripts with commentaries and explanation added by the author. A summary of the sources used may be seen in the subtitle of Calder's single edition as follows:

AURAICEPT NA N-ECES
The Scholars' Primer
Also known as
The Handbook of the Learned

Being the text of the Ogham tract from The Book of Ballymote and
The Yellow Book of Lecan and the text of The Trefhocul
from The Book of Leinster.

Edited by
George Calder

The book, now out of print, runs to 375 pages on the single subject of the Ogham, so I have chosen the extracts below very carefully, as this is not the main focus of our exploration. Calder includes numerous photographs of the original manuscripts and writes the book in the language of the original text as well as in English translation.

The manuscripts of the *Auraicept,* claimed to be seventh-century works, tell us that Fenius the Filí "discovered" four alphabets: Hebrew, Greek, Latin, and finally, Ogham. The latter was considered to be the most perfect and important, as it was discovered last. The filí's role in early society was one of magician, lawgiver, judge, counselor to the chief, and poet. Later, but still at a very early time, these functions seem to have been divided between three distinct scholarly groups: the Brehon, devoting themselves to the study of law and the giving of justice; the Druids, claiming for themselves the supernatural functions, including the art of divination; and the Filí, being principally poets and philosophers, similar in nature to the Welsh bard.

The *Auraicept* tells us that: "The poets filí were a secretive society, with a language peculiar and intelligible to themselves only. According to their tradition, Fenius, at their request, devised this language for them and its obscurity was essential."

Later in the text we are also told that Ogma, son of Elatha and Delbaeth, was the inventor of Ogham (well, maybe?), and as to why it was invented, we are told: "The cause of its invention, as to proof of his [Ogma's] ingenuity, and that this speech should belong to the learned apart, to the exclusion of rustics and herdsmen. . . . The father of ogham is Ogma, the mother of ogham is the hand or knife of Ogma."

We have no fixed date for the emergence of Ogham, though recent research suggests a date somewhere between 100 and 400 CE. Certainly from the phonological evidence, it is clear that the alphabet predates the fifth century. In Ireland and Wales, the language of the monumental stone inscriptions is termed Primitive Irish, with a later transition to Old Irish. Both of these languages predate the arrival of the Celtic influence.

So we have mixed messages regarding the origin of Ogham, but we can plainly see that the alphabet was indeed a coded system of early writing, devised to be read only by an elite section of society. Later history suggests it was also used as a way of recording information about the burial places of prominent leaders and Druids that was unintelligible to the occupying Romans, who may otherwise have desecrated their burial places and physical remains in the name of Roman Paganism and later in the cause of the burgeoning Roman Christian faith.

The major body of text within the *Auraicept* involves an extensive analysis of the grammar and structure of the symbols involved in the alphabet, all of which is irrelevant to our purpose. However, the final sections disclose information that may be surprising to most readers.

One of the closing sections entitled "Forms of the Ogham Alphabet" contains a list of the various forms in which the alphabet may be employed. It lists no less than ninety-three different types, giving detailed explanation of how each one is encoded. The list includes a collection of intriguing form names, such as:

> The Egyptian Alphabet
> The Boat Ogham
> Oblique Ogham
> The Stream Strand of Ferehertne
> Well-Footed Ogham
> Snake Through Heath
> Shield Ogham
> Lively Dotting
> Corn Field Under Color
> Combative Ogham
> Ogham of Uproar of Anger
> Anguish of the Poet's Heart
> Secret Ogham of the Warrior Bands

And my personal favorite:

> Ogham Which Confused Breas, Son of Elatha,
> Who Was under a Prohibition Not to Pass On
> without Reading It

Each form includes a specific coding that further confuses the uninitiated reader. One typically fascinating example, the Fraudulent Ogham, is explained as: "Fraudulent (Ogham) here, each group's defrauding another of the initial letter. It is the second letter of the second group which ends the first group." The description of each of the other forms is equally confusing.

Figure 2.2. Ogham "letters," carved at the edge of an ancient Ogham Stone near the Gap of Dunloe, Killarney, county Kerry, Ireland.

We can clearly see that the Ogham inscriptions are multilayered coded messages designed only to be translated by the initiated reader. The first layer is the horizontal and diagonal grooves that represent the corresponding letters; the second is the fact that they translate into Primitive Irish, a language only read by the learned few; and the third is that the letters were rearranged into discrete forms decipherable only if the reader knew the code of that particular form. The result? A very sophisticated method of writing a secret message that, for the greater part, was simply a person's name.

The use of Ogham progressively declined over the subsequent years, only to reappear during the medieval period, when the romanticized idea of associating each of the letters with an indigenous tree name inspired peoples' imaginations. The most prominent letters, known collectively as Beith-Luis-Nin, are each the Irish for a different tree and together became the favored name for the now simplified Ogham alphabet. This alphabet also became known as "The Tree Alphabet."

It was this tree alphabet and its association of each letter with a tree, viewed in terms of the spiritual aspects of that tree, that developed into the notion of using Ogham as a form of divination.

These days, it is fair to say that the main, if not exclusive, use of Ogham by neo-Druidism is for Tree Alphabet divination. A similar method of divination was mentioned in the *Tochmarc Étaíne*, one of the tales of the Irish Mythological Cycle, where a Druid takes four wands of yew, writes Ogham letters on each, then uses them for divination. However, there is no explanation as to how the sticks are handled or interpreted. It appears that each letter is associated with a tree, and meanings are derived from the attributes of each.

The Wikipedia article "Ogham" sheds light on the more recent development of Ogham as a method of divination, saying that:

> Robert Graves' book, *The White Goddess,* has been a major influence on assigning divinatory meanings for Ogham. Some reconstructionists of Druidic ways use Bríatharogam kennings as a basis for divinatory meanings in Ogham divination. The three sets of kennings can be separated into Past-Present-Future or Land-Sea-Sky groupings in such systems, but other organizing structures are used as well.

In the context of our exploration, all of the Ogham systems arrived at a much later date than the pre-Celtic Pagan methods we will be focusing on, while the notion of using Ogham as a means of divination is relatively modern by comparison.

It is only reasonable to say that all the accounts of the origins of the Ogham systems are taken from an oral tradition that, like most accounts from prehistory, were written down many years later. On the verge of myth and history, the accounts include references to fairy folk and magical lands, but the bulk of the text is verifiable from very real megalithic monuments located in the rural countryside of Ireland and Wales.

It is also worth noting that all the accounts referred to above, as with the *Tochmarc Étaíne,* maintain that the original Ogham were carved onto wooden staves, not stone. This idea was revisited in the late eighteenth century by Edward Williams, better known by his bardic name Iolo Morganwg, an influential Welsh antiquarian, poet, and collector of medieval Welsh literature. He invented an alphabet similar to standard Ogham, which was carved on to short wooden staves of square cross section. These staves were then assembled onto small racks and, when read together, formed the complete text. Morganwg named the system *Coelbren y Beirdd*, known as "Clever Wood of the Bards" or "the Bard's Alphabet" in English. Although Morganwg claimed a definitive provenance for his alphabet in prehistory, he was renowned as a prolific literary forger and was never able to support his claims. For those interested in the Coelbren, Nigel Pennick's book, *Ogham and Coelbren: Mystic Signs and Symbols of the Celtic Druids* (2000), gives an interesting insight.

There is much more to be learned about the Ogham, and I urge the reader to research the numerous sources on the subject. But for our purposes, the brief insight above is sufficient to give a critical overview of how Ogham divination may work and how it evolved.

It may be an indulgence, but I cannot resist ending this section quoting the wonderful closing words of the *Auraicept* itself:

"How is that, pen? And methinks it is good"

The art of divination, however, has frequently been associated with evildoing, magic, and witchcraft. This has never been more evident than in the medieval period, particularly during the time of the Catholic witchfinders, who hunted many wisewomen, nature crafters, and even some female Druids (incidentally, female Druids are not Druidesses, any more than female doctors are to be called doctoresses or female accountants, accountantesses).

To take another extract from the infamous *Malleus Maleficarum*

Diviners (*Divinatores*): Since this noxious superstition takes various forms, with the result that if [the wrong-doing] is well-known and public, the practitioner should be denied Holy Communion. If it is done in secret, he or she is to do penance for forty days *(De consecratione, distinctio)*. Likewise, if he is in holy orders, he is to be deprived of them and imprisoned in a monastery. If he is a layperson, he is to be excommunicated. Likewise, discreditable persons of this kind ought to be censured, as well as those who resort to them, and must not be used as informers at all [The author refers to and quotes from various statutes dating from Roman and Byzantine times to show that diviners and magicians were thereby sentenced to death. The laws also say that anyone may be used as an informer against them]. Anyone is admissible as an informer in this case, just as in the crime of lese-majesty, because Diviners are more or less assaulting the majesty of God. Likewise, they should be questioned under torture. [The law] adds that anyone, regardless of his or her rank, may be put to torture; and whoever is found guilty, even if he lays bare his crime, should be surrendered to the rack, have his flanks torn open with hooks, and endure the penalties appropriate to his crime, as it says in Justinian's Codex. Please note: in the old days, such people were punished by means of a twofold penalty— by death and by animals' claws. Their body was torn to pieces or they were thrown to wild animals to be eaten. Nowadays, however, they are burned, perhaps because of the female sex. (Translated by P. G. Maxwell-Stuart [Manchester University Press. 2007], notes in brackets are Maxwell-Stuart's)

Let's hope that today's Druidic diviners are treated with a little more tolerance.

ON THE END OF TIME

All things must come to an end. This is an inevitability of the cosmos, and our ancestors were well aware of this phenomenon. Every day, they would have witnessed events that confirmed that nothing lasts forever. The passing of their family members, the death of their cattle, the arrival of the winter that heralded the dying of their crops and the plants of the wilderness, and the certainty of death were commonplace parts of their existence. But even as they lived hand in hand with the fact that death is inevitable to all living things, we can see from the above sections that there was, and still is, a belief that death is not the final end to anything. Our personal energy returns to the great whole of the world spirit, many plants are "reborn" in the spring, and our family and clan live on through the newly born, who themselves grow to produce generation after generation through a continuing life cycle.

It may sound naïve, but the Druidic tradition gives no consideration to the fact that all this may someday come to an end. It is, after all, a code for living, not a code for dying. It has no need to consider the end of time, as it does not offer any incentives related to the end-of-time event. The best way to explain this will be for us to look at what other belief systems make of the end of time, even though we can be sure that these comparisons were not available to our Pagan ancestors. We need to look at what religious scholars and theologians have called eschatology.

The Eschatological Myth

It is not surprising that most of the world's belief systems have, at their core, some form of afterlife promise or threat. It's an excellent incentive for their followers to maintain their rules of behavior and worship during their lifetimes. Many Eastern faiths promise their worthy devotees enlightenment and union with the Godhead, while condemning the unworthy to eternal rebirth and repeated lives of suffering until the qualifying conditions are complied with. Similarly, the Abrahamic religions promise eternal salvation and bliss for the faithful or never-ending suffering for those who stray from the path of righteousness. But while these judgments are made upon the individual, the leaders of these faiths also tell us that there is another judgment to be made, only this time upon the whole of humanity (and I assume the rest of nature) when the world comes to an end. It's known as the End of Times, the Omega Point of all existence. Theologians call the study of this concept eschatology, the part of theology that concerns itself with the final death of the human race, the Final Judgment, the destiny of the soul, and the Second Coming of the savior Jesus. The rest of us may think of it as the study of the End of the World, the Last Things, or the End of Time Itself.

For the sake of brevity, if we focus on the Abrahamic faiths, modern-day science now challenges, more than ever before, the idea that humanity, the world, and time will all end simultaneously in the way that we may have been taught.

The final book of the Christian Bible, the book of Revelation, is probably the most cryptic and confusing text in the New Testament. Theologians have spent entire lifetimes attempting to decode its meaning and significance, and we still appear to be not a lot wiser as to how our existing world will finally come to an end. The book of Revelation speaks of the battle of Armageddon, the Four Horsemen of the Apocalypse, and the two hundred million lion-headed cavalry. It becomes more and more cryptic as it involves the lamb-horned beast of the earth, the scorpion-tailed locust, and the Whore of Babylon, all who play their part in the complex tale. Depending on which school of hermeneutics you subscribe to, your interpretation will differ, but fundamentally it tells of the atrocities that precede the Second Coming of Jesus Christ, the final day of judgment of humankind, and the eventual destiny of the human soul.

Today's scientific theory suggests that there may be a massive difference between the end of the world, the end of the human race, and the end of time.

The end of the world has been theoretically calculated to a potential time in the future when our sun and solar system run out of energy and, following a fixed sequence of events, implodes to form another of the black holes that populate space.

Humanity, on the other hand, may well destroy itself long before then, through the destruction of our ecosystem or wholesale annihilation by the various and ingenious forms of warfare we continue to invent. Alternatively, should we manage to avoid either of these forms of self-destruction, there is a much more appealing school of thought that proposes we may transfer some, if not all, of the human race to another planet and continue our existence on a suitable planet in a similar "Goldilocks zone" in another solar system, or even within huge geodesic domes with controlled atmospheres on a less hospitable world. Either way, it seems very improbable that humanity will continue to exist on our world until the day of its destruction.

The end of time, however, is a much more difficult concept to embrace, and the various theories are far too complex to explore within the purview of this exploration. One thing is certain: it will be a long time after the world is absorbed by the expansion of our dying sun. We can, however, suggest, with a high degree of confidence, that its end is not going to coincide with the end of the world or the end of humanity, and it is difficult to imagine that it will involve the efforts of the Four Horsemen of the Apocalypse or the intrigue of the Whore of Babylon.

If we return to the Druidic tradition, we find that it gives no consideration to the end of times, and why should it? There is no promise or threat related to either an individual's end of life or the end of humanity as a whole. Nor is there any need for us to seek salvation from original sin, as we have not inherited this burden from the events in the Garden of Eden. We are born free of all sin, with a blank slate (you will remember the tabula rasa from above).

Significantly, to us there is no God, so there is no supreme being to judge us when our life ends nor anyone to pass judgment on the whole of humanity at the end of times. No Judgment Day, no Messiah, no Second Coming, and certainly no Whore of Babylon. The Druidic belief system is not about judgment or promises and threats to mold our behavior. There are no sticks and carrots goading us on to adhere to any set of manmade rules. Instead, we have a motivation to live correctly within nature, and that includes within human society, which is an integral part of nature. As we have seen, an essential part of our personal energy or force returns to the world force when we cease to live, and this part of us is changed by our behavior, attitudes, and beliefs while it lives within us. When it returns to the collective energy, the changes we have made to it during our lifetime, our influences, and our decisions affect the world force. No matter how small our individual influence may be, it still affects the whole, and it is our individual responsibility to ensure that we only induce positive effects on this, as with all of nature. This knowledge and a life of fulfilment are our rewards for living in harmony within all of nature.

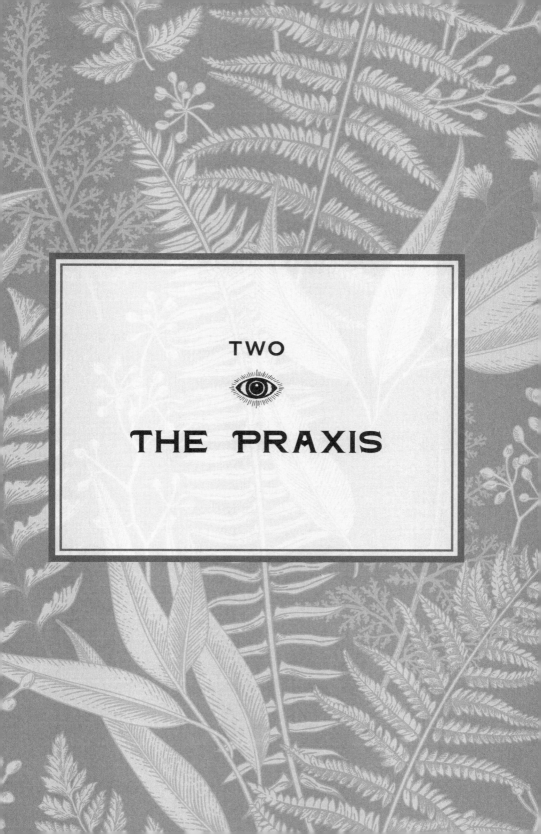

TWO

THE PRAXIS

3

Divination

We know from a range of historical references that divination played a very different role in pre-Celtic Pagan society than it does today. Druidic diviners held a prestigious place in the social hierarchy, consulted by high kings, chieftains, and warlords as well as applying their techniques to the more mundane matters of the everyday life of their kinsmen.

The tradition tells us of ambitious Druids competing for the favor of their tribal leaders by employing increasingly bizarre methods of divination ranging from reading the future in the disemboweled entrails of animals to seeing the future in the flight patterns of wild birds and the smoke rising from their village fires. The invading Romans saw this as the perfect opportunity to discredit and demean the all-too-powerful Druids and sent detailed accounts back to their emperor to show just how brave they were in facing the atrocities of the Pagan priests.

When the Pagan Romans hurriedly converted to Christianity, it didn't take them long to eradicate the Druids, as best they could, and forbid the practice of divination as being an abomination to their newly found God. It may be of surprise to some readers to discover that this ban still remains, and it forms part of the current catechism of the Roman Catholic Church, as can be seen by the following extract.

All forms of divination are to be rejected: recourse to Satan or demons, conjuring up the dead or other practices falsely supposed to "unveil" the future. Consulting horoscopes, astrology, palm reading, interpretation of omens and lots, the phenomena of clairvoyance, and recourse to mediums all conceal a desire for power over time, history, and, in the last analysis, other human beings, as well as a wish to conciliate hidden powers. They contradict the honor, respect, and loving fear that we owe to God alone. (*Catechism of the Catholic Church*)

This all seems a very long way from what is normally considered to be the harmless pursuit of reading the star signs in our daily newspapers or downloading this week's horoscope from our favorite astrological website, but in the eyes of the Catholic Church all are equally sinful.

The Catholic Church is by no means alone in its criticism of divination—many other faiths and political states have outlawed its use—but despite this prolonged, widespread suppression, divination is still widely practiced in most countries of the world, and the most popular method by far is astrology in its various forms.

In simple terms, astrology observes the movement of specific celestial bodies and their positions in relation to one another as a method of divining information related to individuals and terrestrial events. Its history stretched back to at least 2000 BCE, and there is evidence of its use in ancient Egypt, Greece, and the Roman Empire. It also plays a major role in a wide range of religious practices, including Hinduism, Islam, and many of the faiths of China, Japan, and East Asia. But even though it enjoyed a degree of popularity in Europe in the medieval era and earlier, it has had no impact on Druidic lore.

Having said that, the Druidic tradition does use the alignment of celestial bodies and a calendrical system to forecast seasonal progression and thereby predict auspicious dates for influential events, but this is done in a very different way and involves the monolithic stone circles we mentioned earlier in the book.

The main method employed to interpret the relative positions of the celestial bodies into a form of divination is to compile a horoscope, which we can define as a chart illustrating the relative positions of the celestial bodies at the time of a specific event, such as an individual's birth. The horoscope chart is drawn using the zodiac, an area of the sky that extends approximately 8 degrees north or south of the ecliptic (the path of the sun across the celestial sphere over the course of the year). The paths of the moon and planets are also within the zodiac.

In the context of astrology, the zodiac is divided into twelve signs, each occupying 30 degrees (one twelfth of the 360-degree longitudinal plane) of celestial longitude and roughly corresponding to the constellations Aries, Taurus, Gemini, Cancer, Leo, Virgo, Libra, Scorpio, Sagittarius, Capricorn, Aquarius, and Pisces. Most sources seem to agree that the horoscope and the first zodiac originated in ancient Egypt in the many temples dedicated to the Egyptian god of time and the sky, Horus, and in particular the temple complex at Dendera, near the river Nile. Similar astrological charts may be found in many other world faiths, but their compilation and interpretation vary greatly. The compilation and interpretation of an individual horoscope is far too complex and detailed to go into in this exploration, but further research by the reader is recommended.

In focusing on the Druidic tradition of divination, we can see that although the alignments of the celestial bodies and their movements are used as an astral calendar when viewed in conjunction with terrestrial reference points, and the positions of the rising and setting sun and moon (and sometimes the planet Venus) are aligned with portal and reclining stones within stone circles to predict and confirm the changing seasons, the progression of the year, and other important natural occurrences, the planets play no other role in the function of divination.

THE FUNCTION AND OBJECTIVES

The prime function of divination in Druidic lore is to gain an insight into past, present, and future events so that we may understand them through a process of empathy and interpretation.

There are four intellectual components employed:

- **Knowledge of the Past**—experiencing and learning from how past events unfolded
- **Awareness of the Present**—knowing where you are on your journey
- **Anticipation of Events to Come**—using your imagination and insights to help understand how events will unfold
- **Empathy with the Method of Divination Employed**—becoming part of the divination process you choose to employ

All four of these intellectual components are used in conjunction with the divination meditation to achieve our goal, so we need to look at each in some detail.

- **Knowledge of the Past**—Reflecting on our past experiences and drawing on the knowledge and learning we have accumulated over the years is an essential element in helping us understand the insights we are given through our divination meditation. Our past experiences allow us to identify similarities with future events and envisage related outcomes, while our formal learning enables a broader understanding of the ramifications and impact of what may have been revealed to us.
- **Awareness of the Present**—As with any journey, it is essential to know where you are along the way. Without knowing what has happened before and what point you are at now, it is not possible to plan for the future and move forward.
- **Anticipation of Events to Come**—In the vast majority of situations,

it is possible to use our imagination to help understand how events will unfold. Imagination is far too readily banished to the realm of children, whereas in reality it is one of the most powerful tools of divination. As we shall see later, there is a very fine line between imagination, the altered state of mind employed in divination meditation, and the creativity required to anticipate events yet to come.

- **Empathy with the Method of Divination Employed**—We will see in the following sections that to be successful, individuals must immerse themselves entirely in the method of divination they choose to employ. Anything short of complete commitment will result in failure. If we are to be receptive to what is being revealed to us, then we must have empathy with the method being used, and we cannot have this empathy without a full understanding of the principles underpinning these methods.

But before we look in detail at these methods, we need to look at two other important aspects of Druidic divination: the concept of probability and how an individual event impacts the past, the present, and the future.

Despite what some may suggest, there is no such thing as certainty when we attempt to look into the future. All we can suggest is that certain outcomes are probable. Just how probable will vary from event to event.

An extreme but useful example of this is the likelihood of your eventual death. Just because every living thing that has preceded you has died does not make it certain that you will die. You may just be the first living thing to live forever! Admittedly, it is highly unlikely that you will live forever; it is in fact highly probable that you will die like everyone else has done so far, but it is not a certainty—until it happens, that is.

The most appropriate Welsh word for "probable" in this context is *nhebygol*. This word means an outcome that is very highly probable, with a similarly high degree of confidence, but not certain or inevitable. We use this word to avoid the inference of certainty, while not wanting to undermine the high degree of probability involved. The margin of error may sometimes be attributable to the methods used, the interpretation by the diviner, or the ambiguity of the question posed. Frequently, diviners will qualify their response with other aspects that may affect the degree of confidence attributed to each expectation.

The factor of probability or nhebygol must not be ignored but embraced when practicing divination, whether we are using it to understand the past, the present, or the future.

The second and the most important element in understanding the principle and art of Druidic divination is an awareness of how each individual event impacts time itself, and to explain this I shall once again use the simple language of the oral tradition.

Every time something happens, no matter how large or small, it creates a resonance in time, stretching out in all four dimensions. Consider yourself standing on the shore of an infinitely large lake, calm and tranquil, extending beyond sight in all directions. When you throw a stone into the lake, it creates an expanding circle of ripples that move in ever-increasing circles from the point of impact. The waves continue to expand until eventually they dissipate in the vast expanse of water. The larger the stone, the bigger the ripples, the broader the circles, and the longer it takes for the waves to dissipate.

Figure 3.1. Ripples emanating from a dropped stone in Lough Leane (the Lake of Learning), Killarney, county Kerry, Ireland.

This is exactly how events impact time. An event causes the same type of ripple effect as the stone, expanding in all directions equally. The larger the impact of the event, the bigger the ripples, the broader the circles, and the further they travel before they dissipate. Now we consider the fact that these ripples expand in three dimensions, and we have an image of an expanding sphere in space. This is an expansion similar to what we imagine with the big bang theory, with a single event causing the expansion of the universe in all directions. At the final stage, we consider the event within the fourth dimension, time.

To do this, let's return to our two-dimensional model for the moment. Our first line drawing (fig. 3.2) illustrates the expanding impact resulting from the event.

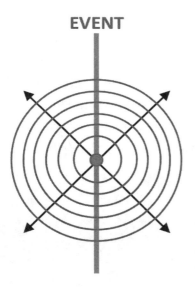

EVENT

Figure 3.2. Line drawing illustrating how when an event occurs, its effect radiates out in all directions simultaneously. In a three-dimensional model, this same effect may be represented by an expanding sphere.

The second line drawing (fig. 3.3) is a simple model of the time continuum, moving forward from the past, through the present, to the future.

The band marked "Time Continuum" represents an individual's progress through time, from our ancestral beginnings, through the present day, and into an infinite future. If you cast your mind back to the previous section titled "On the Passing of Time," this same band

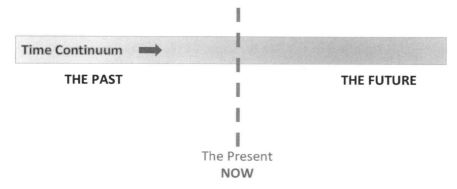

Figure 3.3. An individual time continuum
as viewed from the here and now.

also represents the furrow made by our metaphorical wheelbarrow as we progress through our lifetime, marking the annual cycle as we pass over the uneven path of our existence.

If we now consider an event as it happens in the present and super-impose the event effect illustration over our time continuum diagram, we produce the following (fig. 3.4):

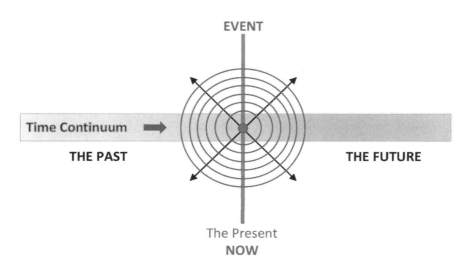

Figure 3.4. An event happening within an individual's time continuum, illustrating the expanding ripple effect in all directions.

The important thing to notice in figure 3.4 is that the effect ripples expand in all directions. We explained this earlier in a three-dimensional universe (as opposed to the two-dimensional illustration shown) by using the metaphor of an expanding sphere, but figure 3.4 also includes the fourth dimension, time. Another thing to note is that the diagram demonstrates the event effect on a single individual's time continuum, whereas in a more accurate model we should include the time continuums of every living individual moving forward in time and space in our parallel journeys from the Alpha Point to the Omega. I will leave this image to your mind's eye, as it is far too complex to illustrate here.

In looking at the detail of figure 3.4, it is not surprising to see the ripple effect radiate into the future; we are all accustomed to the idea that things we do today will affect our future. It is also not difficult to relate to the idea that as the ripples of an event radiate out to each side of our time continuum, they affect the continuums of individuals close to us on a parallel path. We have all experienced this on a day-to-day basis, as we can see below in figure 3.5.

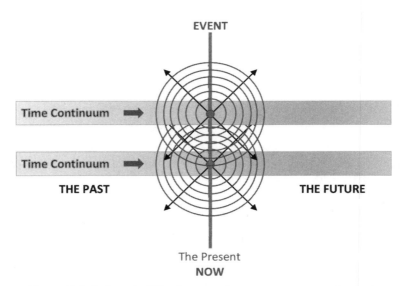

Figure 3.5. It is not difficult to see how two concurrent events in one individual's time continuum radiate out to influence other individuals on a parallel path.

However, if these event ripples emanate in *all* directions, as we can see, then they must also radiate into our past. But how can things that happen today affect our past or, more importantly, how can future events affect us in the present? This is something that we may not have previously considered, but it is imperative to Druidic divination.

So far, we have only looked at events that occur in the present, but to explore this relationship between the future and the present further, we need to look at two more examples: one, an illustration of how past events affect us in the present, and two, how future events affect us in the present. The notion that past events affect us in the present is not unusual to us. We are all accustomed to the idea that our past always catches up with us eventually. Figure 3.6 below is an illustration showing how event ripples from a past occurrence radiate to influence the present.

We know that past events influence the present day. This is exactly how we plan and develop our lives: setting the foundations for our future lives, building families, careers, and a wholesome lifestyle.

But what about the things that haven't happened yet? How can we

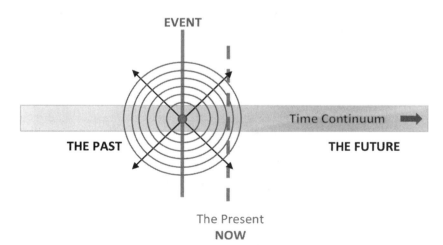

Figure 3.6. An event happening in the past within an individual's time continuum, illustrating how the expanding ripple effect influences the present.

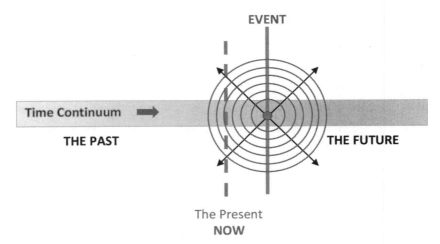

Figure 3.7. An event happening in the future within an individual's time continuum, illustrating how the expanding ripple effect influences the present.

even get to know what they are going to be? Let's look at the same diagram illustrating an event occurring in the future, figure 3.7.

Again, we can see the event ripples from the future and radiates in all directions. Although it feels counterintuitive, this includes radiating back into the present. As improbable as it seems, future events *do* have an impact on the present. At this point, it is important to establish that this phenomenon does not infer a reversal of time or bringing the future back to the present. That is impossible. It simply illustrates that if we can discover a means of becoming receptive to these ripples, attuning our senses to them, and then learning how to interpret them, we will be able to formulate a specific precognition of future events. This is exactly how Druidic divination works.

The oral tradition explains this concept using a sequence of stories involving streams, stones, floating sticks, and flowers. The stream represents the time continuum, thrown stones illustrate the event ripples, and the floating sticks and flowers demonstrate the passage of time. It isn't possible for me to do the same without making this section a much too lengthy instruction manual. This may be an appropriate moment to reflect on why the tradition has always been taught on a one-to-one contextual learning basis, involving an intimate relationship between teacher and learner and using the gifts of nature and the dynamic elements as learning tools. Being able to use the written word and line drawings is a very useful means of communicating, and I hope to have used them effectively in my explanation, but I am left feeling very aware of the difference in the two styles and disappointed that the reader cannot enjoy the same personal, natural experience that I benefited from in my early days. Unfortunately, this is not possible.

What we need, then, is a methodology for training our senses to be receptive to the event ripples of the future, a means of interpreting the information we receive, and most importantly, a means of positioning this information in the context of our specific needs.

We achieve this receptive ability by entering an altered consciousness, and the tradition teaches us that we accomplish this through a form of heightened concentration we call mantic meditation.

Mantic meditation may be described as a process of extremely focused concentration that separates us temporarily from the mundane world and allows us to engage parts of our consciousness that we are otherwise not aware of. One of the results of this opening of our consciousness is the ability to attune our mind to the event ripples of the past, present, and future.

For many years, this phenomenon was associated with the urban myth that we only regularly use around 10 percent of our brain in our everyday lives. This left us with a massive amount of unused brain power to tap into, and the subsequent assumption was that part of this unused and unknown brain capacity was associated with the faculty of mantic meditation. This 10 percent utilization theory was subscribed to by some very prominent individuals of the day, including Albert Einstein, but unfortunately recent neurological studies have proven the theory to be incorrect. It would seem that we use all of our brain at one time or another, for one function or another, but it appears that although we use all the areas of our brain, we may not use each to capacity. We still have the potential to discover new functions for our growing intellect and an additional capacity for as yet undiscovered states of awareness.

It is possible that, through the arcane discipline of mantic meditation, we are engaging a part of this unused mental capacity that may well have been used regularly by our ancestors. It is also possible that we are rediscovering a mental faculty that had been abandoned by most as superfluous to our development, but had been rigorously maintained by the Druidic tradition over millennia.

The oral tradition teaches us how to discipline ourselves to achieve this altered state of consciousness, how to utilize this altered consciousness to attune our consciousness with the event ripples, and how to interpret the insights we gain along with the additional information deduced from the intellectual components we saw above to resolve our query. But first, it will be useful to look at what our current scientific understanding has to say about this altered state of consciousness and what is involved in achieving it.

THE MODERN-DAY SCIENCE

The first phenomenon we should explore is a condition called dissociation. In the context of psychology, dissociation may be defined in one sense as an experience of detachment from our surroundings and sensory experiences or simply a detachment from reality. It also describes the more common everyday event of daydreaming. For our purposes here, it defines an altered state of consciousness.

Daydreaming, in one of its forms, may be described as a short-term detachment from one's immediate surroundings experienced while awake, when a person's contact with reality becomes blurred and partially substituted by mind-created images and sensations, especially those imagined as coming to pass. These images may be positioned in the past, present, or future, with the lines between each often blurred and unclear. The state of daydreaming lies somewhere between waking and sleeping. Research has found that individuals in creative positions such as musicians, artists, writers, and media workers often develop new ideas while daydreaming. Famous mathematicians and scientists claim to have been inspired by daydreaming while pondering difficult problems.

The state of dissociation leading to daydreaming is usually brought about by a simple form of sensory deprivation, which can be the result of boredom. In some cases, it may be induced through planned events such as meditation. In either case, the conditions required are very similar. This is a phenomenon called the Ganzfeld effect, taken from the German word meaning "complete field."

> The effect is the result of the brain amplifying neural noise to look for the missing visual signals. The noise is interpreted in the higher visual cortex and gives rise to hallucinations [mindcreated visions]. . . . This visual effect is described as the loss of vision as the brain cuts off the unchanging signal from the eyes. The result is "seeing black," an apparent sense of blindness. A flickering Ganzfeld causes geometrical patterns and colors to appear. . . in addition to an altered state of consciousness. (Wikipedia, "The Ganzfield effect")

There is nothing new about the Ganzfeld effect, other than its naming, and it has been reported since ancient times.

> The adepts of Pythagoras retreated to pitch-black caves to receive wisdom through their visions, known as the prisoner's cinema. Miners trapped by accidents in mines. . . . [and] Arctic explorers seeing nothing but a featureless landscape of white snow for a long time also reported . . . an altered state of mind. (Wikipedia, "The Ganzfield effect")

If our mind is deprived of external stimulation from our various sensory receptors for any length of time, it changes its mode and closes down its receptors, allowing other functions to take their place. Most of us have experienced the symptoms of daydreaming at one time or another: black vision or temporary blindness (again our receptors shut down with a lack of stimulation); staring or the lack of eye movement and focus, with the resultant eye watering and tears; deafness, unaware of the ambient noises around us; sleep paralysis, the sleep-induced lack of movement that allows us to dream of running through meadows of wheat or swimming in the ocean without actually doing the corresponding limb movements; and occasionally, false awakening, the phenomenon of feeling we are awake when we are actually still asleep (resulting in fear and anguish when we cannot move or speak, even though we think we are awake). But most of all, we experience a feeling of disengagement with the surrounding world, a separation from the mundane, and a freedom from the restrictions and limitations of everyday existence. We explore our imagination, expand our creativity, and become more intuitive and more receptive to inner emotion.

Another state of altered consciousness experienced more frequently than daydreaming is hypnagogia. This is the experience we have when we move from wakefulness to sleep during the onset of sleep. According to the Wikipedia article "Hypnagogia," mental phenomena that may occur during this threshold of consciousness phase include lucid thought (particularly related to problem solving and creativity), visualization, creative inspiration, and even the sleep paralysis and false awakenings mentioned earlier.

The purpose of mentioning these three similar phenomena (daydreaming, Ganzfeld effect, and hypnagogia) is that they are scientifically established events that induce a state of altered consciousness, and as such they are akin to the state induced during divination meditation.

Now we need to look at how the scientific observations fit in with the practices maintained by the Druidic tradition. We must remember, though, that whatever insights we garner from the meditation process must be put into the context of the four intellectual components, which we'll repeat here:

- **Knowledge of the Past**—experience and learning from how past events unfolded
- **Awareness of the Present**—knowing where you are on your journey
- **Anticipation of Events to Come**—using your imagination and insights to help understand how events will unfold
- **Empathy with the Method of Divination Employed**—becoming part of the divination process you choose to employ

THE MARRIAGE OF SCIENCE AND TRADITION

The scientific observations briefly outlined above give us an understanding of how, be it by accident or intention, we can induce a state of altered consciousness whereby we experience thoughts and insights not available to us in the mundane world. Through understanding this process, we can train ourselves to induce this state of altered consciousness while still remaining aware of our experience within it, in a form of lucid altered consciousness, and while doing so focus our intention on attuning to the information emanating from past, present, and future events. We will see that there are eight steps or successions in the divination process: six of which are involved in preparing for and immersing ourselves in this lucid altered state of mind. We will also see that these successions are common to all methods used in Druidic divination. Just how they relate to each of the three methods of divination we will be exploring shall be seen in the following section.

THE THREE METHODS CHOSEN AND WHY

That the reader may explore and experiment with a range of Druidic divination methods, I have selected three different processes from the many more maintained within the tradition with the intention that having experimented with each, individuals will find the most suitable to their needs and personality. Earlier I explained that there are three types of Druid—the Craft Druid, the Elemental Druid, and the Intuitive Druid—each being of equal importance but employing different spiritual and practical attributes to achieve their end results. Because of the techniques they use, each embraces a different form of divination.

There are, in general terms, three different forms of divination; each uses distinctive methods and calls upon different gifts of the diviner.

Interpretive divination is where the diviner induces an action then interprets the results. This includes such diverse techniques as casting dice and reading tarot cards (not that either of these techniques are used in Druidic divination). In all cases, the diviner induces an action, like casting the dice or dealing the tarot cards, and then interprets the outcome.

Inductive divination is where the diviner has no direct involvement in producing the effects that are interpreted. This includes more natural events such as cloud reading, smoke reading, and wind and water divination.

Intuitive divination is where the divined interpretation depends entirely on the intuition of the diviner. This includes such practices as crystal-ball gazing and mirror skrying.

I would once again draw the reader's attention to the fact that none of these techniques involve consulting deities, intercessors, spiritual guides, or mediums. They each depend entirely on the skills and gifts of the individual diviner involved.

I am sure that it has not escaped notice that interpretive divination—using tools and implements to induce actions that can then be interpreted—is most suited to the Craft Druid, who has the gifts to craft the tools and implements needed, while inductive divination—using natural elements like wind, water, and clouds—is naturally in tune with the Elemental Druid, and intuitive divination is ideally suited to the Intuitive Druid.

So that we can look at each of these techniques in turn, I have selected three appropriate divination practices, one for each Druidic type and each utilizing a method most suited to that type. They are summarized here as

- Interpretive Divination—Craft Druid—The Sevens
- Inductive Divination—Elemental Druid—Water
- Intuitive Divination—Intuitive Druid—The Slate Speculum "Speculum Vitae" (The Mirror of Life)

But before we look at each of these in turn, we will focus on the practical processes that are common to all.

PROCESSES COMMON TO ALL
The Eight Successions of Druidic Divination

The foundation of all Druidic rites lies within correct preparation, facilitation, and reflection. The tradition teaches us a progressive sequence that ensures all ritual and practice is undertaken in a way that both achieves the desired end result and, at the same time, ensures the practitioner's spiritual and mental well-being. This is especially important in pursuits that involve such engagement as divination meditation and interpretation. These eight progressive stages or successions have been employed since archaic times, with a long history of their use during the megalithic period and the construction of standing stones and stone circle complexes. Evidence of their continued successful use reinforces the importance of employing them in strict sequence from beginning to end. In the oral tradition, the successions for each individual ritual and practice are taught by rote and are a significant element in the famous memory exercises attributed to the ancient Druid community.

Defining the Intention
The single most important factor in divination is a precise understanding of the intended outcome. This may be extremely specific or more general, but the things that it can't be are vague, unspecific, or ill-defined. If the quest is on behalf of a querent,* then it is the diviner's

---

*A *querent* is an established term for a person proposing a question or quest to a diviner.

responsibility to discuss the quest in detail with him or her, gain a thorough understanding of the querent's intention, and interpret it in such a way that the best outcome may be achieved.

Whether the quest is established through a querent or directly by the diviner, a detailed and specific outcome MUST be defined before a divination process begins. Casting our minds back to the principle of probability explored earlier, it is easy to understand that the less specific the question, the less specific and relevant the answer will inevitably be.

Physical, Spiritual, and Mental Preparation

As in all my books, I cannot overemphasize the importance of proper physical, spiritual, and mental preparation in undertaking any and all esoteric activities. The potential dangers of attempting such an immersive practice as divination will be clear to all, so be aware that leaving out any of the prescribed successions may result in significant spiritual and mental upheaval and disruption.

As you proceed through the various methods below, you will see a detailed explanation of how you should prepare yourself for each different process. I have deliberately repeated some steps in more than one divination process to make each instruction complete in itself and eliminate the need to back-reference instructions as they occur.

Preparing the Working Environment

The working environment is different for each of the methods explored, and a detailed description is given in each case, but the common element is that diviners cannot just enter into a divination meditation without meticulously preparing the environment in which they work. This is done informally as the area is prepared, the working implements assembled, and the querent (if present) is made ready. A more formal preparation involving physical, mental, and spiritual focus is then undertaken in the final steps for the meditation.

Potentializing the Portal

I have deliberately chosen three methods of divination that use different portals to enter meditation so that readers can experiment with each and find the one (or more) that best suits their personality. In each case, the individual potentializing of the portal is explained in detail. The important aspect to remember is that without the correct process of potentializing, no matter which method of divination used, the meditation will not reveal the expected insights. Even though the process of potentializing for each method may differ significantly, each is imperative in achieving the eventual goal.

The Meditation

Once all of the previous steps have been carefully and thoughtfully completed, diviners may begin their journey of dissociation from their mundane environment and attune with past, present, and future emanations. The result will be an insight into future events, a message from the future. Initially, these insights may be perceived as meaningless and confused; this is where the next succession, interpretation, begins. It is important that ALL aspects of the meditation process are committed to memory. In the case of neophytes, or those who have not had the benefit of memory training, it may be useful to write down their insights, no matter how insignificant they may initially appear, so that they may be referred to during the interpretation succession. In all cases, it is important to remember that everything that is revealed is significant, as the interpretation succession will reveal.

Interpretation

Once the meditation is complete, and after a short period of relaxation, the diviner begins interpreting the experiences and insights revealed to him or her. This should be a secluded, quiet experience that is tranquil, calm, contemplative, and measured. No matter which method is used to glean the revelation, the interpretation is common to all. For the purpose of clarity, I have detailed the interpretive succession in each method separately.

Scattering the Working Environment

One of the most common misunderstandings in the entire series of successions is the process of the scattering. It is a time for returning to the mundane, not only necessary for the mental and spiritual welfare of the diviner, but also for the secure disassembly of the working tools and environment so that they are uncorrupted and may be safely used for future facilitation.

Reflection

Sometimes mistaken for the interpretation succession, reflection is when diviners contemplate how well the processes and revelations that they have arrived at have achieved the aspirations and objectives they originally set out. It may also be considered an evaluation process. It is also a time when consideration may be given to changing or augmenting the successions used to improve future facilitation. These subtle changes help to create individuals' unique interpretation of the successions and develop their individual techniques.

4

Interpretive Divination by Learned Wood

The Sevens

We have already seen that, for millennia before the introduction of Ogham inscriptions on standing stones (most commonly known as Ogham stones), similar meaningful inscriptions were carved into wooden staves and passed between Druid scholars. These sigils were coded messages depicting names and other occult signifiers used in Druidic lore. The tradition tells us that over time, a series of seven sigils was derived in order to be used as a divination codex, accessible only to the learned Druidic class. The Sevens, or "Yr Saith" in Welsh, are still the most commonly used means of Druidic divination.

The Sevens consist of seven individual small staves, each engraved with a unique symbol. The small staves are shuffled or mixed by the querent and cast onto a flat surface before being scrutinized by the diviner. There are two aspects that influence the resultant foretelling: the spiritual empowerment introduced by the querent's handling and casting of the staves, and the resulting unique arrangement of the staves in relation to one another. The staves themselves have two elements of influence: the wood from which they are crafted and the sigil engraved on each.

Figure 4.1.
A set of Sevens.

WOODS

Wood, and the trees from which it is harvested, play a hugely significant role in Druidic lore. Most people will be aware of the inseparable link between the oak and the Druid. In fact some would argue that the very name Druid derives from two ancient words meaning "knower of the oak." While there are many references exploring the attributes of the indigenous trees of the Druidic homelands, for the purpose of this book we shall confine our exploration to the two main trees involved in Druidic divination: the yew and the oak.

The Yew Tree (Taxus baccta)

Yew trees may well be the longest-living trees in Europe and populate the vast majority of the Druidic homelands. Left to thrive, they may live for between five hundred and nine hundred years, with some veteran trees surviving for up to twelve hundred to fourteen hundred years. It is because of this longevity that the yew occupies a privileged position in Druidic lore. The ancient pre-Celtic Pagans recognized within their own communities that with age comes wisdom. Knowing that these long-living trees survived many, many generations of their family groups, they ascribed to them the deep knowledge and wisdom that accompanies their extraordinary old age. The fact that the trees had witnessed so many events, both natural and human-made, gave the yew tree the attributes of experience and sagacity, and it is these attributes that contribute to their use as divination tools. Often considered as the learned or wise wood, the yew has given its name to the staves used in the method of divination we are exploring here. Diviners would use this method to seek a wise insight into the future, either for themselves or their querents.

The yew also represents solidarity and permanence, again as a reflection of its longevity. The ancient Pagans carved symbols into the tree in the expectation that they would survive for generations, leaving messages for their successors and descendants. A further attribute of the yew is that of direction and guidance, which we may ascribe to the fact that the trees grew in the same location for generation after generation and were used as markers and signposts for travelers. As such

Figure 4.2. Yew tree forest within Killarney National Park, county Kerry, Ireland.

they may still be found at many crossroads and track intersections.

While it is true that yew trees may be found in many significant auspicious and spiritual places, it is difficult to tell if the locations first became important because the legendary yews were located there, or whether the trees were deliberately planted there to indicate or enhance the spiritual significance of the location. Either way, yew trees are found at most meaningful mystical places throughout the Druidic home-lands. When the newly arrived Celtic Christians began building their churches, they regularly built them near ancient and well-known veteran yews, mainly because they were already acknowledged places of spiritual devotion and well-established gathering points for the local community. Later in the history of Christian church building, yew trees were always planted within the church boundaries and in Christian burial grounds. Some may suggest that this was done because of the poisonous nature of the trees, keeping away scavenging animals and grazing cattle, but it is much more likely the result of the subtle syncretism of the early Christian converts.

The importance of the yew tree within Druidic lore is not to be underestimated, and the use of yew wood as a divining tool is closely linked to the attributes discussed above.

The Oak Tree (Quercus robur)

The oak tree is synonymous with the Druid, particularly when it is associated with the parasitic mistletoe that sometimes grows on its branches. Like the yew, the oak is very long-lived, with some examples surviving for over one thousand years. As a result, the oak is associ-ated with permanence, wisdom, and security. Again, as with the yew, it was a common practice to carve symbols into the bark of the trunk in the knowledge that they would remain there for many generations, and much of what we know today about ancient Pagan sigils was gained from carvings in oak tree trunks. As the wood of the oak is exception-ally hard, the oak also reflects the attributes of endurance and trust. These are attributes derived from the practical use of oak wood in tools, carts, and boats, where the wood proved to be both long-lasting, durable, and trustworthy.

Most people would be aware of the strong relationship between the Druid and the oak. Nearly all representations of Druidic groves show encirclements of oak trees around the gathered Druids, and it is indeed fact that oak groves were, and in some cases still are, the preferred locations for Druidic convocations because of their association with wisdom, security, and strength. It is also a current theory that many of the existing stone circles were originally wooden circles, made from oak wood to test and prove the alignments before the more permanent standing stones we see today replaced them. There are numerous examples of this practice in many of the megalithic circles in Britain, Ireland, and northern France.

Oak Sevens are usually used when the querent is concerned about future issues of trust, relationships, or future permanence/security.

Having looked at the attributes of the yew and the oak, it is not difficult to see that many other indigenous trees demonstrate attributes of their own, derived from their life cycle, practical use, appearance, and physical makeup. Like the yew and oak, many are also used in divination for their spiritual and medicinal benefits, but this is a subject for another time, for now we will concern ourselves with Sevens made from the two trees above.

The yew and oak each bring their own attributes to the staves we are going to use, but we must also consider the sigils or symbols engraved on them. It is the combination of the attributes of the wood and the sigils that make the Sevens so powerful.

SYMBOLS/INSCRIPTIONS

Previously we have looked at the carvings or engravings on Ogham stones, both in the context of the markings or letters used and the methods of encoding them so that only the learned initiates could decipher them. Some have chosen to interpret these alphabets as tree letters, assigning each to a specific tree with the name that, in Old Irish, begins with the letter represented. It is not a difficult step from there to associate each tree letter with the attributes of that tree and use the alphabet in various ways to foretell the future by interpreting each letter's attributes. As a result, we can find various tree alphabet oracles, Ogham tarot decks, and the like.

The sigils used for the Sevens are unique, naïve, and unrelated to the Ogham, although some may be recognized as similar to other Pagan traditions. The meanings attributed to them, however, are individual to the pre-Celtic Pagan usage.

The Sevens symbols are as follows:

THE SUN: The sun symbol represents the giving of life, derived from its association with warmth, light, and the growth of plants, animals, and humans. The symbol of the male.

THE MOON: The moon symbol represents birth, growth, family, and health. The moon cycle defines one of the most significant symbols of pre-Celtic Paganism. The symbol of the female.

EARTH: The earth symbol represents stability, endurance, and permanence.

AIR: The air symbol represents variability, division, and instability. Air, in the form of wind, brings change and unpredictability.

WATER: The water symbol represents fluidity, change, flexibility, and adaptability. Water also plays a role as being revealing, judgmental, cleansing, and purifying.

FIRE: The fire symbol represents cleansing, purification, and rapid change. It stripes away the old and replaces it with the new. Water and fire are mutually exclusive.

WOOD: The wood symbol represents intuition, wisdom, endurance, and tolerance. It's often associated with advice and guidance.

As we shall see, each of the symbols has a variety of meanings beyond the fundamental ones mentioned above. Each meaning is also dependent on its orientation, position in relation to the other staves, and interpretation with regard to the querent's inquiry.

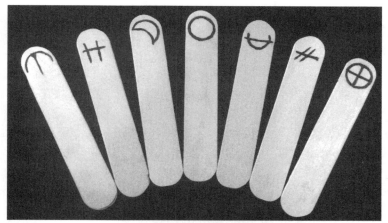

Figure 4.3. Sevens showing the sigils
at the head.

Each symbol is carved or drawn onto the upper end of the wooden stave. The staves are formed from the appropriate wood (bearing in mind the wood's attributes) and are typically five inches long, up to one inch wide, and either around one-eighth of an inch thick or a quarter of an inch thick if used in the rude form.* The sizes of the rude form of staves may vary according to the size of the branches harvested, but each of the seven staves must be exactly the same length, so as not to create a bias in the casting (see fig. 4.4 on page 112).

---

*Some staves are crafted from small branches harvested from the tree and made by carving or planing just two sides of the branch to form flat surfaces, while leaving the remaining surfaces with the bark still attached. Some believe that this minimalist crafting produces rude staves that retain more of the spirit of the original tree than the formally fashioned surfaces of the more familiar form.

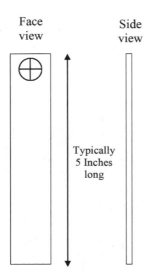

Face
view

Side
view

Typically
5 Inches
long

Figure 4.4. A typical
formal stave with the
earth sigil marked at
the (head) top.

CASTING

We have seen earlier that this form of divination is most often used by Craft Druids who, by definition, are more than competent at crafting the staves they intend to use. The process is one employed by the Druid in what we have defined as interpretive divination. In other words, the staves are cast, as in the casting of lots or die, and the results are interpreted by the Druid reader, who has no direct input or effect on the casting and has not therefore influenced the result. The Druid has, however, cleansed the staves, potentialized the group of Sevens, and prepared them for casting by the querent.

A casting begins with the querent and the Druid sitting facing each other across a usable surface, typically a table. The Sevens staves are released from their bundle, spread out at random, and then gathered and handled by the Druid. During this handling period the Druid concentrates on the image of the future events being queried in the form of the illustration we saw earlier—the effect of the event radiating in all directions along the time continuum. The interpreter concentrates on the event in question radiating into the past (the interpreter's present) and influencing the staves when cast in order to be understood by the interpreter. At some point in the handling the interpreter passes the staves around the periphery of the table's surface, thereby defining the active area of the dispersal of the staves. If any of the staves fall outside of this area, they are deemed irrelevant. When the Druid interpreter feels that sufficient energy has charged the staves during the handling, he or she stacks the staves in an orderly pile in the sequence shown in the description above. This represents the hierarchy of the sigils, with the sun symbol stave at the top. The interpreter then places the stack in the center of the surface, between the Druid interpreter and the querent.

At this point the staves are energized or potentialized and ready for the querent's involvement.

The querent then goes through a similar process as the Druid, beginning by spreading the staves out at random on the table surface, thereby eliminating the order introduced by the Druid during the energizing. To charge the staves with the querent's energy, the querent gathers them up into a bundle and begins handling and shuffling them. While shuffling, querents focus on the inquiry they are pursuing. Sometimes, depending on their focus, they may chant the inquiry to further influence the outcome. When querents feel sufficient energy has been imbued into the staves, they gather them into a bundle in a random order using both hands, raise the bundle to twelve inches above the surface of the table, and drop them. Querents have been instructed that they should not try to deliberately affect any of the aspects of the handling, bundling, or dropping of the staves. Their action should at all times be unintentional and empowered only by the energies of the radiations of the future event of which they seek knowledge. It then becomes the task of the Druid diviner to interpret the positions and patterns of the staves as they appear.

The first task of the diviner is to locate the center point of the array of staves. This may not be the center point of the table surface. In fact it most frequently is not. Only on rare occasions do the staves conveniently fall in the center, more usually they disperse themselves off-center and the center point needs to be defined. The usual method used for this is for the interpreter to describe an imaginary circle around the array of staves and locate the center of the circle (fig. 4.5). Once the center has been located the interpreter then draws an imaginary line through the center point across the surface, parallel to the edges of the table dividing the querent and interpreter. This dividing line is then used as the reference line or datum line for the interpretation.

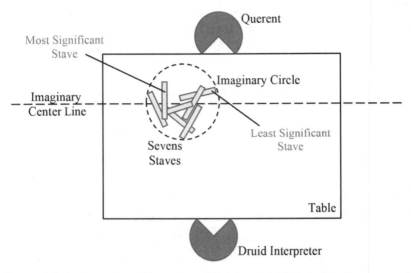

Figure 4.5. Layout of working stone (divining table) showing the array of Sevens staves and the datum line for interpretation.

INTERPRETATION

There are two levels of significance employed to interpret the array of staves.

Primary Significance

1. As the staves are arrayed in order to be read by the interpreter, their meaning is determined from the viewpoint of the interpreter. The top of each stave is therefore furthest away from the interpreter.

2. As the sigil is only engraved on one side of the stave, if the blank side of the stave is showing uppermost then the stave is discounted.

3. The sigil is engraved at the top of the stave. If it appears inverted (upside down), its meaning is reversed.

4. The strength of the sigil is defined by its orientation to the center-line datum. If it sits at a right angle to the datum, it is at its strongest. If it sits parallel to the datum, it is at its weakest. The nearer to the right angle of the datum it lies, the stronger its influence.

5. Associated influences are determined by adjacent staves overlapping or touching each other. If staves are overlapping each other through their center line (forming an even cross shape), their influence on each other is at its strongest. If they are merely touching, their influence on each other is at its weakest. Locations in between are interpreted appropriately.

6. The relative strength of each stave's influence is determined by its orientation to the datum in relation to its neighbors. Again, those at right angles are the strongest, with those parallel at their weakest.

Secondary Significance

1. In arrays where the staves are piled up, the interpretation begins with the uppermost first, with the first or upper staves having the most significance.

2. If staves fall from the surface when they are dropped by the querent, they are deemed insignificant.

The initial insights of the interpretation are determined immediately following the dropping of the array of staves. The subtler, deeper meanings are determined during the meditation and interpretation successions of the process.

THE SESSION

The Nine Successions of Divining with the Sevens

Each session involves the eight successions common to all Druidic divination, and in this particular form of divination we also add the casting succession to give us a total of nine.

Defining the Intention

As we have seen above, the single most important factor in divination is a precise understanding of the intended outcome. This is usually explored and determined some time before the session begins. It will typically either be established by the diviners themselves or through a detailed discussion with the querent.

The more detailed and specific the intention, the more accurate the result may be. If we cast our minds back to the principle of probability we explored earlier, it is easy to understand that the less specific the question, the less specific and relevant the result will be.

It is not helpful to pose inquiries that require a yes or no answer, as this type of divination is usually employed to provide more general insights, so simple binary questions should be teased out to develop a broader inquiry. This softer approach normally provides a more informative insight, giving querents the opportunity to adapt or fit in the response to their overall lifestyle.

In sessions where querents are involved, it is best to arrange a consultation some time prior to the divination session to establish the query. This is best done in a calm and tranquil environment, free from distractions. In such a consultation, the diviner may explain the expected outcomes, including the principle of probability and the simple way in which the insights gained may be used to inform their future endeavors. This initial consultation also provides the diviner with the opportunity to assess the appropriateness and sincerity of the querent. It is futile to proceed with the divination session if the querent is not sympathetic and understanding of the method being employed.

It is imperative that the precise inquiry is agreed to and fully understood by both parties. It may also be useful if a discussion is had about the reaction to any obvious responses and how these responses may affect the querent's future. The anticipation of potentially obvious responses will help both the querent and the diviner position insights into the overall situation of the querent.

Despite the well-known memory training of Druidic lore, it may be helpful for the newcomer to record the salient points of the consultation and the specific inquiry for use in the divination session later.

Physical, Spiritual, and Mental Preparation

Again, I cannot overemphasize the importance of proper physical, spiritual, and mental preparation in undertaking any and all esoteric activities.

The potential dangers of attempting to practice such an immersive practice as divination will be clear to all, so be aware that leaving out any of the prescribed successions may result in significant spiritual and mental upheaval and disruption.

Before entering a divination session (or a querent consultation, for that matter), diviners should be confident that:

- They are refreshed, relaxed, and able to focus intently.
- They are physically prepared for what may be a long, arduous, and taxing period of concentration.
- They are prepared for a period of meditation that should not result in falling asleep. This is a common difficulty in our present-day lifestyles of pressure and overexertion.
- They have freed their mind of everyday, mundane preoccupations.
- They are suitably dressed in appropriate clothing.

Spiritual preparedness is achieved by conventional Druidic cleansing methods, beginning with outer cleansing: bathing or showering and applying cleansing essential oils, or the more natural rain showering if weather permits. Deeper spiritual cleansing is achieved through relaxation meditation, exploring one's spiritual readiness, enthusiasm, and commitment to the task ahead.

Mental preparedness is confirmed when the diviner is confident that he or she can cope with the mental pressures involved. It is important to be mindful of the dangers in immersing oneself in other people's lives and futures and the potential trauma that may result. Often, just being aware of these potential dangers helps to guard against them, but sometimes more formal consideration and preparation may be necessary. Only you will know your capacity for dealing with potential difficulties. It is always useful to establish your own redlines that you will not cross and limit that you will never exceed. It may be that discussing this with colleagues will help you establish your individual capacity for dealing with these matters and recognize warning signs when they appear.

There is no excuse for jeopardizing your mental health in pursuit of any esoteric practice. So always, always, exercise extreme caution in matters concerning your mental well-being.

When you feel that you have achieved your required state of physical, spiritual, and mental preparedness, it is time to progress to the next succession and begin preparing your working environment.

Preparing the Working Environment

Meticulous preparation is essential for successful divination, and creating a suitable working environment with all the essential elements at hand is paramount.

In the case of divining with the Sevens, it is necessary to create a calm, meditative atmosphere without external distractions. The following elements are crucial:

- A lighting scheme that is relaxing and calming. Often dimly lit, minimalizing the surrounding areas while focusing attention onto the working-table surface, which should be of a suitable size to allow the Sevens to be cast.

- Keep the working table (usually called the working stone, as in ideal circumstances the working would be undertaken on the working stone of a stone circle, as done by our ancient predecessors) free of any impediments. It is important that nothing on the table interferes with the casting of the Sevens.
- It is useful to cover the working table surface with a tablecloth or similar. The staves may act too "lively" on a bare tabletop that is wood or plastic.
- The working table should be suitably placed to give freedom of movement to the querent and diviner, while also being clear of any distractions.
- A comfortable chair is placed at two opposite sides of the table; one for the diviner and one for the querent, who face each other. In cases where there is no querent and the diviner is acting alone, only one chair is necessary.
- The temperature of the environment is comfortable for the participants, without being so warm as to cause drowsiness.
- It is helpful if suitable meditative music is played, both to aid concentration and help exclude intrusive external noises.
- Your Sevens have been properly prepared and stacked in the center of the table in readiness.

With all of the above in place, you may now begin cleansing the workspace. This is typically done by calling on the four elements to remove any undue pollution from the work area and the tools within it.

The Druid diviner stands before the work table, extends both arms and calls upon the elements:

I call upon the four prime elements—water, fire, air, and earth—to enter this area and remove whatever harmful or negative forces may impede our working. I do this in the name of the ancients, those who have preceded me and those who may follow me, from the beginning to the end of times.

In the case of the Welsh Druidic tradition that I have been raised in, this request is voiced in Welsh (in fact in Old Welsh), but to do so here would only cause confusion and potential misunderstanding. The Irish, English, and French traditions also each have their own language that they use in similar circumstances, so voicing in English is of course totally acceptable. I maintain the Welsh only in due deference to my ancestors and countrymen.

In other Druidic practices, once the cleansing of the work area is completed the next step is to secure the cleansed area with a protective circle, normally crafted using harvested sea salt and protective herbs, but here, in the case of divination, things differ. To form a protective circle to exclude negative and harmful influences would mean that if there were any negative aspects foretold by the divination, they would be prevented from appearing. So in this practice we will work in what is known as an open circle, allowing both positive and negative aspects to enter.

Now, with everything in place and the working area cleansed, we are prepared to begin the divination session. The querent (if included) and diviner take their places, and the potentializing of the portal begins.

Potentializing the Portal

In this case the portal is the set of Sevens. If the Sevens have been previously used, they will have been cleansed, bundled in order, secured with their tie, and wrapped in their protective cloth, as will be explained later in the scattering succession. As we have seen in the previous succession, they now reside in the center of the work-table surface.

The diviner takes the bundle, removes the staves from their protective cloth, and unties them from their retaining tie. The protective cloth and tie are placed aside, but not on the work surface, which must be kept clear.

The staves are spread out randomly on the work surface. They are then shuffled by the diviner, using both hands to mix them thoroughly by moving them around the work surface.

With both hands spread open and resting on the staves, the diviner says:

I focus the emanations from the future onto these learned staves of yew [or oak, or others depending on which wood is being used]. *We seek knowledge of what the future holds and in particular how it influences* [the inquiry is spoken here]. *We ask this in the name of the ancients, those who preceded us and those who will continue our tradition into the future. We open this portal so that the future may make itself known to us in the present and in the knowledge that we may make the present known to those in the past.*

Having said this, the diviner now gathers the staves together, arranges them in the order of hierarchy (as detailed above), and places them in the center of the table.

The portal is now potentialized and receptive to the emanations from the future. We are now ready for the casting.

The Casting

This is the point where the querent (if included) becomes involved. If no querent is involved, diviners engage in this succession themselves.

The querent picks up the staves and, using both hands, spreads them randomly over the work surface as the diviner did previously. Spreading the fingers of both hands and resting them on the staves, the querent silently recites the inquiry while focusing her energy on the staves. It is useful to explain this step to the querent beforehand, highlighting the mental image of transferring her energy and thoughts from her head, through her upper body, along her arms, and through her fingers onto the staves. The stronger and more efficiently the querent does this, the more receptive the portal becomes and the more the element of probability increases.

Once the querent and diviner consider that sufficient energy has been charged to the staves, the querent gathers the staves together and aligns them into an orderly stack. This must be done without employing any conscious influence on the task. The querent must have a mind clear of thoughts and not try to influence the arrangement of the staves to any extent. The querent now rests one end of the bundle of staves on the work surface, while holding them in the bundle with both hands.

The querent then raises the bundle of staves approximately one foot above the center of the work surface and, having silently recited the inquiry for one last time, drops the staves onto the work surface. Again, it is important that the querent exercises no conscious influence on how the staves fall. The distribution of the staves is determined by the influence of the emanations from the future and not the querent.

The casting is now complete. It is not necessary for the querent to be present for the remaining successions. A detailed interpretation and discussion can take place later.

The Meditation

This is a quiet time, a time for contemplation and reflection. The diviner has the array of staves spread before him or her and, without touching or moving the staves in any way, begins observing just how the array is distributed. Here the diviner also establishes the imaginary circle that encompasses the array of staves and the corresponding center line or datum used to determine the strength of each influence during the interpretation.

If any staves have fallen from the work table, they are collected and the diviner looks at the sigil of each. Although we have already established that these staves will be discounted during the later interpretation succession, it is important for the diviner to know which sigils have been eliminated. For example, if the sun sigil has fallen, the diviner may, and I emphasize *may*, consider that there will be no male influence governing the interpretation. It may also suggest that there will be no growth or progress relating to the future of the query posed. Both of these aspects of the sun sigil could be paramount in questions of future relationships, career prospects, and health issues. If more than one stave has fallen, then the influences of both should be considered in relationship to each other and also borne in mind when discounting them from the final interpretation.

Having considered the fallen staves, if there are any, and placed them to one side, the next consideration should be to look for any staves that may be overlapping or on top of any others.

Generally, the staves either present themselves in a wide array, with very few overlaps, or in a narrower pile or stack, where they present in a bundle piled on top of one another. Of course, as the casting is not ultimately controlled by the human hand, there will be infinite variations on these two presentations. It is for the diviner to assess the individual circumstances. Obvious overlaps are not difficult to identify, and they represent a strong domination of the upper staves over the lower ones. Subtle, corner overlaps suggest a mild control exerted by the upper staves over the lower ones. This is more of an influence than a domination. Once again, the varying degrees of overlap between the two extremes can be considered as illustrating the degree of influence involved.

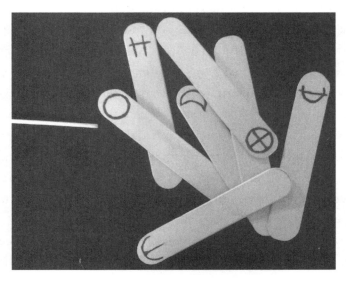

Figure 4.6. A typical array resulting from casting the Sevens, with the reed on the left showing the central line of the casting.

If there are no overlaps, then the influence of each individual stave is considered equal, and the sigils may be interpreted in any order with equal significance.

Where there is one or more overlaps, the upper stave is interpreted first and holds the highest significance.

Remember, at this stage the diviner is only establishing information and observations relating to the array. The actual interpretation begins later in the next succession.

The diviner now begins to build a picture of the main aspects of the array, observing if any staves are presenting face down and therefore having no significance. The diviner also observes if any staves are inverted, having their sigil marking at the bottom not the top. The attributes of such sigils are in this case reversed. Then they take note of the strength of each stave by its related angle to the datum, 90 degrees to the datum having the strongest influence and parallel to the datum the least. Consideration is also given to the relative strength of each stave to its companions, depending on their relative orientation to the datum in relation to each other. Remember that in all cases the staves are read from the diviner's viewpoint.

The purpose of this initial analysis is not to contemplate the meanings of the sigils, but to form a mental picture of the array and the relative influence of each individual stave's positions. The diviner begins to form an opinion of the overall purpose of the array and its complete message, as opposed to the individual meanings of each unique stave and sigil.

The diviner spends as long as is required to formulate what has been called the flow of the meaning, including its direction and combined strength of purpose. Once this is fixed in the diviner's mind, further time is spent in meditation considering how the entire message fits in with the diviner's knowledge of the querent's inquiry.

Only when the diviner is completely confident that consideration has been given to all aspects and ramifications of the array should he or she proceed to the actual interpretation succession and begin the task of interpreting the sigils and their meaning. Before doing this, however, it may be useful for the newcomer to draw or photograph the array as a permanent record that may be referred to later, should the need arise. I suggest this because in the next succession the diviner will dismantle the array as each stave is interpreted and, particularly during the first attempts, it may be difficult for the new diviner to commit the array to memory with so much else to remember.

It is also important to remember that, in this process, the meditation succession does not involve the dissociation technique described earlier. Divination using the learned wood is an interpretive form of divination and as such required the diviner to directly interpret the physical presentation of the Sevens' array without directly influencing the array or employing intuitive insights in the interpretation. It may be seen as akin to the reading of cards, the casting of die, or the reading of tea leaves; the reader simply interprets or reads what is seen, without exerting any direct influence.

Interpretation

It may be advisable for diviners to allow a brief recovery and relaxation period between the meditation and interpretation successions to revitalize their physical and mental capacity.

The interpretation begins with the diviner examining each sigil individually, so that each can be placed within the flow framework discussed above. Here, as in the previous succession, if there are no overlapping staves, each is considered in no particular order and has equal significance. Where there are overlapping staves, the uppermost are read first and have the most significant influence.

Each sigil is considered in the light of the four intellectual components we looked at earlier. For the sake of clarity, I list them again here:

- **Knowledge of the Past**—experience and learning from how past events unfolded
- **Awareness of the Present**—knowing where you are on your journey

- **Anticipation of Events to Come**—using your imagination and insights to help understand how events will unfold
- **Empathy with the Method of Divination Employed**—becoming part of the divination process you choose to employ

We have all used these intellectual components ourselves, whether or not we have been aware of it at the time. It will be useful here to look at a simple example, one that may also demonstrate just how they help in the process of foretelling.

It is unlikely that any of us consider ourselves a diviner or foreteller when we plan our vacations, but we employ nearly all of the same processes or components when we plan our family trips away. Let's take a moment to consider how we decide on what we will pack into our suitcases for our vacations.

One of our first considerations will be what type of clothing we will take. If we are travelling to a destination in a warm climate, we will consider how warm will it be. We will most likely use various media to discover what the temperature and rainfall may be at the present (Awareness of the Present). Then we look to find what the weather will be when we intend be on vacation (Anticipation of Events to Come). We will then think about what we wore the last time we visited a similar resort with the same climate (Knowledge of the Past) and pack the same clothes based on that experience. When we pack we may realize that we are missing a few vital pieces (Awareness of the Present) and plan a shopping trip to replace them (Anticipation of Events to Come), only to discover that they cost twice as much as they did the last time we bought them (Knowledge of the Past). In this simple example we have foretold a number of things to our advantage: the weather during our planned future trip, what we will be wearing, and what we need to shop for.

From this simple and brief example we can see how the intellectual components inform the process of divination and foretelling. When employed along with the imagination and ingenuity of the diviner, they form a major element in the overall process.

It is a useful exercise for newcomers to apply the same analysis to any regular activity they undertake, to see just how often we benefit from them. Travelling to work, cooking a meal, and redecorating a bedroom all involve an element of "foretelling," using the same intellectual components employed above.

It may also be useful to contemplate an even simpler example from everyday experience. If we throw a ball up into the air with the aim of catching it as it drops, are we predicting the future by anticipating where it will drop so that we can catch it? Science would suggest that we are employing our mental ability to calculate its speed, direction, and trajectory; the theory of ballistics; or our animal instincts related to our ability to hunt and survive. These are all intellectual components, as we have seen above.

There is one component we have not discussed: empathy with the method of divination employed. There is no point pursuing any method of divination without the belief that the process can produce the desired results. It is the diviner's responsibility to establish the querent's commitment and empathy with the method being used before beginning the process, otherwise the entire procedure will be invalidated.

Returning now to the interpreting of the sigils in the array, and assuming the array has at least one overlapping stave (as is typically the case), we begin considering the uppermost stave and its sigil.

Let's assume the upper stave has the moon sigil at the top as viewed by the diviner. The stave is at a forty-five-degree angle to the datum, meaning that it is significant but not at its most powerful.

The moon symbol represents birth, growth, family, and health. The moon cycle defines one of the most significant symbols of pre-Celtic Paganism. It corresponds to the female and, in particular, the menstrual cycle.

It is now for the diviner to consider these representations in relation to the query. It is not difficult to see that even the abbreviated description of the attributes ascribed to the moon sigil, laid out above, may be applied in a variety of ways in response to a variety of different queries.

For example, if the query relates to the outcome of a newly

announced pregnancy, the diviner may consider that the sigil could be interpreted as a healthy birth. It could mean the welcoming of a new family member who will thrive and grow physically, mentally, and spiritually. The fact that the moon refers to the female may indicate that the child will be female, but remember that the meaning is moderate in strength, so it may be wise to see what the other staves indicate before making that assumption. The female element may also be present for some other reason; after all, it is impossible to consider any birth without the female element being present. This is why it is important to consider each sigil's meaning in relation to *all* the others.

If the diviner is content that all the potential interpretations of the first stave have been considered, it may be removed to give a clear view of the next.

Again, the diviner observes the position of the sigil on the stave (upright or inverted) and the stave's orientation to the datum. This stave was beneath the previous one, so its strength is inferior to the first. If it is itself overlapping another stave, its meaning will have priority over the next, and so on until all the staves have been assessed.

As a further example for the query above, if the second stave has the air sigil upright and at a shallow angle to the datum, then it may be interpreted as having a weak influence. The air symbol represents variability, division, and instability. Air, in the form of wind, brings change and unpredictability.

The diviner may interpret this as an indication that the birth may bring instability to the home or the relationships involved. It may cause division and upset. It will certainly bring change, as all births do, but as this is a weak influence it suggests that these difficulties will be overcome, yet not without effort, as the result is uncertain and just how it may be done is unpredictable. This uncertainty may be considered in the light of the previous stave, where there was a relatively strong female indicator. This suggests that it could be the female influence that overcomes and dominates these moderate difficulties, as the female sigil dominates the second air stave.

The diviner continues in this vein until all the cast staves have been interpreted in relation to all the others. Only when all the sigils, their influences, and their relationship to one another have been examined can the overall meaning of the casting be determined.

Once this has been achieved, the results are considered in relation to the intellectual components previously discussed. Consider how knowledge of the past may impact the interpretation, how the interpretation is affected by present events, and how the anticipated future events may shape the interpretation.

In the example previously cited, we may consider that knowledge of previous births may impact the physical and mental well-being of the mother and child; maybe the mother's previous medical history has implications? Did the arrival of previous children have any effect on the stability of the family? Does the mother have a history of solving previous family difficulties? Is there a history of baby boys or girls? How do current circumstances impact the interpretation? Is the home situation currently stable? Will the current children be upset by the new arrival? Was it a planned pregnancy? What about planned future events—will they influence the results of the casting? Are there any planned vacations to reduce the stress? Is there a planned home extension to accommodate the new arrival? How will the family budget cope?

These, and many other implications, may color the overall summary of the casting. If the diviner has previous knowledge of these facts, the diviner may ascertain their impact and accommodate them within the interpretation. Otherwise they may be discussed with the querent in the post-casting consultation. Diviners may be able to incorporate these insights and their impact on the casting during the consultation or alternatively arrange a secondary consultation, giving themselves time to reflect on the information and its impact.

Once diviners are confident that all aspects of the casting results have been correctly and meticulously interpreted, they disclose their analysis to the querent.

In conclusion, an evaluation discussion typically takes place to clarify any outstanding points and assess the relevance of the insights and value of the process as a whole.

The interpretation is now complete.

Before any further activities take place, there is a need for a brief period of relaxation and a mental and spiritual cleansing. This is achieved by relaxation meditation, focusing on the light of infinite space. Diviners imagine a bright, white space of infinite dimension, a cleansing procedure for the mind and spirit. Once diviners are refreshed, they begin the scattering succession.

Scattering the Working Environment

It is not sufficient to just place aside the working tools of the casting. They must be cleansed and secured in such a way as to retain their positive influences and exclude any negative intrusions.

Typically the general setting and furniture used for the casting may remain in place or be rearranged at will. It is only the Sevens that need to be cleansed and correctly stored to retain their integrity.

The Sevens may be cleansed either by direct moon cleansing or by washing in moon-cleansed water. The method of moon-cleansing water is described in the final crafting section below. If this is the chosen method, the Sevens staves are carefully washed and dried using clean linen before being bound and wrapped.

The process of moon cleansing begins by spreading the staves in a place where they may be illuminated by a clear bright moon, preferably a full moon or, alternatively, a fat moon, one that is bigger than a half crescent. The stave should remain exposed to the moonlight for as many hours as possible but removed and bound before the sun has any influence. Once moon cleansed, the staves are stacked in order of their hierarchy and bound in place with any natural binding, such as linen ribbon, leather thongs, or similar. Finally, the bound staves are wrapped in an opaque, lightproof, natural fabric of the diviner's choice. They may be stored in any lightproof location until they are to be used again.

Reflection

In the days following, the diviner chooses an appropriate moment for quiet reflection on the casting. This may be considered a self-evaluation, reflecting on the appropriateness of the methods, the results, the benefits for the querent, and particularly the impact the process has had on the diviner's mental and spiritual well-being. This is also a time for consideration of any remedial action that needs to be undertaken in response to any negative residue.

5

Inductive Divination by Water

Captured-Water Skrying

Water, along with fire, may be considered the most potent natural force or element. Its most well-known attributes are that of purification, protection, expiation, revelation, and judgment.

Closely linked to the moon, both are considered predominantly female in their influence.

Water as a force of purification is seen within belief systems throughout the world. It is frequently used in workings of purification as part of initiation, baptism, and the cleansing of sins or violations. It is a purging element often suggesting penance and requital.

Its protective attributes may be seen in its use in isolating threatened entities from danger and washing away contamination. This attribute is frequently a product of water's purifying attribute.

Water's expiating attributes make it an ideal element in workings of atonement, redress, and reparation. It also indicates restitution and recompense.

The revelation attribute of water typically involves its use in foretelling and divination. The idea of water washing away ignorance and revealing truth is commonplace. Its reflective quality also associates it with revelation and insight, and this is the main

Figure 5.1. Feeder stream above Torc Waterfall,
Killarney, county Kerry, Ireland.

attribute that using water as a portal brings to Druidic divination.

Water as a judgmental force has, over the years, contributed to its use in trial by ordeal, such as ordeal-by-drowning and *Ludicium aquae* (trial by water), during the medieval era. Its purity, clarity, and revelatory attributes also contribute to its use as a judgmental element.

This is no more clearly illustrated than in an account in St. John D. Seymour's unique publication, *Irish Witchcraft and Demonology,* where he recounts the tale of one Florence Newton of Youghal, county Cork, in the far south of Ireland.

Seymour's publication contains contemporary accounts of witch trials and the various forms of punishment of the time, including the "swimming of witches":

The account related below, forms the seventh Relation in Joseph Glanvill's *Sadducismus Triumphatus* (Published posthumously London, 1681); it may also be found, together with some English cases of notoriety, in Francis Bragge's *Witchcraft Further Displayed* (London, 1712).

The tale shows that there was a little covey (coven) of suspected witches in Youghal, Southern Ireland, at that date, as well as some skillful amateur witch-finders (Messrs. Perry, Greatrakes, and Blackwall). From the readiness with which the Mayor proposed to try the "water-experiment" one is led to suspect that such a process as "swimming a witch" was not altogether unknown in Youghal.

For the benefit of the uninitiated we may briefly describe the actual process.

The suspected witch is taken, her right thumb tied to her left great toe, and vice versa. She is then thrown into the water: if she sinks (and drowns, by any chance!) her innocence is conclusively established; if, on the other hand, she floats, her witchcraft is proven, for water, as being the element in Baptism, refuses to receive such a sinner in its bosom.

The attributes of water as a vivifying and fructifying influence are more obvious. It brings refreshment to all living things, while returning vital life to nature and promoting growth as the seasons progress. These are some of the more practical and visible attributes ascribed to the water element.

The main virtue of using water in Druidic divination is its reflective quality. Its mirrorlike surface, together with its darkening, undefined depths, have made it a much-used medium throughout the ages.

Using water as a portal for Druidic divination is the demesne of

Figure 5.2. One of the many vivifying streams flowing through the yew forest within Killarney National Park.

Elemental Druids; that is, Druids who, through recognition of their individual gifts, have chosen to use the primal elements as their working medium.

Water may be used in a number of ways for divination and is available in any of its three main working states: as seawater, employed in its natural state; as free water, running in rivers and streams; and as captured water, contained in cauldrons, bowls, or natural vessels such as backwater pools, natural stone basins, and the like.

We shall look at two methods of divination using captured water. The first will look at using captured water as a skrying medium, and the second uses captured water as a portal for pendulum skrying. Unfortunately it is not possible within the confines of this book to explore seawater skrying or free-water skrying, as each is a complex subject in its own right. However, we shall look at harvesting free water and crafting it as a resource for captured-water skrying.

In this section we will examine the process of water skrying by using captured water, contained in an open vessel, as a portal for induced skrying. The water surface, together with any floating botanicals or oils, is manipulated to induce a pattern or signifier that the diviner looks at (or through) to determine the response to a specific query posed by a querent or the diviner himself or herself.

COLLECTING AND STORING WATER IN ITS VARIOUS FORMS

Captured water is obtained by one of five distinct methods. Procure it by:

1. Collecting rainwater directly (in its various conditions/states).
2. Collecting dew formed on a variety of botanical sources.
3. Collecting free water from streams, rivers, and other freshwater sources.
4. Collecting seawater (though we shall not be looking at this in detail, as mentioned above).

5. Distilling hydrosols or hydrolats (floral waters) and essential oils using a variety of botanicals.

We will explore four methods (excluding seawater), enabling readers to choose the one most compatible with their own personality and practices.

Collecting Rainwater Directly

Fresh rainwater is considered the purest form of water used in water skrying, free from all earthbound contamination. Moon-cleansed water, if cleansed properly, is free from spiritual contamination. We can therefore conclude that rainwater that falls and is collected before it touches the ground is considered free from both earthbound and spiritual corruption. This form of captured water is the most pure medium for all types of divination. However, other influences induce alternative positive effects on rainwater.

Thunder water is rainwater collected during a thunderstorm. This is considered particularly effective if pursuing a query related to future conflicts, be they personal conflicts, domestic conflicts, relationships, or even political or national conflicts.

Lighting water is rainwater collected during a lightning storm. This must be done during the periods of actual lightning flashes because the water is then charged with the enormous energy as the lightning discharges. It is particularly useful when searching for responses to questions of power and enlightenment. It is also seen as compatible with questions of motivation, inspiration, and planning for the future,

The most important aspect of gathering all of these types of rainwater is to collect them before they come into direct contact with the earth (once they have, they may well be contaminated by the earth element and its influences). In most circumstances I collect each of these types of rainwater by simply holding a wide, open vessel made of natural (neutral) material, such as a ceramic or glass bowl, in my outstretched hands during the appropriate weather. When collecting rainwater during any type of storm, be careful to stand away from, but in the vicinity of, high buildings or trees. It is much better that they be the lightning conductor and not you.

Each of these types of rainwater may be stored without jeopardizing their integrity within a sealed opaque glass or earthenware vessel. Metal or plastic vessels (including caps, lids, or stoppers) are not suitable. It is also desirable to avoid wooden vessels, as this may influence the water with the unwanted virtues of the individual wood concerned. If thunder water or lightning water has been collected under the light of the sun, it is necessary to moon cleanse them as has been described above to remove any sun element influences before they are used. This is best done just prior to their use, as it then also obviates any other unwanted influences that may have been induced during storage or handling.

Collecting Dew

Probably the most time-consuming form of collecting a water medium, dew is considered an extremely pure, gentle, and delicate medium.

Dew is always collected from specifically targeted botanicals just before dawn, before the sun has an opportunity to influence it, and when it is most prolific and at its most intense. It is only collected during fine weather, never in the rain or during storms, as this pollutes the dew with conflicting aggressive influences.

The main positive influences of dew relate to the botanicals from which it is harvested. It is most often used to seek responses of questions about love, relationships, children, and emotional challenges. In these cases the dew collected from rose petals, snow drop petals, and violet petals is considered the most potent.

As a brief aside, Edward Bach (1886–1936) recognized the power of dew when he visited the Druidic practitioners in northern Wales during the time he was developing his Bach flower remedies. His original remedies were crafted entirely from natural dew before he synthesized the process, using compounds made by macerating the same botanicals

Figure 5.3. A water cauldron (a deep stone hollow formed in the stream) at Druid's Well, Gap of Dunloe, Killarney, county Kerry, Ireland.

in simple water baths. Similarly, the original homeopathic remedies of Samuel Hahnemann (1755–1843) were manufactured from dew in the same way before, again, he eventually replaced the dew with the same botanicals macerated in simple water. One can only imagine that the time-consuming process of collecting natural dew was abandoned and replaced by simple water solutions as the products grew in popularity and the "cures" became manufactured on an industrial scale.

Returning to our main topic, we can see that using dew as a skrying medium invokes a delicate, gentle form of divination that should be taken into consideration when choosing the most appropriate methodology for your purpose.

As with the other water sources, dew may be collected using any suitable vessel made from a natural material, taking care that the dew does not come into contact with the earth. The collected dew may be stored in an opaque vessel (again, of a natural material) to avoid contamination. In this case the dew need not be moon cleansed, as it would have been collected before sunrise and therefore avoided contamination from the sun.

Collecting Free Water from Streams, Rivers, and Other Freshwater Sources

Free-running water is, without a doubt, the most frequently used form of water for divination. Its vitality, clarity, and intrinsic energies make it the most versatile, and its abundance and availability make it the most convenient of sources for the majority of practitioners. It is important, however, that when seeking a source, the following aspects are taken into consideration:

- It is collected at the appropriate time of day or night and stored correctly. Both are explained above.
- The original source has been identified (including tributaries). To avoid collecting polluted water, it is important that we identify the original source and the path of the water to the source, from which it is being collected. If collecting water from an emerging source, thought should also be given to the underground path of the water supply. If it is a high, mountain source, it may not be difficult to see how the water has gathered and percolated from the mountaintop. If the water is collected at a lower source, consideration should be given to its origin and the path it has taken to the source of collection. For example, if the water course travels beneath farmland; has it been polluted by percolating fertilizers or pesticides?
- The flow of water is both prolific and energetic. Fast-flowing water is ideal, but as long as the flow is energetic the impurities and contaminants that coalesce in stagnant water may be avoided.
- Potential contamination, both physical and spiritual, have been eliminated, as mentioned above.

- Collection is possible without physical danger to the collector. Do not be tempted to collect water from sources that may prove difficult to access. Never try that "last little stretch." It could prove fatal.
- Access to, and removal of, water does not infringe on privately owned land or rights. No one wants to face accusations of trespass or theft as a result of overzealous water collection.

Once the water has been collected, it may be stored in the same type of vessels as used above. If necessary, the water may be moon cleansed, as mentioned.

DISTILLING HYDROSOLS OR HYDROLATS (FLORAL WATERS) USING A VARIETY OF BOTANICALS

Using distilled hydrosols or hydrolats is undoubtedly the most advanced and technically complex method of sourcing a water medium for divination. It is used because practitioners can fine-tune the water medium to suit their individual requirements.

Hydrosols or hydrolats are more often known as floral waters and are commonly used in a variety of alternative therapies, such as aromatherapy and aroma massage, as well as in cosmetics, skin-care products, food preparation, and confectionary.

They may be obtained by a number of methods, some of which stretch back to a wide range of ancient civilizations. However, we shall focus on obtaining hydrosols by steam distillation, a method known to have been used throughout the regions of Druidic influence and the one maintained in the oral tradition I received.

The chosen hydrosol is distilled by allowing steam, produced by boiling water, to pass through the collected botanicals. The steam (distillate), when cooled, condenses to produce the hydrosol, along with the essential oil of the leached botanicals.

Both the hydrosol and essential oil "pass over" (to use the alchemical term) the distilling apparatus, and as they cool in the collection vessel the essential oil separates to float on top of the hydrosol. Both contain the virtues of the botanicals used, though they are more concentrated and intense in the essential oil. The benefit of this process, in the case of its use for divination, is that both these mediums are used in the divination working and, when using both together, a much more powerful medium is produced.

The distillation process used, as it is explained below, is a gentle, sympathetic process, carried out at relatively low temperatures, giving two distinct advantages. The first is that both the hydrosol and essential oil produced benefit from the calmness of the process, avoiding any harsh, bruising procedures that may leach other unwanted essences and contaminants from the original botanicals. The second advantage is that, as the process is undertaken at a relatively low temperature, it allows us to adhere more closely to the original Druidic method of distillation. To better understand this second benefit we shall take a moment to look briefly at the history of distillation in the Druidic lore of the region.

It may be generally believed that distilling is a relatively recent discovery, but there is considerable archaeological evidence to indicate that it is indeed a very ancient process. In the regions where Druidic lore would have prevailed, there have been a number of archaeological discoveries of ancient Stone Age sites containing, among other things, communal cooking hearths. Fortunately for me, one of these archaeological digs took place just one kilometer from my home, at a megalithic site now called Aghadoe, where a number of fire pits were recently discovered.

One of the intriguing aspects of these particular fire pits, or *fulachta fia* as they are known in the Irish, is their unique form and construction. Most megalithic fire pits would consist of a round or crescent-shaped depression, usually defined by a surrounding circle of charred rocks and a central core of charcoal residues. However, in the case of the fulachta fia, they are constructed as a rectangular, stone-lined pit containing the expected fire residue, along with a neighboring wood-lined trough that would have contained water. Stones would be placed in the fire pit and, when hot, transferred to the water-filled neighboring trough to heat the water. The hot water was then used to cook meat, fish, and other foods, or sometimes for bathing. Along with the expected animal and fish remains, archaeologists also discovered significant amounts of pottery shards marked with the distinctive patterns of the Grooved-ware Beaker civilization, known to have inhabited the locality at the time. The Grooved-ware civilization was at its peak during the middle period of the Neolithic Age (Stone Age), a time when the Druidic culture was at its most evident. Bearing in mind that this period was a millennium before the Celtic influence arrived in the region, it can be seen to be contemporary with the period of pre-Celtic Druidic divination we are exploring.

The relevance of the discoveries explained above is that during this period people used this form of rock transfer for cooking and heating water for two reasons. There were no metal, heat-resistant pots to use on the fires to heat water until the subsequent Bronze Age arrived. Also, the famous Grooved-ware pottery was not fired sufficiently to make it heat tolerant enough to be placed on a fire because the thermal shock would have shattered the pots instantly, so the pottery discovered could only have been used for storage, eating food, or for drinking from.

However, the Druidic tradition tells us that crude distillation was already happening at this time. Just how this was being done (and how it can be reproduced today) is again explained by the oral tradition.

The first distillation was carried out by placing earthenware pots containing water and botanicals in the cooler embers at the edge of the fire or by surrounding them with warm stones from the fire to heat the water inside. The warm water slowly evaporated and condensed on reeds that had been placed at the top of the pot. The condensed vapor then runs along the reeds and drips into a vessel below. This resulting distillate is a combination of the hydrosol and the essential oil, which later separates when cooled. Incidentally, I still use this method on occasion today. The same result may be achieved by replacing the reeds with large, suitably shaped, smooth-surfaced stones, allowing the same condensation and collection process to be achieved. These were the original mediums used for water divination, so we can see that using steam-distilled hydrosols and essential oils emulate the ancient tradition, as well as being the most advanced and precise method of water divination.

I should also mention here, for the sake of a complete explanation, that we can also obtain floral waters and essential oils by maceration, but I have not included this method because it is less effective and may also create confusion with those who have read my previous publications, describing the extraction of the three cardinals from botanical sources and the comparison of this tradition with that of the early alchemists.

So, having explored the history of the distillation process, we should now look at the most effective way of distilling hydrosols and essential oils using today's equipment. There are two defining principles employed here: first, any equipment must be accessible to the reader, both easily obtained and not prohibitively priced; and second, in using this equipment we are not to compromise the original methodology or the resulting distillates.

As I have mentioned above, occasionally I indulge myself by reproducing the original arcane methods of crafting distillates, but for the greater part I use equipment that, although still associated with ancient techniques of distillation, is readily available and modestly priced, making it well within the reach of those with an interest in exploring this technique.

We are now going to look at the distillation process using an apparatus developed and made popular by early alchemists called an alembic still.

The process of evaporation and condensation at controlled temperatures using a still may be well known to most readers, and it is this same process that we will be using to produce our distillates. The particular type of still we will be using, the alembic still, is readily available at a size and price suitable for our purpose.

An alembic still is a distilling apparatus, now mostly obsolete in commercial production, consisting of a gourd-shaped container topped by an "onion" cap with a long beak and a spiral condenser for conveying the distillate products to a receiver vessel. This process of heating, evaporating, cooling, and condensing is, in both the Druidic and alchemical tradition, called passing over.

Our objective in employing the alembic still is to use the heating chamber, which normally contains the original liquid to be distilled, to heat previously collected free-running water and produce the steam we are going to use to extract our distillates.

So, having the ability to produce the steam in the heating chamber, we need an additional chamber in which to pack our botanicals, through which the steam must flow. To do this, we add a removable chamber above the heating chamber to hold the botanicals. In distilling terminology this is called a split top column, as it is an additional

Figure 5.4. My 500 ml copper split column alembic still.

column that sits on top of the heating chamber and may be split from the still in order to fill it with our chosen botanicals.

As a means of avoiding any form of contamination, we use the traditional material employed for stills since its discovery prior to the Bronze Age, which is of course copper (bronze being the amalgam of copper and tin). This is doubly important, to my experience, as my hometown of Killarney has the oldest copper mine in the world at Ross Island, which was also populated by the Grooved-ware Beaker people mentioned above.

The culmination of all these requirements gives us our still definition as a copper split column alembic still.

Copper Split Column Alembic Still

From a practical point of view, I have found a 500 ml capacity still the perfect size for the quantity of distillates we need. This size also has the advantage of not needing a large amount of potentially hard-won botanicals to pack it for use.

If readers search these specifications on the internet, they will quickly discover a range of ready suppliers. I suggest that the Portuguese and UK manufacturers are the best quality and worth any additional shipping costs.

In addition to the alembic still itself, we will also need a suitable heating source. I have found through experience that, although not traditional, an electric hot-plate heater with temperature control is the most versatile and reliable. Fires, either wood or peat fueled, contaminate the fragrance of the distillates, as do some of the low-pressure gas (LPG) and mains gas heaters.

We will also require a separatory funnel, with a stopcock, and a retort stand to hold it. A separatory funnel is a glass funnel with a narrow top and a stopcock at the bottom. Once the combined hydrosol and essential oil has passed over in the alembic still, it drips into the collection vessel. When we have finished the distillation, the combined distillate is decanted from the collection vessel into the separatory funnel and left to allow the essential oil to float to the top of the hydrosol.

The separation can be easily seen through the walls of the glass funnel, and once the separation is complete the stopcock at the bottom of the funnel is carefully opened to allow the hydrosol to run off. The stopcock is immediately closed once all the hydrosol has left the funnel in order to retain the essential oil that was floating on top. This may then be run off into a separate vessel.

Having all our equipment in place, we must now look at the detailed sequence of events in the distillation of the hydrosol and essential oil.

Selecting Botanicals

First, we must consider the selection of the botanicals we intend to use, and in doing this we must again remember that the choice is driven by the botanical's compatibility with the diviner and not the querent or the inquiry. The botanicals need to be attuned to the personal energy of the diviner, harmonious with the diviner's meditation needs, and able to contribute to the overall atmosphere of the divination working.

We intend to use the hydrosol as the main skrying medium and, in an additional example, we will be using the essential oil as floating agent in the divination working. With this in mind, as well as the overall virtues of the botanicals selected, we should also consider the aspects of color and fragrance. Both of these qualities have a vital significance, as those readers familiar with the workings of aromatherapy and color therapy will be aware. The process of distillation and separation concentrate both the color and fragrance of the resultant distillates and, in the example using floating essential oils, we shall also be slightly raising the temperature of the hydrosol to increase the gentle evaporation of the oil and the release of the oil's fragrances.

As there are a number of sources that the reader may access to research the attributes and virtues of indigenous botanicals in Druidic lore, I shall not repeat the large body of related information here. Instead we will focus on using two botanicals frequently used in Druidic workings of many kinds. We will use herb mint and wild dog rose as the two botanicals in our exploration, as they prove to be compatible with the personal energy of the majority of people. But first we need to look at the various attributes of the two botanicals we have chosen.

⮞ Herb Mint (Spearmint)

Also called garden mint, mentha spicata, mackerel mint, Our Lady's mint, green mint, spire mint, Sage of Bethlehem, fish mint, menthe de Notre Dame, erba Santa Maria, Frauen Munze, and lamb mint.

Botanical: *Mentha viridis*
Habitat: Found predominantly in moist locations, along stream banks and uncultivated lands.

Pliny relates that the Greeks and Romans wore ceremonial crowns and garlands of spearmint at their feasts and decorated their halls and tables with its sprays. They also used spearmint essence as a flavoring in foods and wines. Gerard, in further praise of the herb, tells us: "The smelle rejoiceth the heart of man, for which cause they used to strew it in chambers and places of recreation, pleasure and repose, where feasts and banquets are made." Among the essential oils used in aromatherapy, food flavoring, and alternative/complementary medicine, spearmint ranks first in importance. It typically presents as a colorless or yellowish-green liquid, with a distinctive, highly penetrating odor and a warm, sweet menthol flavor. As such, spearmint oil is the most extensively used of the volatile oils. Distillation from the leaves of the plant, as demonstrated below, yields spearmint hydrosol and essential oil. We will use both of these in the divination example explored later. In these circumstances, using herb mint produces a calming atmosphere, while heightening the ability to attune to reverberations from past events.

⮞ Dog Rose

Also known as wild rose, briar (refers to a prickly shrub), briar-rose, cat-rose, cock-bramble, dike-rose (i.e., hedge rose), hip-rose, and pig-rose. Another vernacular is Ewemack.

Botanical: *Rosa canina*
Habitat: Found growing among hedgerows, wood margins, and on rocky slopes.

Among the essential oils, dog rose is relatively rare. Sometimes used in exclusive perfumes, it may also be used as a delicate flavoring.

Distillation from the whole flower of the plant yields rose water and dog rose essential oil. Using dog rose distillates produces a warming, relaxing environment, while aiding the ability to attune to the more delicate reverberations from future events.

The fruit or hip of the dog rose is more frequently used than the flower or leaves. High in vitamin C, a syrup made from the extract is a popular vitamin supplement, and the fruit itself makes a common tisane.

Harvesting Botanicals

Having selected the botanicals we intend to use and located a suitable renewable source using the information above, we must now consider how we harvest them. Season, weather, location—in the world of winemaking and grape-growing, the impact of these elements is termed terroir. Terroir, as described by Wikipedia, is "the set of all environmental factors that affect a plant's phenotype, including unique environment contexts . . . and a plant's specific growth habitat." Like the grape growers, we need to consider the botanical's terroir influences before harvesting it.

The significance of the season is the most obvious and most visible of these effects. As the seasons progress most botanicals undergo immense structural change. Spring produces buds, new leaf population, rising sap, pollination, growth, and early flowerings. In summer we see major flowering and growth reaching its peak. Autumn brings fruiting, nuts, and the beginning of the plant's preparations for the winter. Winter itself brings with it the shedding of leaves, reduction of sap, dropping of fruits, and seed distribution, both airborne and by herbivorous animals and birds. Each of the seasons, therefore, has a great influence on the individual botanical's appearance, strength, and potency. They also affect the availability of some of the botanical's elements—such as flowers, fruits, nuts, and leaves—all of which are usable elements in divination. The choice of harvesting season is therefore specific to the elements of the botanical we intend to use and the potency of the resultant hydrosols and essential oil.

In the examples we are exploring, spearmint is best harvested when the leaves are mature and at their most fragrant. This means mid to late summer or early autumn. In the case of the example using dog rose, we intend to use the flowers of the plant, so our premium harvesting season will be late spring and early summer, before the rose hips set. Similarly, if we had intended to use the rose hips, we would be harvesting when the hips mature and before they drop, which would be autumn or early winter. Of course all these seasonal definitions are relatively imprecise, and the actual harvesting will depend on the diviner's observations and judgment.

As we saw with the collection of the various types of water used in divination workings, weather has a major influence on the virtues of the botanicals we harvest and must be taken into consideration when planning your harvesting trips. Periods of dry weather have an impact on the botanical's potency, moisture content, and sap content. Prolonged rain produces the high groundwater levels that promote rotting and fungal activity, while moderate rainfall is a necessity for healthy growth and good water content in the plants themselves. Again, the influencing aspects of weather are best judged by the observations of the diviner. In our examples both spearmint and dog rose benefit from modest rainfall and should be harvested either during or immediately following a refreshing rainfall, preferably in the early morning while the plants retain their moisture and before the sun has the opportunity to influence the botanical's virtues or evaporate its internal moisture.

Most types of botanicals favor a particular growing location and habitat. Some favor marshy, damp ground, while others may prefer dry, rocky terrain. Simple research or local knowledge will point readers to

Figure 5.5. A dismantled alembic still showing the individual parts. From left to right: the heating chamber, the split column, the condenser chamber, and, at the front, the alembic head.

the most likely location for the plant they are seeking. The preferred locations for the plants needed for our examples are described in the specification of each, listed above. One consideration not listed above is the influence of the plants surrounding the one we are thinking of harvesting. If the particular plant grows among a group of the same plant, then its influence will be positively increased. In such cases plants should be harvested from the center of the growth group, as those at the group's edge may be influenced by nearby botanicals (in particular by their root growth normally not visible to the naked eye). In cases where individual plants are growing amid other varieties, it is advisable to avoid harvesting and continue searching for other, more suitable locations.

In all harvesting it is important to consider the plant population's ability to regenerate. With this in mind, we should never harvest any more than is essential for our working.

Figure 5.6. The still's split column, filled with spearmint, ready to be assembled with the other parts of the still.

Assembling the Distillation Equipment

While there may be some differences between alembic stills, dependent on the manufacturer, the principle elements are common to all.

The five critical parts of the still comprise the heating chamber (which will contain the water we will boil to produce the steam for distilling), the split column (into which we place our botanicals), the alembic head (the onion-shaped cover with the distinctive long gooseneck), the condenser chamber (a cooling water bath through which the coil containing the steam passes), and the collection vessel (which receives the liquid distillate).

Individual stills will be accompanied by the specific instruction for assembly and use. In this case I am describing the procedure for the alembic still I use and have shown in the accompanying photographs.

Step One

Fill the heating chamber with the contained water of your choice. The various types of captured water are described above. Use the one most suited to your style. The heating chamber should be filled to approximately two-thirds of its capacity and never any more. This is an important safety feature and prevents overflow when the water boils during the steam production process. It is also the correct amount for the size of the split-column capacity.

Step Two

Fill the split column with the botanicals you wish to distill. The split column needs to be packed as tightly as possible to maximize the distillation but not overpacked to the extent that it restricts the passage of the steam. The split column is normally designed to be the appropriate capacity for the heating chamber that it attaches to.

Step Three

The alembic head is firmly connected to the top of the split column, thereby sealing the botanicals in place.

Step Four

The combined split column and alembic head are firmly connected to the heating chamber.

Step Five

The condenser chamber is firmly connected to the end of the extending gooseneck of the alembic-head fitting. If the condenser chamber is of the type that has a flow-through water-cooling system, both the supply and drainage outlets should also be connected at this stage.

Step Six

The assembled unit is placed on the heating plate (or similar) and the collection vessel is placed below the condenser outlet to collect the liquid distillate.

In a well-made alembic still, the fit between the various chambers should be steam-tight when they are pushed firmly together. If this is not the case, or if the joining sections have become worn and ill-fitting through repeated use, then a traditional thick paste of flour and water may be applied to any leaking sections. The paste dries to form a seal once the apparatus has been heated and is easily removed without damaging the joining surfaces when distillation is complete. For safety's sake always apply this sealing paste *before* the apparatus is heated; never when it's hot!

It is always a good practice to test the apparatus with a dummy run without botanicals first. This both cleans and sterilizes the interior of

Figure 5.7. Caput mortuum of spearmint removed from
an alembic still at the end of the distillation.

the apparatus and allows any steam leaks to be located and sealed before the distillation is done.

The Distillation

With the assembled apparatus in place and sealed, we can now begin the actual distillation.

The heating plate is turned on and the water in the heating chamber, reaching boiling temperature, begins producing steam. It will take a few moments for the steam to heat the botanicals in the split column and begin to find its way through the botanicals, up to the alembic head, along the gooseneck, and through the condensing coil in the condensing chamber.

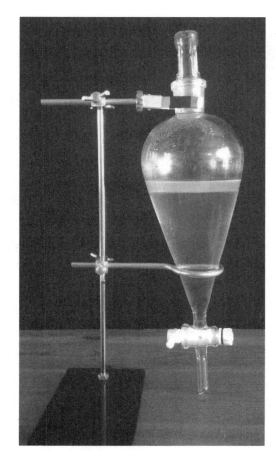

Figure 5.8. Separatory funnel with distillate, showing the essential oil floating on the surface of the hydrosol.

The initial distillate arriving at the collection vessel is called the head. This derives from the ancient alchemical description comparing the entire distillate with a snake, with a head, body, and tail. In this case the head and tail are discarded as being contaminated and not the pure "body" of the distillation. Once the head has been discarded, the distillation continues and produces the main body of the distillate.

Care must be taken not to let the distillation happen at too fast a pace. If the water in the heating chamber is allowed to boil too ferociously, the steam will be produced at too fast a rate, potentially compromising the distillate and risking breaching the seals on the apparatus. We are looking for a moderate, gentle distillation to extract all the desired virtues from the botanicals.

Once the majority of the water has been evaporated, the body distillate is decanted, and the collection vessel is put back in place to receive the tail distillate (to be discarded). As soon as this begins to appear (identifiable by the increased color and density of the distillate and the change in fragrance), the heat is turned off and the distillation is complete.

When the apparatus has cooled it may be disassembled and cleaned, ready for its next distillation. At this point (before cleaning), the apparatus contains whatever liquid tail distillate that may remain in the system, and the split column is full of what is now classed as *caput mortuum* (from the article "caput mortuum" on Wikipedia: "an alchemical Latin term, for materials that have been divested of their virtues and of no further value, whose literal meaning is 'dead head' or 'worthless remains'").

None of this material is of any further use and may be discarded or, in the case of most types of botanical caput mortuum, it may be reused as compost. The distillate may now be decanted for separation.

The Separation

The distillate is now decanted into the separatory funnel, sealed with a stopper, and allowed to stand undisturbed to allow the essential oil to float to the top of the liquid, where it rests on top of the hydrosol.

The separation is complete when no more essential oil rises to the surface. This may take a number of hours or, in extreme cases, a few days.

At this point the essential oil is clearly visible as a separate liquid floating on top of the distillate. A flask is now placed underneath the outlet tap at the base of the funnel, and the drainage tap is opened to allow the hydrosol to drain from the funnel. It may be necessary to remove the stopper from the top of the funnel to allow the hydrosol to flow freely from it.

As the hydrosol leaves the funnel, the essential oil can also be seen travelling down it. When it almost reaches the outlet tap, the tap is closed to prevent any essential oil from draining into the flask of hydrosol. The flask containing the hydrosol is removed, and a second flask is placed under the funnel outlet. The purpose of this flask is to contain the small amount of liquid that borders the hydrosol and essential oil, so that it does not enter the essential oil when it is collected later. The drainage tap is opened, and just enough of this combined liquid is drained off to make sure that only pure essential oil is left. The drainage tap is closed, and the combined liquid flask is replaced with another flask which will collect the essential oils.

Finally the tap is opened for the last time, and the remaining essential oil is drained off.

The separation is now complete, and we are left with three flasks of liquid. The hydrosol from the first flask is decanted into an opaque glass bottle, sealed, labelled, and stored until it is used.

The essential oil from the last flask is similarly decanted, sealed, and labelled.

The small amount of combined liquid in the remaining flask may be used in whatever way preferred (oil evaporator, bath additive, etc.).

The entire apparatus may now be cleaned and stored until its next use.

In the section above we also identified dog rose as a botanical suitable for a more gentle form of distillation and skrying. The process of distilling essential oil and hydrosol from the dog rose is identical to that of the spearmint we have looked at above. It is worth noting, however, that only the flower heads should be packed into the split column of the alembic still. Leaves, stalks, and woody materials should be removed.

Storage

Both the hydrosol and essential oil may be stored indefinitely, if kept in sealed opaque glass bottles, in a cool place, and away from direct sunlight or excessive heat.

We have now seen how we can collect and craft a range of waters that all lend themselves to use as a divination medium. If you maintain an adequate store of each of these water mediums, you will always have whichever type is most suitable for the working you are planning.

TOOLS AND MEDIUMS

Having looked at collecting the various types of water, harvesting appropriate botanicals, and crafting hydrosols and essential oils, we now need to examine the other tools and mediums we will need for captured-water skrying.

Before we begin the divination working we will need to gather all the necessary tools we will be using. The first of these we need to consider is the working stone.

The Working Stone

In all Druidic activities we will need a focal point for our working. Traditionally this was the working stone. This was a large, recumbent stone that was located at an auspicious location and alignment within the circle of standing stones that was the ancient workplace of the Druids. For all intents and purposes the working stone may be considered as the altar, workbench, and laboratory table of the Druid, though most Druid traditions avoid using the name *altar*, as it has complex religious association that are wholly incompatible with Druidic lore.

Fortunately for me, I have regular access to this traditional and

Figure 5.9. A glass divination vessel, shallow enough to be easily viewed from above, accompanied by a jug of hydrosol and two wands.

powerful workplace, in the form of the Seven Sisters megalithic stone circle just two miles from my home, but I appreciate that this privilege is not available to the vast majority of people. So, like everyone else, when I cannot gain access to the Seven Sisters, I use a normal wooden table as my working stone. I use a table made entirely from natural materials to harmonize with the other elements of my work. Typically, this working table is located in my workshop, but it would also regularly be used outside, weather and planned purpose permitting.

For the purpose of this explanation we will assume the working stone is located inside a suitable space—be it a workshop, kitchen, bedroom, or wherever is most convenient—bearing in mind that we will need a quiet location that is free from interruption and may be made dark when required.

Other than the above requirements, the only other specification is that the table is of sufficient size and accompanied by a chair for the diviner to sit in. If there is a querent, then a second chair is placed at the working stone opposite the diviner, assuming the querent wishes to be present and the diviner agrees. If the working stone is suitable, the same working is undertaken with the diviner standing at the stone.

Whether standing or sitting, alone or in the company of a querent, the working stone must be prepared in the same way. For simplicity's sake, in the example that follows we will assume there is no querent present.

We shall be arranging the working stone with candles; the vessel that will contain our divination water (the combined vessel and water is referred to as the water portal); a collection of vessels and containers holding the inclusions, botanicals, and oils we will be using in our working; and, in this particular example, the wands we will use during the divination. We shall look at each of these in detail.

Figure 5.10. A selection of typical essential oils and botanicals to be floated on the water portal. On the *left*, there is a large natural glass inclusion collected from a Welsh coal mine, about a mile and a half below ground.

The Water Portal

The water portal itself is the central point of the divination working, and as such it occupies the central location on the working stone. The empty bowl, cauldron, or other vessel that is to be the portal is positioned at the center of the working stone, usually slightly nearer to the diviner so the diviner may look down into the vessel during the working.

A suitable pitcher—a jug or similar vessel containing the captured water or hydrosol—is placed next to the bowl/cauldron, ready for the water to be poured into it as the working begins. Either two or four candles (dependent on the diviner's preference) in tall candlesticks are located to each side and toward the rear of the portal vessel.

Candles

The choice of the number of candles used is entirely that of the diviner. I typically place two three-candle candlesticks on the working stone, allowing me to control the level of light by lighting as many as I feel is appropriate. I leave the choice of how many I light until the working begins. I always use beeswax candles, but candles made from any natural wax are perfectly acceptable. It is generally not a good idea to use perfumed candles, as this will interfere with any aromas deliberately generated by the portal's hydrosol (if used) or any floating botanicals or oils.

Inclusions

On some occasions it may also enhance the diviner's engagement with the working to place various "inclusions" into the water of the portal. When using captured seawater for example, it may be useful to place one or more beach stones into the cauldron or portal. If the diviner can find and feel a connection to a specific, single beach stone, then this would be particularly appropriate. In my experience this would typically be a stratified, decorative beach stone, formed by natural forces into an appealing shape. This would be placed at the base of the portal cauldron or bowl, then covered with the cleansed, captured seawater so that it sits well below the surface. Exactly how this enhances the divination is explained in detail below. In contrast to this single-stone approach, some diviners prefer a collection of smaller beach stones, arranged in a harmonious way at the base of the portal.

Other inclusions may be river stones (used in a similar fashion to the beach stones mentioned above), driftwood, foraged wood, crystals, mineral stones, natural glass deposits (blocks of glass formed naturally and popular in the Welsh tradition, as they often appear among coal deposits), or other sympathetic materials. In addition to inclusions positioned below the water in the portal vessel, other materials may be floated on top of the water for a similar purpose.

Floating Botanical

A variety of botanicals may be floated on the water contained in the portal: appropriate herbs, flowers (complete flower heads or petals), leaves, barks, or any other suitable floating botanicals. The purpose of

Figure 5.11. Two types of wands used in Druidic divination. On the *left,* an embraced wand, on the *right,* a simple rude wand.

floating botanicals on the portal water's surface is described in detail below. A similar result may be obtained by floating oils on the surface of the water.

Floating Oils

The most common oils used for this purpose are the essential oils of herbs, flowers, or those extracted from any of the other botanicals mentioned above. If distilling hydrosols and essential oils as described in the section above, it is ideal to combine both as skrying portal mediums.

The Purpose of Inclusions, Floating Botanicals, and Floating Oils

There are two reasons why diviners use the three aids described above. The first is to enhance their ability to attune their senses with the working. We will see that, in preparation for the divining working, the water for the portal is gently heated. The reason for this is so that when the botanicals or oils are floated on the water, their fragrance will be released and free their influence and virtues into the air. Diviners benefit from these influences and virtues during the meditation and interpretation successions. The second reason is that when diviners begin the meditation, they initially consider the shapes and patterns made by the botanicals and oils on the water's surface, then, as part of the process of dissociation with their surroundings, they focus on the infinite plane below and beyond the water's surface, deep into the portal's pathway. The floating materials on the water and the inclusions at the base of the portal vessel help define the periphery or boundary of the portal in the mundane world and lead the way to the place where the diviner becomes receptive to the emissions from future events. By intense concentration on this focal point beyond the mundane and maintaining a lucid awareness of their situation, diviners achieve the altered-mind state required to search for the revelation they seek.

Skrying Wands and Their Use

The final tool we shall look at before exploring the successions of the divination working is the skrying wand (fig. 5.11). The skrying wand differs from other wands, as it is used to disturb or stir the surface of the portal water for the same reasons as the items described above. In other words, it is initially to produce any indications or patterns that inspire diviners in their endeavors and, later, to define the boundary of the mundane portal used by the diviner.

Skrying wands are usually crafted specifically for a planned divination working. As such they are, for the greater part, rude wands (simply crafted in a crude or rude fashion, they are unsophisticated and therefore possess more powerful virtues of the tree from which they are harvested). They are intended for one use.

Instruction on harvesting and crafting this type of wand is detailed in chapter 9, "Crafting Your Own Tools."

As one would imagine, these skrying wands are used to disturb the portal water surface by the simple actions of the diviner. Small, focused movements of the wand by the diviner produces ripples and movement in the water's surface that produce the indicators that assist the diviner. Some diviners choose not to use skrying wands as, arguably, the movement and concentration required to create the desired patterns distract them from achieving the state of dissociation they need. It is worth experimenting with both methods to discover the best for each individual.

Having looked at the tools needed, we shall now move on to explore the successions of the divination working.

PREPARING THE WORKING ENVIRONMENT

Once again it is important to stress the need for meticulous preparation of the working environment. I will remind readers of the dangers, both mental and spiritual, in beginning any working without properly preparing themselves and their working tools.

The working stone is laid out as described above sometime prior to the working. Diviners MUST prepare themselves in the way described in the previous chapter before beginning any aspect of the working. Once confident that their own cleansing and preparation is complete and effective, work may begin on preparing the working environment itself.

The Protective Circle

As with all Druidic workings, no matter where they are enacted, it is important to prescribe a protective circle enclosing the work area. Beginning at the front of the working stone and moving in a clockwise direction, pour a continuous, unbroken line of sea salt onto the floor to form a circle encompassing the entire work area. As you return to the starting point, it is advisable to leave an entry point (a gap in the circle) to allow entry and exit until the working begins. We need to use natural sea salt, preferably salt that has been evaporated by ourselves from a known, unadulterated source of seawater, to ensure its purity. Be careful, if using purchased sea salt, that you can vouch for its provenance and purity.

Figure 5.12. My divination cauldron being prepared for use.

Once we have entered the circle, in order to begin the working we stand at the entry, holding sufficient salt to close the circle. Extending our arms, we say:

I call upon the four elements to cleanse this circle and remove any unfriendly influences from within. I do this in the name of all those who have preceded me.

With this, we use the remaining sea salt to close the entry gap and seal the protective circle.

This cleansing process, though necessary as the initiating point of the working, is deliberately brief and simple. It reinforces the fact that nature, in its normal state, is good, and anything bad will need to be a deliberate, conscious decision to deviate from this natural state of goodness. As nature itself is not able to make conscious decisions, we can assume the status quo of goodness remains unless human activity intervenes. Our cleansing, therefore, is a safeguard against any unknown human interference or interventions that may have been deliberately or unintentionally evoked on the working.

Cleansing and Purifying Your Tools

Before beginning our working we must be certain that all our tools and equipment are thoroughly cleaned. Although all our tools would have been cleaned prior to storing them for subsequent use (see "Scattering the Working Environment" in the previous chapter and in the succession below), we must cleanse them again before they are used.

We have examined the cleansing of the skrying mediums above (moon cleansing and distillation as appropriate), so once physically cleaned, if the tools are placed within the protective circle as it is closed and purified, the tools will benefit from the same purification as everything else enclosed within the circle.

POTENTIALIZING THE PORTAL

Once the protective circle has been purified and sealed, we can progress to potentializing the portal itself. The portal cannot be considered useful until it has been potentialized; prior to that it is just a vessel of water with a variety of things immersed in it or floating on its surface.

We begin the potentialization by bringing the portal vessel to the front or center of the working stone. If we are using any inclusions, we arrange them inside the vessel.

Next, we fill the vessel with our skrying medium (the preferred form of captured water or hydrosol), which, if we are choosing to use floating botanicals or oils, we have previously gently heated to just above blood temperature in readiness.

We then sprinkle any chosen botanicals on top of the water or we drop small amounts of the chosen essential oil onto the surface of the water. Our skrying portal is now assembled and ready to be potentialized.

Diviners now take a moment to organize and focus their thoughts. This is the point where the physical gathering together of the working environment is finished, and diviners begin their journey toward their spiritual involvement. Secure inside the protective circle, the first step is to put all the considerations of the mundane world to one side to focus on the task ahead. This may be done by any method the diviner prefers. Some compartmentalize their mundane concerns by placing them into imaginary mind boxes, mind rooms, or other favored compartments. They make a conscious effort to close the door behind them to seal their concerns inside until the working is complete. Others have told me how they mentally bury their concerns, making sure to firmly pat down the earth to secure them. Yet others seal their concerns into jars or boxes using string and sealing wax in their mental efforts. I am sure there are many other processes that individuals choose to separate their mundane, everyday issues and concerns from their spiritual journeys, and diviners should feel free to use whatever means they prefer.

Once diviners are confident that they have placed the mundane to one side, they then look toward their working and make sure they have a very clear understanding of the successions they shall be working through and the query they are pursuing. They must establish a precise, unobstructed path from the beginning of the divination working to the end, clear in their understanding of what will be undertaken and what the final intention may be. Mentally stepping through every stage of the working before it begins ensures the diviner fully anticipates every obstacle that may present itself, focuses the mind fully on the journey ahead, and elevates the mind beyond the mundane.

Only when diviners are confident that they have achieved the various stages outlined above should they proceed to the potentialization of the divination portal.

The diviner now stands before the portal vessel, which we recall is at the front and center of the working stone and has been charged with the chosen inclusions, captured-water medium, and/or floating botanicals/oils.

With one hand resting on each side of the portal vessel (left and right), the diviner speaks the following:

I call upon the infinite forces of nature to help me in my quest, open my mind and spirit to receive whatever the future may behold, and let my energy attune to the emanations I seek, as the many have done before me and the many who shall follow.

If diviners intend to work seated, they now sit in preparation for the working. If standing, they distribute their weight comfortably between their feet and ensure their body is at ease.

With hands resting on the working stone on each side of the portal vessel, the diviner now begins the journey beyond the mundane.

SKRYING MEDITATION

The first focus is on the floating botanicals or oil. The intention is to draw the image of the floating array into the mind. Even at this early stage of the working, receptive minds may gain insights into their quest. It may be possible to interpret the array as a portent or message and envisage shapes or patterns that may express meaning or be signifiers for future revelation.

At this point, the diviner may choose to use the wand to influence the arrangement of the botanicals/oil floating on the water portal surface. Remember that this is the method most often used by the Elemental Druid, and we have identified it as an inductive form of divination, one where the interpretation is induced by the diviner so the Diviner "makes it happen." Typically in this case diviners delicately touch the surface of the water portal to induce a reaction helpful to the eye and mind. They may use a series of gentle touches around the water at the portal vessel's edge or use a more active intervention by delicately stirring the water's surface. In either case the purpose is to induce new images and impressions that will assist the diviner in the first stage of the quest (the First Grove or *llwyn*).

The harvesting and crafting of two appropriate wands is discussed in the crafting section below.

If using an inclusion instead of floating botanicals/oils, the diviner first focuses in on the inclusion. This is done for the same reason as above: the inclusion may suggest meaningful signifiers informing the remaining divination.

In both cases focus must be maintained as the mind and spirit journey on. Diviners progressively relax their body and becomes aware of their breathing pattern, slowing their breathing to induce further relaxation. In time, depending on the intensity of focus and the receptibility of the diviner, the focus moves to another plane. This is the beginning of the dissociation. As the mind is progressively deprived of stimulation, the brain cuts off the senses one by one.

Usually, as the eyes focus intently on the floating items or the inclusion, they lose definition and react to the lack of stimulation; the diviner sees only blackness. Most of us have experienced this in what we commonly call daydreaming, but we are seldom aware of it until it is over and we suddenly realize that we have been unconscious, unaware of the world around us. The difference is that, instead of being unaware of the phenomenon while it is happening, in this case we must maintain our total awareness while in the dissociated state. This is common to the practice of intentional lucid dreaming, where individuals are fully aware that they are present within their own dream and can control events as they wish.

One of the first indicators of this state is that the eyes begin to water as additional tears are produced to moisten the eyes as we stop blinking. This is a totally natural and necessary occurrence.

As dissociation proceeds, the diviner's other senses are diminished. Hearing, touch, and the other senses become numbed as they quite normally shut down in response to the lack of external stimulation. Eventually the diviner becomes totally unaware of the surroundings and achieves an altered consciousness. The diviner becomes completely dissociated from the mundane world.

This state can be achieved unintentionally, due to lack of stimulation and daydreaming when quietly looking out of a window or intentionally, as explained above. With practice and concentration, controlled dissociation can be achieved at will. The difficulty is in maintaining awareness while doing so and avoiding falling asleep or entering a state of ennui.

With practice the diviner can become aware of the suppression of each sense as it happens. As I mentioned previously, typically the diviner's sight is the first to be suppressed, followed by hearing, touch, and smell. If diviners can identify each of these changes as it happens, it is also possible to confirm their awareness of their conscious presence at each stage.

First, as their eyesight diminishes, they become aware that they have ceased seeing the actual portal and, at this same moment, consciously reaffirm their awareness of their condition and presence within their altered state while slowly beginning to "look around" and discover their new world.

Then the same process unfolds for hearing, again reaffirming awareness of their situation and listening for the sounds within the new environment.

And so on for the remaining senses until diviners are fully conscious of their transposition to their altered-mind state.

Achieving this awareness gives diviners control of themselves and many other elements within their alternative environment.

A moment of validation is then taken when diviners confirm their complete awareness of themselves within their new dissociated world. This awareness includes a verification of their consciousness being relocated and their spirit being present, but elevated to a more receptive state, since they are removed from mundane concerns and focused on the quest.

Diviners should now be aware that they are actively conscious within their transcendental state. Here we may define this transcendental state as being beyond ordinary or common experience, thought, or belief. It is fundamentally supernatural, abstract, or metaphysical and entirely dissociated from the mundane world.

Each of the stages of progress toward the final revelation is called a grove (llwyn in the Welsh) and is compared to a physical grove within a forest, giving security and sanctuary on the journey. This grove of dissociation is the most significant. Diviners enter the llwyn at a certain point, at which time it may be useful to memorize a marker of their point of entry, one they may identify on their journey back to the mundane. This is particularly useful for neophytes, as there will be comfort in being able to find their home marker within the llwyn as they return.

Within the llwyn diviners will find a diverse panorama of paths available to them, and, being in a lucid state, they will be capable of making their own choice. We can see that this form of meditation may be used for an almost infinite variety of purposes. The goal here is to search for emanations from future events, and it is up to the individual diviner to elect a specific method of doing this. Typically diviners may search the grove (using mental imagery of a physical grove) until either events or portents are revealed to them. Or they choose to sit quietly within the grove and consciously open their mind and spirit to make them receptive to emanations. In either case diviners need to be selective of the revelations they receive and may need to fine-tune the insights that are revealed in order to determine and retain the important elements, while eliminating the insignificant and irrelevant. It is imperative that diviners relate their insights to the signifiers they observed within the water portal at the outset of their journey (signifiers indicated by the floating botanicals, the floating oil, or the inclusions).

This method, as readers will recall, is used by Elemental Druids as a form of inductive divination. They are therefore looking for revelations signified by their own inducement, which have been made to happen by the diviners themselves. So signifiers and indicators from the water portal are paramount. In addition, as this is normally employed by Elemental Druids who receive their inspiration and power from the natural elements, they are also looking for signifiers and portents revealed or related to the elements. This begins with the captured water element of the portal and is continued with the natural llwyn of dissociation, where all the natural elements are in evidence.

The focus of diviners is intense because, in the diviners' transcendental state, they are totally removed from their surrounding environment, have opened their consciousness, and have attuned their mind to their quest. If all the preceding steps have been completed earnestly, diviners become ever more receptive to the emanations from the future events they are searching for, and any number of signifiers and portents will, in time, be revealed to them.

A strong conscious effort must now be made to secure these revelations in the diviner's memory. Every minute piece of information must be remembered in as much detail as possible. Again, this is a skill that comes with practice and one attributed to the well-known memory training of the Druidic tradition.

Only when diviners are confident that they have acquired all the information that is available should they begin their journey back to the mundane.

This is done by raising their awareness of their lucidity within the llwyn and seeking the path for their return. This would normally be identified by a familiar indicator within the llwyn, the marker they memorized at arrival, an image from the mundane, or one the diviner may otherwise relate to. This shows the path home, and once the diviners trigger their journey home by passing or touching this marker, they simply return to the mundane environment from where they began their journey. This should not be hurried; a gentle, slow return of the senses is essential for the success of the next succession.

When diviners are confident that they are in total control of their physical and mental faculties and are fully returned to the mundane state, then they are ready to progress to the next succession: interpretation.

INTERPRETATION

It is now the diviners' task to incorporate the three contributory factors in their consideration of the interpretation. The three factors are as follows: (1) the four intellectual components as we saw above; (2) the indications given by their observations of the water portal, its floating botanicals, oil, and/or the inclusions beneath the water's surface; and (3) the insights revealed during their transcendental journey of lucid, altered consciousness. It is the combined interpretation of all three factors that allows the diviner to arrive at a holistic understanding of the foretelling.

If diviners find it helps, it is a good first step to record their experiences during the divination meditation so that they may refer to them as they develop their interpretation. It is useful to use two pieces of writing paper, one to record their memory of the signifiers they experienced during the period of the meditation on the water portal's surface and the other to list the revelations they acquired during the transcendental altered state of consciousness.

The first of these will include images that might have revealed themselves through the floating botanicals/oils or the submerged inclusions. The diviner records *everything* that can be remembered. Notes and drawings illustrate all the impressions the diviner recalls, no matter how insignificant they may seem at the time. Recollections of particularly powerful images should be underlined or circled. Once the listing is complete it may be useful to review the listing and mark the various entries, with some form of ranking using a priority marking ranging from one to five. This will help later in the interpretation process.

The second page will contain a similar listing and ranking as above, but this time of the insights gained during the transcendental phase. This is typically much longer and more detailed than the previous listing and will be much more focused on the objective the diviner is pursuing. With these analyses complete we can now explore the interpretation succession in detail.

The objective of the interpretation succession is, as the title suggests, to interpret the insights gained from all three contributory factors (as listed above) in the context of the quest the diviner or querent posed. To do this we must first look at each of the contributory factors individually, relating each to the quest, then combine all three to arrive at the best possible interpretation. The conclusion of what may at first seem a complex series of activities should be a simple, direct response to the query. It should be easily understood, concise in its explanation, and unambiguously related to the inquiry.

We begin this by considering each of the four intellectual components we looked at earlier. For the sake of clarity, I list them again here:

- **Knowledge of the Past**—experience and learning from how past events unfolded
- **Awareness of the Present**—knowing where you are on your journey
- **Anticipation of Events to Come**—using your imagination and insights to help understand how events will unfold, without reference to the revelations obtained during the divining meditation (these will be incorporated later in the process)
- **Empathy with the Method of Divination Employed**—becoming part of the divination process you choose to employ

Responses to each component's inquiries are either obtained from the querent during an interview preceding the divination or fashioned by the diviners themselves. In either case the information is recorded in detail to be correlated later in the process.

It would be useful at this point if we consider a fictitious example, so that we can follow the process as it unfolds:

The diviner is consulted by a thirty-five year-old male who has been married for ten years and is worried because his marriage has not yet produced any children. He wants to inquire if he and his wife will eventually have children. If so, will the child be male or female and will she or he subsequently enjoy a successful and fulfilling life?

As a brief aside I have taken this example from one that I discovered on a visit to the temple at Delphi in Greece some years ago. A similar question was posed in antiquity to one of the many oracles at Delphi. In that particular case the oracle, following much ritual imbibing and contemplation on the question of whether the queen's imminent issue was to be a boy or a girl, pronounced her revelation in three simple words, expressly with no punctuation:

"BOY NO GIRL"

Depending on where precisely you place the comma, you may choose whichever response suits you best. Needless to say, the oracle was proven correct. We will plan to achieve a more unambiguous prognostication.

Returning to our exploration, we shall now place the querent's request within the framework of the water portal interpretation succession.

First, how does the querent's situation and his inquiry relate to the four intellectual components? This is established during the consultation prior to the divination working.

- **Knowledge of the Past**—We know the querent is at an age where he should quite reasonably expect to be capable of having children with his wife. We also know that they have been regularly attempting to conceive over a period of many years without success. Repeated consultations with medical experts have suggested that there are no medical conditions interfering with their efforts. From questions posed by the diviner, we may also add that they have for some time been in a suitable socioeconomic situation (this is not a judgmental observation, but an attempt to discover any impediment that may be present) and that there have been no continuing conflicts in their relationship. We have also established that both parties' siblings have successfully produced offspring.

- **Awareness of the Present**—Both the querent and his partner are aware of the continuing and mounting pressure on their relationship as a result of their circumstances, and both feel that the ongoing strain is contributing to a potential breakup in their marriage. The matter is becoming increasingly important. They are both aware that there are no medical reasons for their dilemma.

- **Anticipation of Events to Come**—The couple fully intend to continue trying to conceive. They may well split up if they do not have a child.

- **Empathy with the Method of Divination Employed**—The querent is convinced that the divination working will reveal a response to his query and is committed to becoming involved in the working. He is fully aware that the diviner cannot and will not influence future events on his behalf and is content to accept the results of the working.

The diviner now has all the information required to both pose the specific question needed to enter the divination working and understand the context and motivation for the quest. It is now for the diviner to determine if the quest is justified, if the querent is credible, and whether the question is of a type that may result in a useful and constructive result.

If the diviner is content that the quest is a suitable one, then the diviner proceeds to plan the working in detail. The diviner decides when and where the working will take place and if the querent is to be present or not.

The diviner will then need to decide on the type of working that feels most appropriate. Assuming the diviner is an Elemental Druid and has decided to use a water portal for the working, the diviner now considers the most sympathetic combination of working tools. It is necessary to bear in mind that the water type, inclusions, floating botanicals/oils, and wand are all intended to harmonize initially with the diviner and secondly (but importantly) with the type of quest being pursued.

In our example, the diviner chooses to use a combination of simple, moon-cleansed rainwater and rose hydrosol (rose flower water, distilled as explained previously). The rainwater is chosen because of its simplicity and purity, reflective of the uncomplicated style of the quest, and the dog rose hydrosol to introduce a subtle, loving, contemplative aspect to the working. A compound wand is chosen, crafted from a wand of oak for wisdom, insight, and tolerance and with an ivy embracement* to signify the family bond and sincerity of the quest. In this case the diviner selects dog rose essential oil as a floating oil to enhance the working.

With everything in place, the diviner begins the working. Remembering that this is an inductive form of skrying, the diviner initializes the working by inducing a reaction. To do this, the diviner gently stirs the surface of the liquid portal to induce any form of signifier that engages with the quest.

As the diviner begins the meditation and becomes more receptive to images and signifiers relating to the quest in our example, the floating oil forms fleeting images that resonate with the question posed. An image that suggests the flowing movement of a child's play invokes the primary reason for the quest. The movements, full of energetic color and vivacity, project a rainbow of cheerful good fortune that the diviner accepts as positive resonances from the future. As the diviner's focus intensifies and the diviner begins the stages of dissociation, the induced

---

*An embracement is the botanical chosen to wrap around (embrace) the shaft of the wand to complement or enhance one or more aspects of the working (such as ivy, holly, and mistletoe).

images of the floating oil continue to produce shapes and patterns that indicate the positive aspects of the quest, giving confidence in the validity and eventual results of the quest. Now the diviner begins to focus beyond the surface of the water portal, and the images of the oil start to fade away.

Soon the diviner enters the first llwyn of dissociation and, having validated the lucidity of their presence, starts the process of opening his mind to resonances from the future. In the case of our example, this first points toward a llwyn emanating from the relatively near future. Here the diviner sees and hears signifiers of children playing and, among them, a glowing image that could only be understood as that of a much-loved and cherished child: a young girl, contented in the company of her playmates. A sound emanating from an adjoining llwyn attracts attention. Pushing through the hedgerow and emerging into the second llwyn, scenes of a graduation swirl in front of the diviner. The glowing child is now a radiant adult, preoccupied in her qualifying celebration. Continuing the journey within the dissociated landscape, the diviner enters the next llwyn in the quest. Here the diviner witnesses a quiet scene of a mother and father watching on as three young children play happily next to a shimmering pool. The mother, visibly content and enjoying her family, has an incandescent glow surrounding her.

Feeling confident that the emanations from the future being sought have been revealed, the diviner begins the return journey to the mundane. Finding the familiar location of the portal and initiating the return, eventually the diviner acknowledges being present at the working stone where the journey began.

Having taken a moment to relax and regain his worldly equilibrium, now is the time for the diviner to record all the events of his meditation: the insights revealed at the entry portal and the received emanations of the transcendental meditation. These are reviewed in conjunction with the intellectual components acquired at the preworking consultation.

Any interpretation must be dependent on the correspondence of evidence derived from *all three* contributory factors mentioned. Only when there is undeniable correlation of all three can the revelations be confirmed and coalesce into a dependable interpretation.

In this example the diviner concludes that there is an undeniable yearning by the querent and his partner to become the loving parents of a much-wanted child. The subsequent evidence of the divination working initially reveals the warm, loving signifiers shown at the portal, which are reinforced by the revelations of the emanations from future events during the diviner's altered state of consciousness.

Further, detailed consideration and analysis of the working leaves the diviner with a confident interpretation.

A child will be born in the near future, a female in good health who enjoys a loving and sociable infancy. The querent's partnership continues to be productive and loving. The child grows to marry and have children of her own. In short, the family's future seems happy, productive, and enjoyable. There is nothing to suggest that the family will experience anything other than what may be considered the normal problems and minor setbacks that every long-term couple may endure.

The interpretation being complete, the diviner will, at some time in the near future, consult again with the querent and explain his interpretation, giving the querent ample opportunity to ask questions; the diviner will answer those questions, where possible, with reference to his experiences during the working.

Although an imaginary example, it is indeed very typical, and everyone experiencing a divination working of this type will recognize most aspects of the interpretation succession as it is described above.

An important element of this working is that the diviner chose to remain in his natural form during the meditation, walking through the various llwyn as his own self. This, however, is not always the case. We shall see in one of the other examples that follow how, on occasions when it is appropriate, the diviner may choose to shape-shift, assuming the shape and personality of another creature to facilitate a more apposite interpretation. This second methodology is much older that the first and, as we shall see, explains one of the enduring mysteries of Druidic divination.

SCATTERING THE WORKING ENVIRONMENT

Once the working is complete, it is essential that the working tools and materials are dismantled, cleansed, and stored in the proper manner so that they are available for the next working. Each item is carefully washed, dried, and placed back on the working stone. When all the tools and materials are returned to the stone, a simple invocation is spoken over them by the diviner:

> *Within the security of the circle of protection I reaffirm the purity and integrity of all these tools and materials. I do this in veneration of all those who have preceded me and all those who will follow.*

With the cleansing finalized, the protective circle may be opened, the tools enfolded in their storage wrappings, the remaining materials secured in their storage vessels, and the working scattered.

REFLECTION

The final succession is, from the diviner's point of view, the most important. It is imperative that diviners allocate sufficient time to reflect on the entire working. This provides an opportunity to evaluate their techniques, beginning with their role in the initial consultation. Where the correct questions asked of the querent? Was sufficient opportunity given to the querent to explain his or her concerns? Did the diviner pose the correct query before entering the working? Was the best possible combination of water, floating botanicals and/or oil, and wand used? How effective were the diviner's efforts during the dissociated altered state of mind? How inclusive was the interpretation? Was the balance between all three contributory factors correct? Diviners ask these and whatever other questions they think may be relevant to their development and growth as diviners.

As a closing consideration diviners MUST take a moment to reaffirm their mental, spiritual, and physical well-being. This is imperative in acknowledging the dangers that individuals expose themselves to in practicing any *esoteric art.*

This is also the time to consider and plan any remedial actions the individual may feel necessary to address any shortcomings exposed by the evaluation process detailed above.

6

Intuitive Divination by Slate Skrying

The Slate Speculum

Intuitive divination is, by some, considered to be the purest form of divination, where the divined interpretation depends entirely on the intuition of the diviner. This is the exclusive realm of the Intuitive Druid. No one in the history of the oral tradition has yet been able to manufacture intuition. As far as we understand, intuition is an inherent gift present at birth for a very small number of individuals.

The tradition maintains that there is never more than *one* Intuitive Druid born to each generation. It also tells us that many generations may pass without this individual being identified, occasionally leaving gaps of hundreds of years between the death of one and the elevation of the next.

At the time of writing this book there is a single Intuitive Druid within the Welsh tradition. By definition she was born with an innate knowledge of the laws of nature and how they relate to the Druidic tradition. She is, at present, the Prime Druid* who instinctively interprets all aspects of Druidic lore.

---

*In the Welsh tradition, female Druids are equal in all aspects to male ones, and historically, female Intuitive Druids have been recognized in virtually equal numbers as male

This being the case, and with the Intuitive Druid being such a rare occurrence, one may ask, "Why are we going to explore two techniques for intuitive divination if it is restricted to such uniquely gifted individuals?" Well, the simple answer is that we all have intuition to some extent or another, and for those who feel it may be appropriate for them, we need to explore it in some detail. Also, even if individuals happen to think that they do not have sufficient intuitive power to engage with this method, it is important for every reader to gain an understanding of divination at all its levels and in its varied methodologies.

We will look at two techniques of intuitive divination: the first is divination by slate skrying using a slate speculum, and the second is divination by cupstone skrying, using the *bullaun* (Irish tradition) or *cerrig cwpan* (Welsh tradition).

Mirrors are familiar objects in our everyday lives, and their use stretches back to the beginnings of most civilizations. They have always had a dual function; the most prominent as a functional household object and the less well known as an instrument of the occult.

A speculum is simply a mirror. A slate speculum is a sheet of slate polished to a specular, meaning *mirror,* finish. Probably the oldest form of mirror, the fine grain of slate lends itself to being polished into a highly reflective surface and, although examples have been found in archaeological digs, it is difficult to prove that the examples found were actually used as mirrors. The oral tradition, however, identifies slate speculums as being used long before the use of polished copper or bronze in the Egyptian and Roman cultures.

The regions where Druids would have exercised their influence are replete with plentiful supplies of ancient slate. The Scottish island of Lewis, for example, has deposits of Lewisian gneiss that have been dated at three hundred million years old. The majority of slate deposits in Wales and Ireland were formed around 400–459 million years ago, and the slate used in our working is of this generation.

(*cont.*) Intuitive Druids. The Welsh tradition does not recognize the term "Archdruid," but uses the title "Prime Druid" for the incumbent Intuitive.

Slate is the finest-grained form of what is called foliated metamorphic rock. The foliation describes the layers formed in the sedimentary rock as it is compressed. These layers of foliation in the slate are called slate cleavage, and when expertly split using thin, specialized chisels, the slate divides into smooth flat sheets. This property is called fissility, and it is the property that allows slate to be used, not only for speculum, but also for roofing, floor tiles, and many other purposes. For millennia the slate quarries of northern Wales and western Ireland have provided building materials that are still exported all over the world.

The slate used in our working was sourced from one of these ancient quarries on the island of Valentia,* off the western coast of Kerry in the southwest of Ireland, and is somewhere in the region of four hundred million years old. The method of crafting the slate speculum is described in detail in the crafting section (see chapter 9).

The ancient age of the slate contributes, of course, to its qualities of wisdom and knowledge. Much has happened in the world during the time the slate became compressed and formed. It will have witnessed much change, and the emanations of these changes will have been recorded in its structure. It is therefore the ideal medium for crafting divination tools, and its fine-grained nature makes it perfect for producing the highly polished, specular reflective surface of the speculum.

We will look at the techniques of using the slate speculum below.

TOOLS AND MEDIUMS

There are a variety of tools and mediums employed in divination using a slate speculum. These will need to be assembled, cleansed, and potentialized as they are arranged on the working stone. Again, assuming that

---

*Valentia Island was the reputed home of the famous blind Irish Druid, Mug Ruith (or Mogh Roith, meaning "slave of the wheel"). He could grow to enormous size, and his breath caused storms and turned men to stone. He wore a hornless bull-hide and a bird mask, and he flew in a machine called the *roth rámach,* meaning "the oared wheel." (Wikipedia, "Mug Ruith")

the average reader does not have access to a recumbent stone within a standing stone circle, we shall be using a simple wooden table as our working stone.

The Working Stone

The working stone must be of sufficient size as to allow us to arrange all the tools and mediums we will need for the working. If using a wooden table (whatever size or shape it may be, it is imperative that it is made exclusively from natural materials), it should be positioned in a quiet location against a background that does not interfere with the meditation process. A blank wall, a window looking out onto a tranquil scene, or any other background that will not disturb the quiet, contemplative atmosphere of the divination meditation works best.

Candles

We will need strategically positioned candles to create the subtle reflection needed for the meditation. My preference is to use two three-candle candlesticks, which allows maximum flexibility and control over my lighting and reflection balance.

Meodyglyn and Gruit Ale Libations

I have chosen this point to introduce the use of libations* as, although they may be frequently used in all forms of divination and other workings, they are particularly influential in the practice of intuitive divination.

In the crafting section we shall look at the crafting of two different libations used in the Welsh oral tradition. Either of the two may be used for any working, although it is recommended that only one is used for each, as mixing them is never a good idea. Although some of the

---

*In its more formal use a libation is an offering to the gods, however here we are using the word in a more informal definition as a spiritual drink or offering. We will see that although its main purpose is to influence the diviner's consciousness during the working, a respectful offering is made to the memory of those people who undertook similar workings in the past and those who may continue to do so in the future.

names of the libations may seem familiar, never be tempted to buy or use mass-made products as a substitute. The ingredients and crafting of the libations are not only important aspects in making sure the finished libation is all that it should be, but the actual harvesting and crafting processes are important skills every Druid must master.

Meodyglyn (also known as metheglyn) is a form of alcoholic short mead, fermented from honey and a combination of influential herbs, barks, or flowers. Short mead is similar in style to sherry or port, a form of fortified wine, even though it does not contain grapes but uses honey as its source of sugar starch. As such, it is thought to be the oldest form of fermented alcoholic drink.

Gruit ale is the original ale of the regions influenced by the Druids. Nowadays many people are confused by the common misuse of the word ale and its regular interchange with the word beer. There is a historic and important difference.

When we first discovered the process of fermenting the sugars released from grains like wheat, corn, and barley to produce alcohol, we also decided that the result was way too sweet for our taste. This inspired our ancient forbearers to introduce a bittering agent into the drink to make it bitter and therefore more thirst-quenching. They used a combination of indigenous herbs, barks, and other botanicals to produce this effect, some of which they quickly discovered had additional psychotropic effects, and it was those that interested the Druids the most. It was this original brew that was given the name *ale*.

As time progressed, a new bittering agent, hops, arrived in the region and changed many of the recipes overnight. These hops were imported from central Europe, and for a number of reasons including taxation and social control, these new brews containing hops were called beer. In later history the brewing of ales became illegal as governments controlled (and taxed) the importation of hops into the region and, therefore, the production and sale of beer. The argument was made that the old ales had intoxicating effects that interfered with all aspects of everyday life, including the ability to work in the most productive manner, while the new beers were equally as refreshing without the additional psychotropic effects of ales. In relatively recent times the distinction has been lost, and it has become popular to call all sorts of beers *ales* in an attempt to give them the credibility and appeal that comes with the idea of an ancient brew. There is also a similar argument based on the difference between top-fermented and bottom-fermented beers and lagers, but that is beyond out purview.

We will be crafting one of the many true ales from the oral tradition in chapter 8. It is called gruit ale (*cwru llysieuol* in the Welsh), and it contains a collection of the same indigenous herbs used to craft the early true ales. A number of these herbs are also known to have psychotropic effects that are intensified when combined with alcohol.

In this section we will simply explore the presentation and use of these libations during the divination working.

The Slate Portal—The Speculum

The slate speculum is to be our meditation portal and will be the focus of working. The speculum we shall be using has been crafted from slate harvested from the slate caverns on Valentia Island, off the coast of West Kerry, Ireland. I chose to polish the reflective area at the center of the slate shard in the traditional manner, using finer and finer abrasive stones and then ground seashore sand mixed with vegetable oil to make a fine-grade cutting compound to achieve the final specular finish. I chose this method as the polished-slate artifacts unearthed at sites in Kerry are dated to the megalithic age, predating the use of metal chisels and tools, so only stone tools would have been used to produce the original speculums.

PREPARING THE WORKING ENVIRONMENT

As with all workings, preparing the working environment in the proper manner is essential. Assuming the working stone is in position as described above, the next stage is to assemble all the tools and mediums needed for the working. The slate speculum that is to be the divination portal is positioned at the center of the working stone. The slate portal is usually held by an easel, tripod, or similar accessory that secures it in a position where the diviner may look straight into the reflective area.

It would be typical in most domestic situations for the diviner to be sat (rather than stood) facing the speculum for the working, so a suitable, comfortable chair is put in place. If the working is in response to a querent, it is not normal practice for the querent to be present at the time. All the necessary information regarding the working quest will have been obtained during a preworking consultation with the querent, so only the diviner's chair is required.

We now position the candlesticks in a nominal location to each side of the speculum. They will be adjusted to the optimum reflective position during the initial potentializing of the portal.

A wand, an essential oil, and a small cloth are positioned on the working stone beside the portal. With everything in place, we are now ready to begin the potentialization of the portal.

A libation vessel containing the chosen libation, along with a suitable goblet, are positioned near the portal on the working stone.

Before we progress to the next succession I will once again remind the reader of the importance of correct preparation of the diviner's spiritual, mental, and physical awareness, with a further warning about the dangers to the individual's well-being if he or she is not suitably prepared for any esoteric working. (Refer to the preparatory procedures detailed in the previous workings.)

POTENTIALIZING THE PORTAL

As is usual, the first stage of potentializing is cleansing the tools and mediums to be used and securing a protective circle to encompass the working stone. A salt circle is created around the working stone using recently evaporated pure sea salt, preferably self-crafted. A small entrance gap is left at the front of the circle, allowing the diviner to enter and leave the area before the protective circle is sealed.

The diviner lights the candles on the working stone and adjusts the seat and the candles to achieve the optimum reflective view.

Looking into a slate speculum for the first time can be a strange and upsetting experience, and neophytes should prepare themselves accordingly. A dark mirror is an ancient and profound portal that often reveals more than the diviner anticipates. The depth and darkness of the ancient black slate easily draws the diviner into a reality beyond the simple, polished surface of the speculum, and as such many workings often involve some form of conflict or battle between what the speculum reveals and what the diviner is searching for. Using a slate speculum is typically a convergence of what the speculum naturally reveals and what the diviner is seeking. This convergence is achieved through the diviner's intuition, but the journey is often a difficult and troubled one.

To achieve the optimum reflective position, the diviner sits immediately in front of the reflective area of the slate speculum. The candles are then adjusted so that their light illuminates the preferred image of the diviner.

Some diviners prefer to look at the reflected image of their own face and choose the illumination positioning they feel most comfortable with. Others, including myself, prefer a blank reflection, one that reflects no image. This is achieved by adjusting the speculum so that it reflects a blank space with no reflective image. In this case the candles are positioned to produce a bloom or glow on the reflective surface. I find that the blank reflection offers a deeper, more contemplative reflection, but I appreciate that looking at one's own reflection gives a very personalized experience, and focusing on the eyes allows diviners to delve behind and through the image they see.

I suggest that readers experiment with both techniques and adopt the one they find most compatible with their personality.

With the speculum appropriately positioned and illuminated, diviners create the protective circle by pouring a continuous line of sea salt in a circle encompassing the working stone, leaving an entrance space at the front if they need to exit and enter the circle before it is secured. If diviners are ready to begin the working immediately, they close the entire protective circle, stand before the working stone, raise both arms, and say:

I call upon all the potencies of nature to cleanse this working and dismiss any harmful or destructive influences from this circle of protection.

In the Druidic tradition, this type of spell is called an intention, and it has a twofold effect. First, it appeals to the primal forces of nature to assist in the working, and second, it arouses one's inner force to the working at hand, focusing and intensifying the spirit and consciousness to the task, to the exclusion of all other matters.

Once the first intention is complete, diviners pour a serving of libation from the libation vessel into the goblet, lift it high with both hands, and say:

I offer this libation in pursuit of my quest. Given from nature, made by nature, and for the use of nature. Guide my journey, protect me from that which wishes me harm, and aid me in my pursuit. In the memory of all those who have made this journey before me and in anticipation of all those who will follow. The first portion to nature, the remainder to nature through my pursuit.

With this, diviners pour a small amount of the libation onto the ground in an offering to nature, then take a sip of the libation for themselves.

Now diviners may take their seat before the speculum portal and make themselves comfortable for the working.

Picking up the small cloth, a small amount of essential oil* is

---

*The essential oil may be any that the individual prefers. Sage is a common choice, as it introduces a wise and contemplative influence. The fragrance also relaxes the diviner and induces a calming, focused atmosphere.

dropped on the material. Diviners then briefly polish the reflective surface. This is seen as a means of cleansing the speculum, wiping away any contaminating influences and making the speculum's surface even more reflective.

It is recommended that diviners now take a period of relaxation before beginning the meditation succession. Taking occasional drafts of the libation, diviners relax their body and clear their mind of all mundane affairs. Slowly and in their own time, their focus on the working intensifies, and anticipation gives way to an overwhelming desire to begin the journey. Only the diviner will know when the time is right to begin, and this will vary not only with each individual person but also with each individual working.

When fully prepared, diviners confirm that their position before the speculum is correct and comfortable. Then, holding the wand in their right hand, they place the wand along the bottom of the speculum.

In a slow and definite movement, they lift the wand from the bottom of the speculum to the top in a diagonal wiping motion (similar to a windshield wiper on a car). This opens the portal, removes the veil of obscurity, and allows the diviners' journey to begin.

MEDITATION

Having looked at the theory and practice of the meditation in detail already, I will concentrate here only on the particular aspects of the meditation particular to intuitive divination.

Here the diviner seeks an altered consciousness by dissociation through the intense focus on and through the slate speculum.

At first it is instinctive to focus the eyes on the surface of the speculum, and the mind looks for superficial images appearing on the external plane of the reflective surface. Slowly, with practice, diviners unconsciously alter their focal plane to the infinite depths below the reflective exterior and are drawn deeply into the dark interior of the black slate.

Here there are no extraneous sensory stimuli, no interfering noises, images, or smells. As the focal intensity increases, to the exclusion of everything mundane, the diviner delves deeper and deeper into the dark interior. The speculum is no longer reflecting images of the mundane world, but now becomes the gateway, the portal, to the altered consciousness. This is where the diviners' corporeal state gives way to their intuition, and consequently their intuition becomes receptive and attuned to reverberation from the past and, more importantly in this situation, emanation from future events.

The Intuitive Druid does not look to witness future events in the same way that the Elemental Druid seeks, through inductive divination, to induce images and scenes from the future. Nor does the Intuitive Druid construe signs and messages as the Craft Druid does during the interpretive divination. Rather, Intuitive Druids enable their intuition to provide their understanding of the response to their (or the querent's) quest.

To a great extent intuition defies explanation or definition. One view on intuition suggests that it is a process that gives us the ability to know something directly, without analytic reasoning or bridging the gap between the conscious and nonconscious parts of our mind, between reason and instinct.

If we take this definition to be somewhere near the truth, then the Intuitive Druid bridges the gap between the conscious and the unconscious, the rational and the irrational, the mundane and the transcendental, and our everyday world and the altered consciousness of divination meditation.

As diviners travel deeper and deeper beyond the speculum's surface, they eventually arrive at a plane of enlightenment. It is a hidden place, where Intuitive Druids experience an awareness of all that they seek and, as noted above, they "know directly, without analytical reasoning." That is not to say that what is revealed to them is by definition irrational, just that it is arrived at without using their powers of reason. They just know it. The process is beyond reason.

By becoming attuned to the radiating emanations from the future events that will influence and respond to their pursuit, the answer to their quest is revealed to them in its entirety.

It is important that each individual who attempts this form of intuitive divination appreciates that a certain amount of experimentation and practice is necessary to discover the personal aptitude for the technique. For some people, those gifted with a powerful intuition, the whole process will be instinctive; for other, less intuitive individuals, the technique may be difficult but not impossible. For those many, many individuals who have a low level of intuition, by far the majority of the population, it may be better to pursue one of the other techniques of divination that is potentially more compatible with the virtues they have been gifted.

When the Intuitive Diviner is confident that all of the information sought has been revealed, the Intuitive Diviner begins the journey back to the mundane. This is typically the reverse of the entry, often explained as walking backward through the portal and stepping back into the everyday.

The final step in this succession is for the diviner to close the portal. Again the diviner holds the wand in the right hand and, in the opposite action to the opening movement, moves the wand in a sweeping movement from the top right of the speculum to the bottom left in a wiping movement, signifying the closing of the portal. The wand is then placed aside.

INTERPRETATION

As with the other divination techniques, when the diviners return to the mundane a brief period of relaxation is essential, during which time they reaffirm their self-awareness in their worldly location and confirm their physical, mental, and spiritual well-being.

For Intuitive Druids the interpretation succession is a similar process to the meditation. They quietly reflect upon their meditation experience, relating their newly gained insights to the intellectual components they had garnered during their preworking consultation or, if there is no independent querent to consult with, their own preworking contemplations. The diviner's intuition guides the way to the overall interpretation of the working, and invariably a meaningful conclusion is arrived at.

SCATTERING THE WORKING ENVIRONMENT

With the working complete and the sought-after conclusion achieved, the diviner begins the task of scattering the working.

The candles are extinguished, and the candlesticks are placed aside. The various tools and mediums are sealed for storage. The wand is wrapped in its protective cloth, and finally the slate speculum, the most important element of the working, is also wrapped in its protective cloth to be stored. At this point it is safe for the diviner to breach the protective circle, by brushing away the salt to create an exit gap so that all the tools and mediums may be removed and stored.

REFLECTION

At a convenient moment, not too long after completing the working, the diviner takes a quiet moment to reflect on the working itself: evaluating its effectiveness, considering the significance and appropriateness of the outcome in relation to the original objective, and assessing the effectiveness of the techniques employed. This is the time that diviners reaffirm their methods, effectiveness, and how well they have maintained their obligation to adhere to the practices and philosophy of the tradition.

If faults are detected, this is the time to plan reparation and think about revisiting their basic beliefs or realigning their methods and techniques with the teachings of the tradition.

Time must also be taken to consider their well-being in light of the working. Are there any light effects on their spiritual being? Is their mental condition what it should be, and has there been any impact on their physical welfare?

This, of course, is an ongoing practice of every Druid, as it should be with anyone who involves themselves in occult or esoteric activities. It is foolish and very dangerous to assume that people can involve themselves in any of these types of activities without knowingly or unwittingly exposing themselves to dangers of all kinds. Continuous, ongoing health checks are imperative.

It will be useful too if we take a moment here to reflect on the entire process that I have explained above.

Intuition, however it is employed, is a gift. I have never come across an example of someone who has deliberately acquired it through conscious effort. Many have discovered their innate ability, some at an early age, others later in life. A number of my colleagues have discovered their vast intuition had been lying dormant and it is awakened, often to their great surprise, by their exploration of the various techniques of the Druidic tradition. Individuals with an intuition of the magnitude required to be elevated to the rank of Intuitive Druid do not need to be told about their gift; it is invariably inherent in their personality, and they wear it with confidence and a degree of pride.

We are all gifted with some level of intuition, and I am sure that all readers will have experienced or employed their own at some time or another. These normal levels of intuition can be nurtured and developed, and with training they can become useful assets that individuals may learn to use for the benefit of themselves and others. However, you will see, from the description of the technique of intuitive divination laid out above, that the technique just does not work without the required level of innate intuition. Unlike the description of the process of inductive divination, where the various successions may be described in detail and examples cited that illustrate the specific aspects of each stage and give the reader a shared experience of the working, in the case of intuitive divination this is just not possible. The insights revealed are simply intuitive, defying reason and, frustratingly for me, defying explanation.

Readers exploring this technique should persevere and maintain their determination. As I mentioned previously, small amounts of intuition can be nurtured and developed to significant levels by training, application, and regular practice. Focus on concentration and practice only when the time feels right. Nothing will be gained by forcing your intuition. Leave time for meditation and, very importantly, become intimately familiar with your portal, getting to know every inch, every notch, every chip, every indent, and every imperfection. Polish it often; this raises awareness of its physical presentation and its spiritual worth.

When you choose to meditate, no matter what the focus of your meditation may be, take the opportunity to look deeply into your speculum and use it as a medium to intensify your concentration. On these occasions do not try to use the speculum as a portal or search randomly for revelations. Simply use it as a focal point; looking deeply beyond the surface will invariably help your meditation and help bond you to the speculum as a working tool.

Finally, do not set yourself too difficult a quest when you first begin exploring any of the divination techniques. Thinking you can begin by predicting the results of the national lottery or foretelling the winner of the derby is only going to result in disappointment, disillusionment, and may just end up with you prematurely abandoning a gift you had not allowed enough time to develop. Searching for these types of outcomes is rarely successful and never beneficial in the long term.

Similarly, giving yourself the objective of foretelling an unknown querent's precise examination grades will prove impossible, and these types of quests should be refused or redefined before any working begins. For example, while precise result numbers are impossible to predict (if you have read what precedes this, you will know that that's just not how it works), you may have measured success in foretelling the general outcome of the exams and how this influences future life decisions, which, after all, is much more important than the actual numbers.

7

Intuitive Divination by Cupstone Skrying

The Bullaun

lthough this is a further form of intuitive divination, I have chosen to include it to place all the techniques described above in the historical and cultural context of our overall exploration of Druidic divination.

Here we shall explore the oldest but now least-used form of Druidic divination: cupstone skrying.

The focal point or portal for this ancient technique is the cupstone, which is an ancient ritual artifact found not only in Wales and Ireland but also in England, Scotland, much of northern Europe, and as far afield as Scandinavia.

The oldest examples are identified as originating sometime during the Neolithic Age, which dates them somewhere in the region of 10,200 BCE, over twelve thousand years ago. However, the majority of examples have been dated to sometime around 4000 BCE, making them at least six thousand years old.

As the name suggests, cupstones, in this context, are medium-sized, smooth stones hollowed out at the top. There are some instances where such stone hollows have been formed naturally, either by the motion of the sea or by river eddies, but the cupstones we are considering are most definitely man-made for a specific use.

Known in the Irish as *bullaun* stones and in the Welsh tradition as *cerrig cwpan,* their significance (if not their precise use) extends from Neolithic times.

In general appearance these stones may be thought to have been used as querns for grinding grain, herbs, or similar food preparation, but the locations at which most of these bullauns have been discovered, such as high rocky outcrops and other ritual sites, make their use for domestic tasks such as food preparation look unlikely. More significantly, the oral tradition of Druidic lore and the long-standing local folklore of the region attach spiritual or magical significance to the bullaun. One such belief in the Irish tradition that persists to the present day is that the rainwater collected in a stone's hollow has healing and curative properties, and history tells us that the ritual use of some bullaun stones continued well into the Christian period. Many are found in association with early Christian churches. It is also worth noting that a number of recumbent stones* lying within stone circles in Ireland, Wales, and England, have cup hollows carved into their surface. These recumbent stones have been the focal point of the many workings and rituals that have taken place within the circles, further illustrating the use of cupstones and cup hollows as essential ritual artifacts.

As the Christian saints entered the territories of the pre-Celtic tribes and encountered the bullaun being used in Pagan ritual, they demonized the stones and condemned their use. They quickly renamed them cursing stones or tormenting stones and drew them into the confines of the newly built churches so that they could be closely supervised. Finding that their Christian converts still held on

---

*Recumbent stones are part of the significant alignment references within all stone circles. Often found lying on their side surfaces, they are the working stones for all Druidic workings. They are similar to altar stones, but without the religious connotation.

to many of their Pagan beliefs and traditions, the Christian fathers worked to adapt and assimilate the old ways into their Christian practices. One of the many, many rebranding projects they undertook in their efforts toward religious syncretism was to invent a new history for the bullaun. They now became praying stones and blessing stones, originating from a tale of an Irish saint, who, when dropped on his head as a child upon such a stone, became instantly saintly. At the same time, his now saintly head created a hollow in the stone, which henceforth was destined to collect and retain healing rainwater with miraculous curative qualities.

We can observe this absorption of the bullaun cupstone into the early Celtic Christian church, with a prime example at Muckross Abbey, Killarney, count Kerry (see fig. 7.1 on page 200). Topping the wall surrounding the cloister at the abbey is a smooth twelve-inch-wide capping stone balustrade. At one side of the cloister's rectangle we can see a bullaun cup carved into the stone, alongside a compass defining the cardinal points.

It may seem difficult to imagine that Pagan Druidic workings were actually being carried out regularly within the abbey's cloister, but this layout is identical to that of a Druidic working stone usually found within a stone circle, and there are no known recorded Christian ceremonies that utilize these particular features.

The bullaun had found a new history and a welcome new home in the confines of the increasing numbers of Christian churches covering the landscape of Ireland and Wales. We will encounter such a stone convert later as we familiarize ourselves with the Neolithic bullaun at the ruins of Aghadoe Cathedral, which was the first cathedral in Ireland and is less than a mile from my home in county Kerry.

Many bullaun were, and still are, used in conjunction with curse stones, small rounded stones placed inside the hollow of the bullaun. These would be used by turning them while invoking an intention (a Druidic prayer) or, more often, while focusing the senses on a divination working. It would also be common to add essential oils, other oils,

Figure 7.1. Bullaun and cardinal points carved in the balustrade of the cloisters, with the twisted yew tree in the background at Muckross Abbey, Killarney, county Kerry, Ireland.

Figure 7.2. Close-up of a bullaun cup and a compass carved into a cloister balustrade at Muckross Abbey, Killarney, county Kerry.

or even butter to the hollow to create an unctuous, sensuous quality as the stones are turned within the bullaun, relaxing the diviner and strengthening their bond with the stones during the working.

In Cornwall, England, another area of Druidic influence, bullaun have been discovered that are unmistakably womb-shaped and have a distinct channel carved in the position of the birth canal. The tradition tells of the use of these womb stone bullaun in fertility rituals and birthing rites in Wales and Ireland, as well as on the Cornish peninsula in the UK. But we will return our attention to the simple bullaun and its curse stones, as used in the Irish and Welsh tradition, and in particular to the ancient bullaun mentioned earlier, located at Aghadoe Cathedral.

Aghadoe (Irish: *Achadh an Dá Eo*), is a townland sitting high above the town and lakes of Killarney in county Kerry, Ireland. It takes its name from *Acha Dá Eo*, which is Irish for "the place of the two yew

Figure 7.3. The bullaun (stone bowl) at Aghadoe Cathedral, Killarney, county Kerry, Ireland.

Figure 7.4. The two yew trees at the ruins of Aghadoe Cathedral. One is in the foreground and the other is at the far side of the cathedral.

trees." Earlier we explored the significance of the yew tree in early Pagan culture, its importance within Druidic lore, and how the ancient traditions associated with the yew were carried forward into the developing Christian practices. Accordingly, we see that it is still traditional for Christian churchyards to have a solitary yew tree growing within its perimeter. Aghadoe is uniquely distinguished by having *two* yew trees growing in close proximity to its ruined cathedral, within the confines of the cathedral's burial ground. The reason for this has been confused by history, but the presence of these yews is irrevocably linked to the cathedral's location.

There is abundant evidence of a number of Stone Age settlements at the broader site of the ruined cathedral, where undoubtedly the vast panoramic view over the Killarney valley and lakes offered security to its early inhabitants. These early inhabitants left formidable evidence of their activities that include fire pits, dwelling remnants, and a number of cultural and ceremonial artifacts, including the bullaun currently located next to the cathedral ruins. Undoubtedly they would have planted their culturally important yews in and around their expanding settlements.

When the Christian monks arrived, at a much later date and having established their religious communities elsewhere in the Killarney valley, they understandably sought tranquil, inspiring locations to build their churches. They needed places conducive to religious contemplation and meditation, and as anyone who may have visited the site will contest, there are few more inspiring locations than Aghadoe.

The setting is famous for its views of the lakes and islands, including Lough Leane and, at the lake's center, the famous Innisfallen Island.* On the island are the ruins of Innisfallen Abbey, originally a Druidic center of learning attracting students from all across northern Europe, that like the megalithic age site at Aghadoe, was commandeered by the growing Christian converts and transformed into a Christian abbey.

Arising from this connection, legend has it that the yew trees located at Aghadoe Cathedral ruins have a common ancestry with not only the one growing at Innisfallen Abbey (the two locations are visible to each other), but also the yew in the cloister at Muckross Abbey ruins, the mature yew at Saint Mary's Cathedral, and the Franciscan Friary cloister yew in the center of Killarney town.

These are very visible examples of the significance of the yew in binding together the sites of Christian religious importance and how the new faith attempted to absorb not just the physical manifestations of the old Pagan beliefs, but also the metaphysical elements of its predecessor.

As we saw above, one of the artifacts found at the Aghadoe site was

---

*The abbey on the island of Inisfallen is where the famous "Annals of Inisfallen" were composed. Now housed at the Bodleian Library, the annals are a chronicle of the medieval history of Ireland. There are more than twenty-five hundred entries spanning the years between 433 and 1450. The manuscript is thought to have been initially compiled in 1092.

Figure 7.5. The vintage yew tree within the grounds of Saint Mary's Cathedral, Killarney, county Kerry, Ireland.

the bullaun that is now located next to the outside wall on the north-western corner of the cathedral; during Christian times it has been used to gather holy water and is also believed to have brought great heal-ing powers. We know that this bullaun was hollowed out between five thousand and ten thousand years ago, meaning that it was crafted using hard stone implements, probably at the same site where it now resides. We also know that for the vast majority of its existence, it has been used by Druids as a Pagan working vessel, until it was sequestered by the burgeoning Christian church as a curiosity.

At the peak of its importance, the bullaun would have been regu-larly used as the focal point and portal for divination workings. Along with its accompanying *cerrig tyfu* (tumble stones), it was the most powerful portal for the Intuitive Druid, requiring the highest degree of ability and concentration.

There is little question that ancient bullauns or cupstones are not available or accessible to the majority of readers, but it is possible to undertake a very similar working using well-chosen modern substitutes.

These are the most important factors to take into account when selecting a substitute vessel for the bullaun:

1. The vessel should be of a suitable size or, more to the point, the vessel's hollow should be of a suitable size. It needs to have low side walls and be big enough for your closed hand to sit inside the hollow along with the tumble stones, with just enough room for you to be able to turn or tumble the small stones over in your hand without restriction. You should be planning to use no more tumble stones than can sit in the center of your cupped hand, typically ten to fifteen small stones. Tumble stones are discussed in more detail below.

2. The vessel should be made of natural, nonmetallic material. Earthenware bowls, marble mortars, or similar are well suited.

3. You should, whenever possible, be able to account for the provenance of the vessel. For example, I have two earthenware bullaun made for me, to my own specification, by a local artisan potter who both enjoyed the challenge and was intrigued by the bullaun's eventual use.

4. The vessel must be of sufficient overall size, weight, and proportion to make it stable when it is being used. If it is too light, or its center of gravity is too high, it will move around when you try to tumble the stones. This will interfere with your concentration during the divination meditation. Both the eventual size and the overall weight and stability of the vessel will be influenced by the material it is crafted from, so be sure that whether you are commissioning your own design or choosing from a premade range, the stability is ensured. Heavy vessels with wide bases and

Figure 7.6. Using a mortar as a bullaun. This one is seen with its tumble stones inside, ready for use.

a low center of gravity that are made from natural materials are ideal.

5. The vessel surfaces should be smooth, nonporous, and easy to clean.

Having selected a suitable vessel, we then need to turn our attention to the other tools and mediums required for the working.

TOOLS AND MEDIUMS

Tumble stones are usually harvested from riverbeds or seashores. They need to be smooth and rounded (but not perfectly symmetrical) so that they turn comfortably in the hand. The intention is that they intensify concentration during the meditation, but the sensation should not be so tedious that you become desensitized to it. There is a balance between the point where the banal turning of the stones becomes monotonous and the point where the shape and texture of the stones distracts the diviner's attention from the working. Water-shaped and smoothed stones are ideal. Their random size, shape, texture, and mineral type perfectly suit this use. Although the size of each stone will naturally vary, it is important to select stones that are between one-half inch and three-quarters inch in overall size. This will give you a reasonable number of stones to fit comfortably inside your bullaun vessel. It is always advisable to harvest more stones than you think you will require, giving you the opportunity to mix and change until you arrive at your individual preference.

When you place the tumble stones into the bullaun's hollow and move them around with your hand, you will notice that, in their natural state, the stones can feel abrasive and make a noise as they are tumbled in the hollow. To make the tumbling experience more conducive, we add a lubricating oil to the stones and vessel. Fragrant essential oils are ideal and provide a relaxing aroma as they warm up during the working. They can sometimes, however, prove to be thin and too liquid for some stoneware surfaces. Vegetable oil or other natural oils are also very suitable. A balanced combination of both of the above can prove ideal.

On some occasions I have used another traditional lubrication in the form of fresh butter. This was commonplace in the prevailing agricultural culture of the original practice, and in fact in rural Scotland bullauns are still referred to as butterball stones as a result. There is a corresponding legend that Scottish bullaun were used to hold offerings of butter or milk (both have purifying properties), but this does not appear in the Irish, Welsh, or English traditions.

Whichever lubricating medium you choose to use, the important factors to consider are

1. That you do not use too much of the medium; it is only meant to form an unctuous bond between the tumble stones, bullaun, and the diviner's hand. It is not intended to be a pool in which the tumble stones are immersed.
2. That the medium provides a smooth, sensual sensation, eliminating any abrasion and noise as the stones are tumbled.
3. That, if an essential oil is being used, the aroma must be a soothing and relaxing one to reinforce the concentration during the working and not a stimulating or arousing one that may prove to be distracting.

BULLAUN PREPARATION

If using a bullaun (or substitute) for the first time or after a long period of storage, it is essential that it is cleansed before use. This is particularly important in a substitute vessel that is selected from a predesigned retail range where their provenance is not known. This may be done by moon cleansing, as described in the crafting section, or more often by washing in moon-cleansed water. If using the tumble stones for the first time, a similar cleansing is required. Both may be cleansed simultaneously by placing the tumble stones in the bullaun's hollow before cleansing.

PREPARING THE WORKING ENVIRONMENT

In general terms this working is the most simple to prepare, while at the same time being the most powerful technique of divination. The reason for this is that the working depends mainly on the intuition of the diviner and not primarily on the tools and mediums like we have seen in the previous workings. This being the case, we are attempting to prepare the workplace as a suitable environment for the diviner to work in.

In cases of all workings of intuitive divination it is recommended that, if the inquiry comes from a querent, all the necessary information be garnered during a preworking consultation and the querent is *not* present during the actual working.

The location should be tranquil and relaxing. It must be as quiet as possible, and the ambient lighting should be subdued. Assuming the diviner to be right-handed, a comfortable chair is placed facing either a blank wall or a window with an outlook onto a serene, calming vista. A table is place alongside the right-hand side of the chair. The table is positioned so that when the diviner is seated, facing the wall or window, it supports the right elbow as the hand is tumbling the stones in the bullaun. The bullaun is positioned in the corresponding location on the table.

The tumble stones, contained in a suitable vessel (not the bullaun, but a storage vessel), are placed on the table near the bullaun.

Figure 7.7. The mortal bullaun, tumble stones, and libation prepared and ready for the divination working.

The lubrication or bonding medium, contained in its bottle, is positioned on the table next to the bullaun.

The libation is placed with a suitable goblet (if the diviner chooses to use such).

A clean white linen cloth is placed over the bullaun and will be used to wipe the hollow as the working begins.

The diviner begins by describing the protective circle and cleansing the working, as explained in the previous examples.

If the diviner chooses to use a libation, it is poured into the goblet; the diviner raises the goblet into the air with both hands and pronounces:

Born from nature I submit this libation to this working, and in commemoration of all those who have preceded on this journey before me I offer the first to nature and the second to the working.

At this point a little of the libation is poured onto the ground at the foot of the working stone, and then a little is poured into the bullaun, and then the diviner drinks the rest.

Once the circle is sealed and the libation offered, the diviner proceeds to the next succession.

POTENTIALIZING THE PORTAL

The next step in the working is potentializing the bullaun portal. This begins by the diviner picking up the linen cloth covering the bullaun and wiping the inside of the hollow to ensure there are no unwanted particles contaminating the inside that would later prove abrasive to the stones and bullaun.

Placing the linen to one side, a small amount of the lubricating medium is poured into the hollow. The tumble stones are gently dropped into the hollow, and a few more drops of medium are placed on top of them. Using the right hand (again, assuming the diviner is right-handed), the stones are initially turned in the medium inside the hollow, beginning to establish the unctuous bonding of the stones, the bullaun, and the diviner's hand. Having primed the bullaun the diviner sits on the prepositioned chair, places his elbow on the adjacent table, and places his hand into the bullaun's hollow. A conscious process of relaxation begins.

With everything in place the diviner begins the slow, gentle tumbling of the stones in the hollow. As the stones and lubrication oils begin to warm to the temperature of the diviner's hand, a sensuous bond starts to develop and the diviner begins the process of dissociation prior to establishing the meditation succession.

SKRYING MEDITATION

Intuitive diviners approach the meditation in the same way as we have seen in the above examples. The dissociation progresses, and as a result of the lack of external stimulation the senses begin to shut down. Typically vision is the first of the senses to close down. If diviners sit with a low-stimulus or completely stimulus-free outlook, as described above, their vision will diminish quickly, usually followed by hearing, touch, and smell. At each stage, diviners reaffirm their awareness of their lucidity within their dissociation and their relocation to the environment of their altered state of mind.

As we discovered in the previous example of intuitive divination, there is no typical experience of the divination of the Intuitive Druid. Every Intuitive Druid has an individual technique, and each may vary according to the query that is being pursued.

Most emphasize the need to attune to the emanation from future events by establishing an open, receptive mindset and feeling the radiations of energy that disturb the time continuum extending from the future, through the present, to the past. It may be useful for the reader to revisit the relevant sections where we explored the time continuum and event radiation to expand this explanation.

As a starting point, it may be productive for neophytes to employ the following journey to develop their meditation technique.

Having completed all the above successions and arrived at a state of altered consciousness where diviners are fully aware of their presence within their transcendental state, it is important to begin a lucid and intentional journey within the meditation to become attuned to the emanations from the future that the diviner seeks. Having reaffirmed your presence in your dissociated environment, look beyond the confines of your location. This may be done by employing a tunnel technique, which means visualizing the entrance to a dark, black tunnel with no visible exit at the other end. Enter the tunnel with confidence, even though there is no apparent end or exit. Walk into the endless dark with controlled confidence, the path ahead invisible, but keep walking in the knowledge that you will achieve your goal. As your intuition kicks in, you may see the distant signs of an exit, a pinpoint of light. It may be that a dim light also starts to illuminate your path. As you progress, you know you will eventually arrive at a place where your intuition rules and you will become intimately attuned to the emanations you seek. Your confidence *must* grow as you proceed; there is no room at this moment for modesty or timidity! As you proceed you are rapidly approaching the tunnel's end, until you eventually arrive at the exit point.

You find yourself standing in a place with no confines, illuminated with a pure white light that strips away everything except your focus and intense concentration. You have the single-minded purpose of opening your mind and senses to becoming attuned to the radiations from the future, and you maintain this focus until your intuition reveals the insights you strive for. This is the place and time of intuition. Your achievements here depend entirely on *your* intuition. There is no other source of information, no great well of knowledge; it's just intuition.

Once the diviner is confident that he or she has achieved all that can be achieved, the return journey to the mundane begins. This is the simple process of retracing the steps of entry and journeying back through the tunnel to the place of origin, the mundane.

The tunnel process is only one meditative model that employs the intuition. It is possibly the simplest, probably the most frequently used, and the one that proves most successful for the majority of newly engaged diviners.

It is also a means of developing one's intuition, which, like all our other practices, improves with repetition and correction in light of meaningful ongoing evaluation of our progress.

There are, of course, many other techniques for intuitive divination. My recommendation is that you begin with the method described above. It presents an understandable and achievable goal and may be easily repeated, evaluated, and developed. It is also a means of gaining additional insights into which may be the best techniques for you. I suggest that when you have a working understanding of the tunnel methodology, you may just use it to pursue an insight into what alternative techniques may be more suitable for you and seek revelation of the method you can best attune to.

Once diviners have reaffirmed their presence in the mundane, following a brief period of recovery and relaxation they begin to recollect the revelations and insights they obtained before beginning the next succession, interpretation.

INTERPRETATION

For Intuitive Druids the interpretation succession is a similar process as the meditation. They quietly reflect on their meditation experience, relating their newly gained insights to the intellectual components they had garnered during their preworking consultation or, if there is no independent querent to consult with, their own preworking contemplation. The diviner's intuition guides the way to the overall interpretation of the working, and, invariably, a meaningful conclusion is arrived at.

SCATTERING THE WORKING ENVIRONMENT

With the working complete, the protective circle is erased. The bullaun and the tumble stones are carefully cleaned and stored, along with the other tools and mediums ready for the next working. Finally, the working environment is returned to its normal state.

REFLECTION

It is imperative that sufficient time is allowed for the diviner to quietly reflect upon the working, evaluating the effectiveness of the process from start to finish. Every aspect of the working should be examined, appropriate remedial actions put in place to rectify any shortcomings, and changes to working tools, mediums, and techniques planned.

It may be useful for those new to this technique to make a to-do list as their skills develop and their methodology is fine-tuned.

The Praxis

Having looked at the three fundamental areas of Druidic divination—interpretive, inductive, and intuitive—it may now be easier for readers to understand their close relationship to the three classes of Druid.

Interpretive divination is the ideal technique for Craft Druids, who are gifted with the skills and practical ability to craft their tools from the natural resources that surround us, empower them, and empathize with their use. Interpreting the insights revealed through the use of their self-crafted tools is inherent in their gift.

The Elemental Druids are intimately entwined with the elements of nature and therefore in the ideal position to use the natural element to induce the insights revealed to them. Their relationship with nature and the elements inspires their workings at all levels, and it is appropriate that their divination techniques focus on the use of water, fire, earth, and air.

Intuitive divination depends entirely on the personal gifts that the individual has identified, nurtured, and developed. In some cases this gift of unique, powerful intuition is inherent at birth. Such people are rare, but even rarer are the individuals whose inherent intuition is inextricably tied to the Druidic tradition and its place within nature. These extremely rare individuals are the Intuitive Druids, who appear no more than once in each generation. The Welsh tradition tells us that they appear equally as males and females. They display an innate knowledge of the workings of nature and a comprehensive understanding of how this relates to Druidic lore.

Our history tells us that many have claimed the gift, but not a single one of these claimants has been acknowledged as an intuitive. It is invariably the case that true intuitives have been recognized from within their community and elevated through the common consensus of their fellow Druids.

It is sometimes the case that an elevated Intuitive Druid also holds the position of the Prime Druid, but it is by no means a common occurrence. Most frequently, both roles exist in parallel.

There are two major considerations readers should take into account as they search for the most suitable technique for their own use. The first consideration is that no single technique is superior to the others. Each is equally insightful, and each yields equally meaningful results. The second is that individuals must adopt the technique most compatible with their gifts and abilities, and the only way to discover the best technique for you is to experiment with each in turn, allowing yourself enough time and sufficient practice in each technique to discover which best suits you. The tradition tells us, as does my own experience, that all individuals will know when they find the technique that they best harmonize with.

Whichever method best suits your gifts, it is better to persevere, develop, and nurture your ability rather than seek to use a technique that you may not be compatible with. Many people have said to me that they feel there is some form of hierarchy leading from interpretive divination, through inductive divination, and finally to intuitive divination; this is most definitely *not* the case. I believe the theory is born from two erroneous ideas. The first idea is that because the Intuitive Druid is such a rare and precious occurrence and it is quite rightly considered the most authoritative and insightful class, then it must also be the case that intuitive divination is equally as senior to the other two forms.

At the risk of repeating myself once again, this is most definitely not the case. The second source of misunderstanding originates from a number of neo-Druidic organizations or modern orders who suggest that there is a hierarchical scale of "Druidism"* progressing from bard, through ovate, and eventually arriving at Druid. These various grades are invariably achieved through completing progressive levels of training from very expensive online courses that issue certificates when each stage is completed. This is, of course, absolute nonsense. The unfortunate result of these grading systems is that neophytes, and even some mature individuals, naturally assume that there are hierarchical grades of Druid, which there are not.

Each of the classifications I have explained above is no more than a recognition of each individual's particular gift and a description of the gifts and abilities they choose to employ. There is no progression through grades, although some people will find that as they develop their gifts and explore their individual potential, they may naturally cross from one classification to another. Indeed, many have discovered that their abilities allow them to span more than one classification and may be both Craft and Elemental, or Elemental and Intuitive, or any combination that best suits their talents. It may also be worth pointing out that there are no real Druidic qualifications to be awarded, even if some individuals and orders seem pretentious enough to assume they may do so. In the Welsh tradition and, to my knowledge, all other traditions not associated with neo-Druidic orders, Druids become Druids when they are recognized by the community they live in and serve. At that point they are accepted by their peers and expected to respond to the needs of their community. There is no initiation rite; there is only this natural acceptance and recognition. There are only two stages of ceremonial significance. The first—and for most Druids the only—

---

*There is no such thing as Druidism. Despite what these various online orders promulgate, the Druid is the learned class of an ancient and arcane worldview that nowadays we choose to call Paganism. To call this belief Druidism is akin to calling Christianity "priestism" or the Jewish faith "rabbi-ism."

progression ceremony is the name-giving, where individuals are given their Druidic name (the significance of this I have explained in a previous book, and it is a little lengthy to enter into here). The second ceremony would, for a few individuals, be the elevation to Prime, as discussed above.

In conclusion, I advise each and every individual to experiment freely with all the techniques explored above. Quite simply this is the only way to explore your individual spirituality and discover your natural gifts. Do not be tempted to go beyond the confines I have detailed above, as there are obvious and not-so-obvious risks and dangers in going too quickly or irresponsibly into any aspect of metaphysical practice.

Enjoy your exploration, allow plenty of time for experimentation, and practice. Be prepared for setbacks and amazing revelations. Persevere and take the time to develop your gifts to their full potential. Above all, open your mind and spirit and seek to attune your personal energies with the world force, then you may achieve whatever you seek.

THREE

CRAFTING

INTRODUCTION AND GENERAL GUIDELINES

The single most important aspect of Druidic divination is to work *within* nature, and this means forming the closest and purest connection with all the other characteristics and attributes that nature holds.

In the crafting of the mediums and tools that you choose to use in your workings, three considerations outweigh everything else: purity, provenance, and responsibility.

The search for purity means that we use only natural, unadulterated materials.

So that we can guarantee that we are using only pure, uncontaminated materials, we must be sure of their provenance.

Only by knowing the provenance of our materials can we be sure they are obtained from responsible sources. We must ensure all the materials we use are derived from renewable, sustainable resources.

None of these things can be truly guaranteed if we buy mass-produced materials or premade tools where we have no evidence of their origin or background. If you are entirely sure of the provenance of the materials and production processes of a local craftmaker, then there is a case for commissioning certain pieces of equipment, particularly if they require specialist crafting techniques or processes—for example, accurately fired pottery or earthenware. In other cases, specialist laboratory glassware or copper alembic stills require dedicated manufacturing equipment and expert skills that are beyond the ability or resources for most individuals.

However, this does not mean that we should ignore or abandon the principles and considerations detailed above. Where equipment is purchased from a third party, the usual cleansing and potentializing workings are even more essential and really must be carried out meticulously.

8

Crafting Your Own Mediums

Because of the intense, personal relationship that exists between diviners and their working mediums, it is *always* the case that they should be crafted, harvested, and blended by the diviners themselves.

Diviners need to take into consideration each of the following aspects when harvesting and crafting their materials.

1. In every case the materials used—whether botanicals, oils, minerals, or waters—are chosen for their attributes to harmonize with the diviner more than the working itself. The materials are selected and crafted to enhance the diviner's abilities. Having said that, it adds further energy to the working if materials also harmonize with the intention of the working. So, in every case, diviners should ensure that their selection of materials empowers both the diviner and the working, acting as a catalyst to enable the most effective outcome.

2. When harvesting botanicals, the diviner must be absolutely sure that the plants are accurately identified. Many of the plants employed have a number of look-alikes, and incorrect identification may at best result in inhibiting the working and at worst could poison or otherwise harm the diviner. A confirmed ability

to identify your native wild plants is imperative, as is a thorough understanding of the nature and use of the botanicals you employ.

3. If you choose to purchase botanicals from a third party—be it a retailer, grower, or other individual—no matter how reliable or reputable, be aware that you can never guarantee the origin of any botanical that you have not harvested yourself.

4. When harvesting botanicals, it is important to consider the effects of the terroir in which they are growing. The virtues and attributes of surrounding plants may well influence the attributes you anticipate from your harvest. No plant grows in isolation, and every neighboring plant influences the attributes of every other plant close to it. Be sure that you are aware of the attributes not only of every plant you intend to harvest, but also of every plant that may be growing close to it.

5. When harvesting botanicals, be aware of the change in potency related to their age, size, and the time of day they are harvested. As you will have read above, the weather at the time of harvest also exerts an influence on the botanicals.

6. The aspects of harvesting the various forms of water are discussed in chapter 5 (page 132).

7. The various methods of storing botanicals have a powerful influence on their potency. Using newly harvested botanicals imbues the virtues of freshness, energy, and vitality, while using dried or otherwise preserved botanicals may instill the virtues of maturity, strength, and wisdom.

8. It is important to be aware that if you are crafting botanicals, oils, waters, or any other medium, the vessels and utensils you use may have their influence on the material you are crafting. Never use any vessels or utensils that may be made entirely or partly of man-made materials. Whenever possible avoid the use of metal implements or vessels and, where it is impossible to find an alternative, ensure the metal is a natural single element such as copper (never steel, aluminum, etc.).

9. A range of issues relating to brewing and fermentation are discussed below but, as a general consideration, be aware that fermentation can produce poisonous products, and readers must have a full understanding of the process and subsequent results of any fermentation process they employ, especially if the result is for human consumption. You may also wish to consider the legal aspects of producing and/or consuming alcoholic beverages in the location where you live, as these vary enormously from place to place.

Having considered these general aspects, we may now proceed to the individual items involved in the divination working.

MOON-CLEANSED WATER

Whatever type of captured water is being used—be it from lakes, streams or seawater—its collection and storage was explained above. Here we will look at the process of cleansing your choice of water using the energy of moonlight.

As in most other worldviews, the moon is considered female and one of the most significant and powerful influences available to us. Moonlight is both pure and purifying, and therefore it is considered to be the strongest cleansing agent we have access to.

Although it may seem obvious, it is worth underscoring that moonlight is at its most abundant and influential when the moon is full. To help understand the significance of the moon's cycle, it will be useful here to examine the progression in some detail, as it is important to understand the significance and procession of the phases of the moon and how to employ the moon's influences during its cycle.

The Moon's Cycle
The moon completes a single cycle of waxing and waning approximately every twenty-eight days, a lunar month. There are approximately

thirteen lunar months in a solar year, more commonly known as a calendar year. We will start at the first phase of the moon: the waxing crescent moon.

When the moon is a waxing crescent, the dark side is typically to the left and the lighter crescent is to your right. When it is waxing the moon only appears briefly as the sun sets. As an indicator, it sets soon after sunset and rises after sunrise. It is therefore the moon you sometimes see during the day, when weather conditions allow.

As the cycle progresses, the thickness of the crescent fattens and the moon rises a little later each day, until eventually it appears around noontime and sets around midnight. This is generally known both as the waxing halfmoon and the moon's first quarter.

The next phase is possibly the strangest. This is the phase Druidic lore associates with the female cycle and gestation. The moon appears to be perfectly rounded on the right-hand side with a pregnant bulge in the middle of the left-hand side. This phase has the strange name of the waxing gibbous moon. As the cycle moves on, the moon continues to rise and set later, rising midafternoon and eventually setting well before the morning sunrise.

We then progress toward the full moon. In around fourteen days from the beginning of our cycle, the moon grows or waxes to a complete circle, the full moon. It is at this center point of the cycle that the full moon rises as a complete bright circle, just as the sun is setting. The full moon will set perfectly at the following sunrise.

After taking half its cycle to achieve a complete circle, the moon now begins to reduce in size as it starts to wane. It starts by progressively getting darker on its right-hand side, while the left-hand side appears to remain in its full moon configuration. This phase is called the waning gibbous moon, and while it still appears round and full on the left, a protrusion appears on the right. The moon rises well before sunset and sets well after the sunrise.

As this waning gibbous moon gets progressively thinner, it arrives at the half-circular moon we saw earlier. This is the third-quarter moon or waning half-moon, and it appears during the last quarter of the moon's cycle. This time it appears as dark on the right-hand side and bright on the left-hand side. It eventually progresses to rising at midnight and setting at midday.

The moon continues to reduce and now becomes a waxing crescent moon, with the dark side on the right and the bright side on the left. Now it rises in the very early dawn and sets at sunrise.

Approaching its smallest image, the moon eventually wanes completely and vanishes altogether. This is the time of the dark moon, more commonly known as the new moon. The moon now rises at sunrise and sets at sunset and is therefore invisible, as it is obliterated by the brightness of the sun. The dark moon continues for three to four days until eventually a thin sliver of moon appears at sunset, just where the sun has set. This is known as the first crescent. The moon begins to wax again. This moon rises just after the sun sets and sets just after sunrise. Following this the moon begins to fatten again as it continues its waxing cycle.

By using the moon mapping described here, with practice it is possible to identify when the moon is at its fullest and most powerful. If you plan your cleansing workings to coincide with the full moon, it is possible to maximize its influence.

Choose a cloud-free night nearest to the full moon and place the item you want to cleanse on a firm surface, away from wind and anything else that may disturb it. Before you position the item make sure the sun has set completely, as otherwise it will influence the cleansing. The moon will traverse the sky from left to right, so position the item in a location where it will receive the longest exposure to the moonlight possible. Be sure to remove the item and place it in a darkened place before the sun rises again.

In the case of moon-cleansed water, the water should be contained in a transparent vessel, typically a glass bottle or demijohn, and sealed firmly with a stopper.

Other items that are not transparent, such as earthenware or wooden items, may be moon cleansed in the same manner. There is no need to rotate them to expose all sides directly to the moonlight, as its influence will permeate the material and cleanse every part of it.

BOTANICAL COMPOUNDS

Whether simples (consisting of one component) or compounds (consisting of more than one component), botanicals play a major role in the divination working. They are selected and harvested (and sometimes blended) so that their attributes enhance the gifts and personal energies of the diviner and influence the working at hand.

The most significant aspect in selecting the most appropriate botanicals is the effect their attributes may have on the diviner and how they will enhance the diviner's gifts within the working. Here they are seen primarily as enabling rather than purely influencing mediums.

Within the Welsh tradition, there are three significant botanicals that are most regularly and successfully used for the divination working, both as simples and blended into compounds. Of course many others are similarly appropriate and powerful, and individuals should make themselves aware of which botanicals are available and suitable in the range of indigenous botanicals in the region in which they live. Here, though, we shall look at the three major botanicals in the Welsh tradition: dog rose petals, spearmint, and oak bark. We have considered both dog rose and spearmint earlier, as we used them as examples for the distillation of hydrosols and essential oils, but for the sake of completeness I shall repeat some of this information here.

ᇬ The Dog Rose

Botanical: *Rosa canina*

Habitat: Found growing among hedgerows, wood margins, and on rocky slopes. Most of the dog rose I use is harvested from the hedgerows of the fields surrounding my home.

The dog rose is relatively rare. Sometimes used in exclusive perfumes, it may also be used as a delicate flavoring. When using it as a floating botanical for a divination working, we use only the petals of the blooming flower. These may be used freshly harvested or stored as whole dried flowers, detaching the dried petals once the working begins. If intended to be dried and stored, the flowers should be laid out with sufficient space between them in a warm and airy place. Depending on the ambient temperature and humidity, the flowers will be dried in four to five days. They may then be stored in a sealed, lightproof vessel for up to a year.

When using them as floating botanicals, the petals are gently removed from the flower head and carefully sprinkled on to the surface of the water portal.

Using dog rose petals for divination induces a gentle, harmonious portal with a strong feminine aspect. This may relate to the feminine aspect of the diviner or to any female associations of the quest of the working. I use dog rose frequently, either on its own as a simple or blended with spearmint as a complex. I find it most powerful when used fresh, harvested on the same day as used. The dried flower is equally potent, but sometimes lacks the enthusiastic, energetic properties of the fresh petals. When harvesting, ensure that only a small proportion of the available flowers are taken, as they are an essential element in maintaining the bee population. You may wish to return to the same site to harvest the dog rose hips later in the season, so be careful not to deplete the standing stock in any single area.

The fruit of the dog rose is the more frequently used than the flower or leaves. High in vitamin C, a syrup made from the extract is a popular vitamin supplement, and the fruit itself makes a common tisane.

❧ Herb Mint (Spearmint)

Also called garden mint, mentha spicata, mackerel mint, Our Lady's mint, green mint, spire mint, Sage of Bethlehem, fish mint, menthe de Notre Dame, erba Santa Maria, Frauen Munze, and lamb mint

Botanical: *Mentha viridis*

Habitat: Found predominantly in moist locations, along stream banks, and in uncultivated lands.

Pliny relates that the Greeks and Romans wore ceremonial crowns and garlands of spearmint at their feasts and decorated their halls and tables with its sprays. They also used spearmint essence as a flavoring in foods and wines. Gerard, in further praise of the herb, tells us: "The smelle rejoiceth the heart of man, for which cause they used to strew it in chambers and places of recreation, pleasure and repose, where feasts and banquets are made."

Spearmint is extensively used in aromatherapy, food flavoring, and alternative and complementary medicine, where it ranks first in importance. It has a distinctive, highly penetrating odor and a warm, sweet menthol flavor. Spearmint essential oil is the most extensively used of the volatile oils. Spearmint produces a calming atmosphere while heightening the ability to attune to reverberations from past events.

The herb may be harvested by cutting the stem while leaving the root, which will regrow. If intending to use as a dried herb it is best to leave the leaves attached to the stem, spread the stalks out with plenty of room between them, and leave for one to two weeks in a warm, dry, airy place away from direct sunlight. The herb stalks may be stored in an airtight, opaque storage jar or box for up to six months.

To use either the fresh herb or the dried version, remove the single leaves from the stalks just before use and sprinkle delicately on the surface of the water portal. Again, I find the dried herb less energetic than the fresh, though both have an invigorating yet reassuringly calming influence on the portal, equally compatible with male or female influences.

Spearmint leaves blend well with dog rose petals as a complex. To do this, simply mix two parts dog rose petals with one part spearmint leaves in a small bowl before carefully sprinkling the combined complex on to the surface of the water portal. Used in combination, these two botanicals complement each other well, particularly if the both are used freshly harvested.

ᘏ Sessile Oak Bark
Also called Cornish oak or durmast oak

Botanical: *Quercus petraea*
Habitat: Commonly found in rocky, upland areas with high rainfall and shallow, acidic soil. Its ability to grow in stony, shallow ground gives rise to the name *petraea* which means "of rocky places." The sessile oak is the national tree of the Republic of Ireland and the unofficial emblem of Wales and Cornwall in the UK.

The oldest oak in the United Kingdom was, until recently, the Pontfadog Oak in northern Wales, which was understood to be more than twelve hundred years old and had a girth of 42 feet 5 inches (12.9 meters).

The most noted use of oak bark is as a constituent in the tanning of leather and as an ancient dying agent for a variety of fabrics.

Harvesting oak bark is a huge responsibility and should only be undertaken by those who are aware of the pitfalls and are prepared to do so in a reverent and respectful way. The first and most important factor is to never harvest in a way that completely encircles the trunk of the tree. Bark should only be taken in vertical strips, no wider than one inch and no longer than five inches. Only a mature tree should be harvested.

Each tree should be harvested not more than once per year. The optimum time for harvesting is early spring to mid-spring (April to June), when the tree is at its most vital stage and the spring sap is rising.

Harvested bark may be used fresh or dried by placing it in a dry, warm place with ample circulating air. The dried bark may be stored in any airtight, lightproof container for up to a year.

When being used, the bark pieces are crumbled into small flakes and carefully sprinkled onto the surface of the water portal.

Oak bark has the attributes of wisdom, experience, and judgment, and it brings the benefits of its extreme age to whatever working it is used for. It is an excellent floating botanical and recommended to be used whenever possible, ideally in every divination working.

The crumbled oak bark may be blended with either or both the botanicals mentioned above. The ideal proportion is two parts dog rose petals, two parts oak bark, and one part spearmint. The components are mixed dry, before floating the complex on the water portal.

OIL COMPOUNDS

The most important aspects to consider when using essential oils are, as we saw above, purity, provenance, and responsibility. With this in mind, it is difficult to justify the purchase of premade essential oils unless you are completely convinced of the legitimacy of their sourcing and production.

The crafting and distillation of essential oils was described in detail already, so I will not repeat it here. Instead we will consider the best botanicals to use, together with how and when to best harvest them. There is a large selection of fresh herbs, flowers, tree barks, berries, and fruits that may be used effectively in the crafting of essential oils to use in divination workings. Depending on where readers live it will be best to select suitable ingredients from their indigenous fresh varieties. In the British Isles and Ireland, and particularly in the Welsh tradition, I have selected three of the most appropriate botanicals. Each may be crafted and distilled in the method described in the water skrying chapter. I have selected the three with the most powerful attributes for divination: wild herb rosemary, gorse flower, and Scots pine needles.

⮜ Wild Herb Rosemary

Botanical: *Rosmarinus officinalis*
Habitat: Grows abundantly in most woodland and hedgerows, and it is a commonly grown garden plant, both for its appearance and as a culinary herb.

Rosemary has a striking, pungent aroma produced by one of its volatile compounds, cenole, which has recently been shown to be a stimulant to the central nervous system.

The narrow herb leaves grow along long stalks, and both the herb leaves and stalks may be added to the alembic to distill the essential oil. Rosemary is best harvested in the spring and summer, when the plant produces the most of its volatile compounds. Harvest it by cutting the stalk near the base, and use immediately after harvesting. As the herb has many other uses it may also be dried and stored for future application, but it is by far better to use the fresh herb for distilling.

Gorse Flower

Also known as common gorse, whin, and furze flower

Botanical: *Ulex europaeus*
Habitat: Abundant in open barren land, mountainsides, moors, heathland, waysides, and hedgerows.

The gorse bush, or furze as it is known in Ireland, is both a gift and a curse to the rural farmer. It may be planted to create cattleproof hedges but spreads quickly to populate pastureland. It is the subject of regular annual burning-back to clear for winter grazing. The prickly, thorny plant produces abundant small, bright-yellow flowers that cover vast swathes of mountainside and wild moorland with its vivid, brilliant color.

The flowers are difficult to harvest, as they sit well within the thorny bush and are well protected by the plant's prickly stalks. The small, bright-yellow flowers appear in the early spring; some may even bloom in midwinter depending on their terroir. They are best harvested between two to three weeks after they first bloom.

The flower petals are closely packed and may be individually removed as soon after harvesting as possible. Only the flower petals should be included in the distillation alembic.

The gorse flower's essential oil has a distinctive coconut-like fragrance and offers calming, relaxing attributes that help focus concentration during the working.

☙ Scots Pine Needles
Also known as Scots fir or Scotch fir

Botanical: *Pinus sylvestris*
Habitat: Found mainly on poorer, sandy soils, rocky outcrops and peat bogs. The Scots pine is known to have been present in Ireland over 88,000 years ago, and it is still abundant both in the wild and cultivated within commercial nurseries.

Only the mature needles are harvested as the juvenile needles are less effective. The needles are harvested on the light-brown branches and must be used fresh. The needles remain on the shoots and may be cut into short lengths to fit within the alembic's column.

The essential oil is extremely popular. It is used extensively in aromatherapy and as a domestic fragrance. When used as a divination floating oil it evokes calming, cleansing attributes. It is particularly beneficial if the divination working is likely to be a long one, as it's fresh, invigorating virtues increase the stamina and concentration of the diviner.

Blending essential oils for use in divination workings is commonplace, and the choice of oils is extensive. Care should be given when blending oil complexes as, although many of their attributes may be complementary, the fragrances that play a major part in their benefits may not be so compatible.

All essential oils should be stored immediately after distillation in a sealed, lightproof vessel or bottle. The oils will typically retain their potency for up to a year if stored in a cool, dark place.

In all cases, when the essential oil is ready for use, it should be gently dropped onto the surface of the water portal. The oil will float on the water's surface and, if preferred, may be stirred with a wand to create more imaginative and revealing images.

CRAFTING LIBATIONS

There is a long history of brewing and distilling alcoholic drinks in all the regions of Druidic influence, and we can say with confidence that the community's Druid would have played an indispensable role in their crafting.

The history of brewing tells us that ancient brewers did not introduce yeast as a fermentation agent into their brews, but instead depended entirely on natural airborne yeast to ferment their meads and ales. However, the Druidic tradition tells us that all Druids had their own individual brewing wand or mead stave. At the request of each family in turn, they would visit a home for a stirring, which involved stirring their brew with the wand to magically induce the fermentation. No one, not even the Druids of the time, knew that because the brewing wand was never washed, it transferred the natural yeast from one brew to the next, and there was nothing really magical about their method.

Although this produced a very hit-or-miss result and a very unreliable process, either the Druid's brewing wand or other airborne yeast did eventually kickstart the fermentation. The resultant brews were of very unpredictable and inconsistent result, and there was no real understanding of the fermentation process or how the natural sugar and starch content of the fruits, berries, and vegetables they used affected the alcoholic strength and taste of the resultant drink.

One probable exception to this was the use of honey in the making of meads. Meads, both long (similar to cider or ale) and short (more akin to sherry or port), are believed to be the first fermented alcoholic drink discovered in the region. Honey, the principle ingredient of all meads, was a very common and highly revered commodity used in a wide range of Druidic remedies. Honey produced the most reliable results, as it retained a consistent level of sugars and was free from the molds and other contaminants that could easily affect the reliability of fruit- and berry-based drinks. The tradition recalls that on one occasion, a preoccupied Druid gathered a batch of honey, diluted it with spring water to craft a remedy, and stored it, only to forget about his potion for a number of months. When he eventually rediscovered it, the honey had fermented with natural airborne yeast. When he drank the liquid he discovered the charms of alcohol and added the potion to his regular workings from that day forth. This is one explanation for the discovery of alcohol by the Druids.

We know that alcoholic drinks were made for both recreational and ceremonial use and that the ancient pre-Celtic tribes also distilled alcoholic spirits, as we saw earlier.

The use of alcoholic libations, sometimes supplemented with psychotropic herbs, was and is common in Druidic workings. They are used as a relaxant and to induce alternative states of mind more receptive to spiritual experience. Here we shall explore the crafting of two of the most regularly used libations: meodyglyn, an herbal honey short mead of the Welsh tradition, and gruit ale, a honey-based long mead or ale that incorporates a complex mix of particular psychotropic herbs found growing wild in Ireland, Wales, and most of the UK.

Brewing Meodyglyn

Meodyglyn, also known as metheglyn, is an herbal mead, basic to so many Druidic workings and rites. Like all meads, its main ingredient is honey, which is the sole source of sugars for the fermentation. Traditionally all Druidic fermentation depends on random airborne yeast, with help from the druid's brewing wand as explained above.

This method, although wholly traditional, is both unreliable and unpredictable, producing brews with inconsistent strength and flavor. It even occasionally results in spoiled brews due to contamination from unwanted fungus and molds. While the ancient Druids considered this uncertainty inevitable and unavoidable, we can now eliminate the prospect of ruined brews by applying just a few simple scientific rules, none of which compromise the resulting brew's integrity.

Readers who have previous experience in fermenting and brewing will see that we will be applying fundamental principles and techniques in the recipes that follow. For those readers who have not yet experimented with fermentation, it will be useful to explore simple brewing and fermentation methods from the many sources available worldwide.

We shall, as always, attempt to use fresh ingredients with known and trusted provenance whenever we can, but as the fermentation process fundamentally changes the attributes and virtues of each ingredient, the use of dried herbs is allowable. Similarly, that we may expect reliable and consistent results, we will be using brewer's yeast instead of depending on whatever strains of airborne yeast may be abroad in the region where the reader lives.

Although I have mentioned the advantages that gaining an insight into the general techniques of brewing will offer, it is necessary to emphasize the importance of cleanliness throughout the entire procedure. Sterilizing each and every piece of equipment, container, and bottle is imperative. Proprietary sterilizing agents are readily available from any reputable home-brew supplier, be it on the main street or online, and should be used as instructed by the manufacturer. Alternatively, sterilizers produced for baby feeding equipment are equally effective.

In both of the following recipes I have used the following standard measurements. These may be easily converted to other standard measurements using conversion tables available either in most regular cookbooks or online.

Standard LIQUID measurements used

- There are eight fluid ounces in a cup.
- There are two cups in a pint.
- There are two pints in a quart.
- There are four quarts in a gallon.

Standard WEIGHT Measurements used

- There are sixteen ounces in a pound.
- There are fourteen pounds in a stone.

Meodyglyn Ingredients

1 gallon spring water

1 quart honey

1 ounce wood sorrel herb

2 ounces strawberry leaves

2 sprigs rosemary

½ ounce thyme

2 ounces fresh cowslip flowers

brewer's yeast

METHOD

Place one gallon of spring water into a large saucepan; add the wood sorrel, strawberry leaves, rosemary, thyme, and cowslip flowers. Bring to a slow boil and allow the herbs to infuse in the hot water for at least half an hour, longer if you require a stronger herb flavor. Strain through a fine sieve and return infused water to the saucepan. Make volume up to one gallon.

Add one quart of honey and bring to boil. Allow to boil for up to twenty minutes, skimming any scum from the surface of the liquid as it appears (do not allow scum to boil down into the liquid). When no more scum appears during the boiling, remove the pan from heat and allow to cool. When the liquid reduces to 70 degrees F, add the yeast (unless your yeast has a different working temperature, in which case follow the instructions provided with the yeast), pour into a demijohn, seal with an airlock, and place aside in a warm place to ferment.

Fermentation will be complete when no more bubbles escape from the airlock and the yeast has fallen to form a sediment at the bottom of the demijohn. Carefully syphon off the clear liquid, leaving enough at the bottom so as not to disturb the sediment. Pour into sterilized bottles, seal, and leave for at least two months to mature.

Brewing Gruit Ale

Gruit ale is a real ale by the original definition, meaning that it does not include hops as a bittering agent and depends on a complex of other indigenous herbs to counteract the sweetness of the fermenting sugars. Like the meodyglyn above, gruit ale uses honey as its only source of fermentation sugar, but because gruit is an ale, additional honey is added during the bottling process following the main fermentation. This honey priming enlivens a secondary lesser fermentation within the sealed bottle, resulting in the sparkling effervescence we are accustomed to in most ales, beers, and lagers. In this aspect gruit ale is more often classified as a long mead, due to its high honey content.

Because of the secondary fermentation within the bottle, care MUST be taken to ensure that all bottles used are appropriate to contain pressurized drinks and are sealed in a way that retains the pressure (and therefore the fizz) within the bottle.

Gruit refers to the bouquet of fresh herbs used to infuse the ale. There are many variations, and, as with the meodyglyn above, gruit ales are crafted with certain combinations of herbs for particular workings, rituals, and remedies.

As well as being regularly used as libations, both of these drinks have a particular standard recipe considered as the best possible combination for use in most workings, and it is those two recipes that are described here.

The following gruit ale is a honey-based drink that, in common with most ales, also contains malted grain to provide additional fermenting sugars. Malts are available in many strains, each having a distinctive flavor and character. It is well worth exploring the variations with your local home-brew supplier or researching the subject online before you select your strain. The quantities set out in the recipe may be adjusted to suit the malt variety and your individual taste. Malt is not a contributory attribute, and variations in strain or quantity do not affect either the fermenting process or the final virtues of the brew.

The three main botanicals in the brew are myrica gale, yarrow, and wormwood; the influences of each of these is amplified significantly when combined with alcohol though the fermentation working. As a result, the properties of the gruit ale are highly intoxicating: they are narcotic, aphrodisiacal, and psychotropic when consumed in sufficient quantity. The ale stimulates the mental process, creates euphoria, and enhances sexual potency. Most importantly it expands mental receptiveness and activates previously dormant mental capacity, enabling the mind and spirit to attune to the external emanations so important in Druidic divination. The botanical components may not be readily available in some regions, but most are available, in their dried form, from reputable herbalists either in stores or online.

Please be aware that some of these ingredients may be restricted to registered herbalists and medical prctitioners.

The reader may also find some regional constraints due to local legal restrictions.

Gruit Ale Ingredients

1 gallon spring water
1 quart honey
1½ pounds pale malt
1½ pounds malted barley
1 ounce bog myrtle (*Myrica gale*)
1 ounce yarrow (*Achillea millefolium*)
1 ounce wormwood (*Artemisia absinthium*)
1½ ounces wild rosemary (*Ledum palustre*)
½ ounce wild sage (*Salvia officinalis*)
2 ounces raspberry leaves (*Rubus idaeus*)
2 ounces gorse flower whole tops (*Ulex europaeus*)
2 ounces nettle leaves (*Urtica dioica*)
1 ounce of oak bark (*Quercus petraea*)
ale yeast

METHOD

Place both malted grains into a large, nonmetallic container. Heat the spring water to 175 degrees F, then pour enough of the heated water on to the malts to make a stiff mash. Cover and leave to mash for three to four hours. Pour mash through a fine sieve into a large saucepan. Leaving the malts in the sieve, reheat water to 175 degrees F, and pour over malts in sieve to remove malts' flavor until the liquid mash is made up to one gallon. This part of the process is called sparging, and the sieved liquid is now referred to as the wort.

Boil the wort, honey, and herbs for two hours to infuse the botanicals' flavors and attributes. Skim any scum from the surface until no further scum is produced. Cool to 75 degrees F then pass the liquid once again through the fine sieve.

Decant into fermentation vessel (usually a demijohn), add yeast, seal with an airlock, and place in a warm, dark place to ferment. Fermentation is complete when the brew stops producing bubbles through the airlock and the liquid clears, with a firm sediment forming on the bottom of the fermentation vessel. Siphon fermented brew into a sterile vessel, leaving sufficient liquid to prevent the sediment from being disturbed.

Prime pressure-proof bottles with ½ teaspoon of honey, fill with brew, and seal. This secondary fermentation will produce an effervescent ale. Store for at least four to five months before drinking. Open with care!

9

Crafting Your Own Tools

HARVESTING AND CRAFTING SKRYING WANDS

Wands, rods, and staves are the most regularly used tools within the Druidic tradition, and as such they should be harvested, crafted, and maintained in the most assiduous way possible. They are an extension of the Druid's personality and a channel for the Druid's personal energies. They are selected carefully, with much contemplation and consideration, and then cherished more than any other of the tools of the Druid. Great care is given to harmonizing the attributes and virtues of the woods with the personal energies of the user, and here once again I will reinforce the philosophy that the tools of Druids are attuned to the Druids themselves, rather than to the working.

There is no suggestion within the tradition that the ornamentation of wands, rods, or staves enhances their power or effectiveness in any way whatsoever; in fact most accounts imply the exact opposite. By decorating or altering the appearance of the natural branches, we may be reducing their natural energy, and how can we improve on nature's work in any way whatsoever?

The teachings of the Druidic lore emphasized the concept that the less that is done to change the branches we select to harvest and craft, the more the tree's innate attributes are maintained. As a result most Druidic wands, rods, and staves are "rude," meaning natural, unadulterated, and naïve, used in their natural state. Having said that, it is typical to remove some of the bark from the wood and expose the heartwood at the tip, as this amplifies the channeling ability of the tool.

Having introduced wands, rods, and staves I should now explain their physical differences and the various uses they are put to.

Wands are normally around twelve inches (thirty centimeters) in length and in the Welsh tradition are crafted into three kinds:

1. The simple rude (Welsh: *chrai*) wand, is comprised of a single length of wood, with the bark stripped away from between a quarter to three-quarters of its length. The tip is pointed in order to reveal the heartwood.

2. The embraced (Welsh: *cofleidio*) wand, also known in English as a caressed wand. The wooden wand is wrapped with, or embraced by, an additional botanical to enhance, amplify, or otherwise augment the wand's attributes and virtues. The augmenting botanicals are typically ivy, mistletoe, holly, or similar.

3. The more complicated entwined or plaited (Welsh: *wedi'u cydblethu,* meaning "has been interwoven") wand. This wand is made from two or more entwined branches of different woods. Typically these wands comprise between two to five woods, carefully selected to complement each other's attributes and virtues.

Rods are less used in the Druidic tradition but still have a part to play. Normally around thirty-six inches (ninety centimeters) long, the bark is removed from the first six inches (fifteen centimeters) of each end. This allows users to hold the exposed wood while placing the bare wood of the other tip on the surface they intend to influence, thereby creating a direct link or conduit for their personal energy to flow through. The dark-barked wooden rod with the exposed white wood at each end is said to have given rise to the stage-magic wands of latter-day conjurors.

Staves are synonymous with the idealized, romantic image of the Druid. Again, the intention is to make the stave the conduit for the user's personal energies. In Druidic lore the stave is crafted to be exactly the same height as its user. Most staves are crafted in the rude fashion and are simple lengths of the appropriate wood, occasionally with naïve patterns carved into the bark and sometimes taking the form of the Druid's own unique identifying mark, known as that Druid's "touch." Staves are both functional and ceremonial, and anyone who has taken a stave along with them when walking in woods or mountains will appreciate its value as a multipurpose tool. Similarly, if the Druid is conducting ceremonial rites or large-scale workings, the stave is a very visible and powerful ceremonial tool. Most popular with Elemental Druids, staves are often held aloft to invite or invoke the elements, their base-tip thumped hard on the ground to awaken dormant energies flowing from the earth element. Needless to say, none have Gandalfian magic crystals embedded at their heads. It is also commonplace for Druids to tie various botanicals, thongs, and pouches to their staves. Their pouches may contain their Sevens or tumbling stones, botanicals may be attached to enhance the stave's energies for workings, and thongs may be tied to commemorate workings, ceremonies, and rites from the past.

Whether it be a wand, rod, or stave, the single most important factor in its ability to function is the wood from which it is crafted. Each is harvested and crafted in the same or very similar manner, so the selection of the most appropriate wood is the prime consideration.

There are four stages in creating each wand, rod, or stave:

1. Deciding on which wood is most appropriate
2. Finding the best donor tree
3. Harvesting the wood in the correct fashion
4. Crafting the tool so that it works most effectively

The Woods—Their Attributes and Virtues

Selecting the Most Appropriate Wood

Depending on where you may live, there will undoubtedly be local traditions related to the virtues and attributes of the indigenous trees of your region; there certainly are where I live in southwestern Ireland. These folk traditions will most likely have been maintained over many ages of experience and experimentation, handed down through generation after generation. It is imperative that they are not ignored or cast aside for other traditions that may not be as apposite for your locality.

My experience, from the localities in which I have lived, tells me that some woods have virtues that are best suited to certain uses. For the sake of simplicity, I have selected three to explore as suitable woods for tools to be employed in divination workings. Bearing in mind that in each case it is the intention to match the wood primarily to the Druid and secondly to the working, I have selected the three local woods in a way that allows us to look at how each best serves both the Druid and the intended working.

The Welsh tradition attributes certain Druidic virtues to the yew, the hazel, and the quicken or rowan tree.

Rude yew wands are frequently used in divination, hazelwood wands are the preferred choice for making embraced wands, and quicken wood is commonly married with yew and hazel to craft compound or entwined wands for divination workings. I have deliberately chosen these three woods because, as well as being the most effective, they may not be the woods most frequently associated with the Druidic tradition.

We have already explored the history of the **yew tree,** its relationship with the ancient Pagan Druids, and how the various traditions related to the tree have been carried forward to the Celtic Christian religious practices of the present day. Many of the attributes we associate with the yew stem from its long life and evergreen foliage. There are examples of yews that have survived for well over one thousand years, and when standing in the presence of one of these veteran trees there is no disputing the fact that they invoke a powerful feeling of endurance, wisdom, vitality, and longevity. It is the virtues of wisdom and longevity that make the wood particularly attractive for crafting wands. The yew has left its imprint as a prominent actor in the history of Ireland, Wales, Scotland, and England by lending its name to important individuals and places in mythology and folklore that remain with us to the present day.

The history of the yew extends back, beyond the evolution of the current languages of what we now sometimes call the Celtic peoples, to the proto-Celtic language. It was known as the *eburos,* which is very close to the first-known Druidic name. In the subsequent Old Irish it was known as the *ibar,* and in Modern Irish *iur.* As for other Celtic-derivative tongues, it is known as the *iubhar* in Scots Gaelic; *ivinenn* in the Breton language of northern France; *euar* in Manx, the language of the Isle of Man; *ewen* in the ancient tongue of the Cornish people; and in my native tongue, Welsh, it is called the *ywen.* Comparison may be made with a number of these names, and the relationship between the individual cultures may be observed by the similarities of their name for the ubiquitous yew tree.

When you consider the selection of the yew for your own workings, you should think first of your own personal energies. If you feel that the attributes of wisdom, maturity, vitality, and experience reflect and enhance your energies, then consider using the yew wood as a simple rude wand. Do not forget that if you wish to augment these attributes even further, you may craft your yew wand as an embraced wand or even more strongly as an entwined, compound wand.

The **hazel tree** may not be one that springs to mind when most people think of the Druidic lore, but the entire tree—its leaves, branches, wood, and nuts—are important assets to any Druidic divination working, particularly in the Welsh and Irish traditions. As Druids often carried rods of hazel, the tree was considered as an important symbol of wisdom and was never knowingly burned in home fires, particularly those used for cooking. The Druid's brewing rods were always crafted from hazel wood in reference to its attributes of wisdom and whole-someness. The tradition of hazel as the tree of wisdom and foresight has been carried through the indigenous witchcraft and wisewoman history, and it is still evident in modern Wiccan and neo-Druidic practices.

There is also a strong tradition associated with the edible hazel-nut, known throughout the Druidic regions as "the nut of wisdom" (Welsh: *cnau doeth*). It is often included in ceremonial feasts and eaten by Druids prior to auspicious workings, as a sign of respect for the tradition and to enhance their energies.

Again, the history of the hazel stretches back into prehistory and pre-dates the use of the Celtic languages. The ancient proto-Celtic name for the hazel was *collos*. It evolved into the Old and Modern Irish word *coll*, which is once more very close to the ancient Druidic name. In the Welsh tradition it is called *collen*, and in the Cornish tradition it is *collwedhen*.

If you think that the hazel's attributes of wisdom, foresight, and wholesomeness acknowledge the personal energies you intend to employ in your divination, then you may consider using hazel wood as a simple rude wand. Alternatively, as with the previous analysis, you may wish to employ it along with other botanicals and woods as an embraced or entwined wand.

The last of the three trees I have selected here is the **quicken tree,** more commonly known as the **rowan tree** or the mountain ash, an even more enigmatic tree than the previous two.

The rowan tree has long been known as a magical tree of protection and is present in a wide range of traditions. It is known to protect against evil and malevolent energies. In the Welsh Druidic tradition it is best known as the Wanderer's Tree or Tree of Guidance for its ability to protect travelers from becoming lost and for offering guidance to those who may have lost direction in life. It is a dense, hard wood, and as such it is often used in crafting bowls, goblets, and other household vessels. It is also commonly used in crafting farming tools and carts, as well as in hut and boat building. The rowan berries (or quickening berries) are frequently used to make foods, jams, and preserves, as well as in fermenting alcoholic beverages and ceremonial meads such as the methyglyn described earlier.

The traditions of the tree have been embraced by the Wiccan community even though it is historically renowned as a tree of apotropaic power, particularly cherished for its power to ward off witches. For this reason it was often planted around houses and on each side of gateways to protect against unwanted spells and incantations. In Irish mythology the quicken tree is known as the Faire Tree, again for its association with magic and protection. In neo-Druidism the rowan is known as the portal tree as it gives access to "other places."

In Old and Modern Irish the rowan is known as *caorthann*, while in Welsh it is called *yr coeden griafol*, neither of these names correspond with the Druidic name.

If you feel that the rowan's attributes of apotropaic power, its ability to ward off malevolent influences and ill fortune, and its reputation as a powerful divination facilitator are attuned with your personal energies, then you should use a simple rowan rude wand. The rowan wood is, however, most frequently used in conjunction with the yew and hazel as an entwined compound wand, particularly for divination workings.

Having considered the attributes and background of each of the three trees, we now turn our attention to selecting the most appropriate donor tree from which to harvest your wood. Whether you intend to craft a wand, rod, or stave, the imperatives employed for selecting the donor tree are the same. These may be listed as:

- the health and vitality of the individual tree
- the terroir the tree has grown within
- the surrounding botanicals and their influences

Whichever tree you are intending to harvest your donor branch from, it is essential that you are confident that the tree is in the prime of health with the capacity to regenerate replacement branches.

Consideration must also be given to any parasitical growth on the tree and the branch you are targeting. These include mosses, lichens, ivy, or similar, as each of these will have an impact on the attributes of the tree branch. When surveying the prospective tree, look carefully for any wildlife that may depend on its integrity. Birds, squirrels, insects, and other creatures all have a right to retain their homes and habitat, so make every effort to be as considerate as possible and make your harvesting as inobtrusive as you can.

The terroir refers to the environmental conditions in which the tree has grown. These include the effects of climate (temperature, humidity, and rainfall), the soil in which it grows, winds, floods, and seasonal changes. All have an influence on the tree's attributes, as well as its ability to regenerate the wood you plan to harvest.

It is very unlikely that the tree you are planning to harvest from is growing in isolation from other botanicals. Each of these surrounding botanicals will have an influence on the attributes of the donor tree. The neighboring plants will exert their influences in relation to their proximity to the donor. It is advisable to research the energies and influences of any surrounding plants when you are surveying for a suitable donor tree. There are far too many variants for me to list them here, but there are numerous resources that provide suitable descriptions of the plants that may be growing in your particular locality, together with the energies they may exert on the donor tree.

Once you have decided on the most suitable donor tree, you must then plan the harvesting of a suitable branch for your wand, rod, or stave. But before you finally decide on your branch and start harvesting, there are a number of aspects that you will need to consider.

Harvesting

The first thing to consider when selecting a donor tree is the orientation of the branch you are targeting. The second consideration is the time of harvesting. The fact is that they are so closely related that, in reality, both must be considered together.

The ideal time to harvest your branch is as close as you can to the sun rising at the end of the night of a full moon. The reason for this is that, as we have previously seen, the moon has an unrivalled cleansing influence. This influence is at its most powerful when the moon is full. I have examined the phases of the moon previously and suggest that readers make themselves familiar with how these phases manifest themselves in their locality and plan their harvesting accordingly. If it is not possible, for any reason, to harvest on the full moon, this may be used to the advantage of the harvester. If a branch is harvested during a fattening moon (waxing moon), when the moon is growing toward its full state, its influence will be one of rising energies. However, its cleansing power will be reduced accordingly, so the harvester will need to select a donor tree that is as free as possible from surrounding botanicals' influences. If a branch is harvested under a skinny moon (waning moon), its influences will be one of diminishing energies and the moon's cleansing power will also be reduced.

The branch must be harvested just before the sun appears so that the moon's influence is at its greatest.

If possible, a clear, cloudless night is best, but the most important factor is the moon's phase, so a cloudy full moon is preferable to the clear night of a waning moon.

If we take the moon's cleansing power to be paramount, then we must look at the branch's orientation in relation to the moon's influence to maximize its effect. The moon, like the sun, rises in the east and sets in the west. So at various times, if we wish to make sure that the branch has grown under the greatest influence of the moon, we need to select a branch that has been exposed to the moon for the greatest period of its growth. This may mean that the branch is oriented to the northern aspect or the southern aspect, depending on the time of year and the location of the reader. It is important for individuals engaging in Druidic lore to acquaint themselves intimately with the movement of the moon and the sun and the cardinal points of the compass in relation to where they live and where they conduct their workings. It is not possible within the confines of this book to expand on each and every different orientation of potential readers, but with a little research and some concentrated observations, it is not too difficult for readers to position themselves accurately and gain a detailed understanding of their orientation within the cosmic pattern. In fact this is a basic necessity for anyone who plans to be involved with any aspect of Druidic lore.

Having selected the branch to harvest and planned the most effective time and date for harvesting, all that is left is for harvesters is to get up early, at the predawn of their selected day, and harvest their branch. Using a sharp knife, cut the branch as close to its junction with the donor tree as possible. Once cut, the first thing to be done is to seal the wound on the tree with wax to prevent any loss of its energies or the fluids that continually flow through its structure. Typically I carry a beeswax candle for this purpose and melt a copious amount of wax onto the wound to seal it.

This done, it is now best to trim all the excess twigs and leaves from the branch and leave them at the base of the donor tree to decompose and reenter the tree's life cycle. Now is the time to return home and begin the crafting of your tool.

Crafting

Many people's idea of a wand is an intricately carved or turned magical accessory. That's not surprising given the exposure such things have on the big screen, TV, and the range of these elaborate items available from most Wiccan and mystic suppliers. From childhood onward, we are exposed to the idea of these magical wands, used by a multitude of characters ranging from Mickey Mouse to Harry Potter. In the Druidic tradition, however, nothing could be further from the truth.

The whole purpose of Druidic wands, rods, and staves is functional, not decorative, and there is never any suggestion that crafting elaborate, highly decorated wands is either advantageous or desirable. None of these everyday, functional tools are considered to be status symbols or prestigious pieces of art; their worth is measured by their effectiveness and the harmony the diviner develops with them.

The first step in crafting a wand, rod, or stave is to finely trim any twigs or other blemishes or growths that may be apparent. Using a craft knife, penknife, or similar, small blemishes are removed from the surface of the branch. The piece is then cut to the required length, which in the case of the wand is around twelve inches (thirty centimeters), for a rod this is around thirty-six inches (ninety centimeters), and for a stave, the length equals the height of the user. The only variance on these lengths may be when the crafter decides to cut the branch to the nearest convenient branching—at the point where a smaller branching or sprouting junction may appear. Normally, the crafter cuts the base or handle end of the branch first to establish a solid, well-proportioned base point. The required length is then measured from that point, and the branch is cut at the closest appropriate length.

For a simple **rude wand**, a cut through the bark (only) around the circumference of the wand is made about six inches (fifteen centimeters) from the base end. The bark is then carefully stripped from the length of the wand to expose the bare wood, leaving the first six inches with the bark remaining. This is the wand's handle. A guidance mark is made on the bared wood approximately two inches from the tip end (the other end to the handle base), and the tip is pared away to a point to expose the heartwood of the wand. If we think of the wand as a similar conductor of energy as an electrical wire may be for electrical energy, then the handle represents the outer insulating covering, the bared wood represents the inner insulating covering, and the heartwood itself represents the conductor metal at the center of the wire.

If the branch is to be crafted as an **embraced wand**, then the crafting process is exactly the same, with the exception of the length of the wand that is stripped to expose the bare wood. For these wands, only half of the length of the wand is stripped of its bark. The selected botanical that will embrace the wand is then attached to the handle of the wand and wound around the length of the wand's shaft to the tip, where it is secured with natural twine of cotton string.

Figure 9.1. Two Druidic skrying wands. On the *left,* an embraced wand, on the *right,* a simple rude wand.

In the case of an **entwined wand**, two, three, or four individual wands of exactly the same length are prepared in the fashion of the simple rude wand. The individual wands are then bound tightly and securely together at their handle base with twine of natural cotton string. The separate wands are then plaited together (entwined) to form a single compound wand. When the plaiting is complete along the length of the wand, the compound wands are again secured in the same way at the tip end. It is imperative that newly harvested, green branches are used for this purpose and that they are plaited as soon as possible after harvesting, while they are still supple and flexible. If the branches have dried and become brittle, they will break or split during the plaiting, compromising their ability to act as a conduit for the diviner's personal energies and rendering the wand useless. By entwining the individual wands together, we combine their attributes

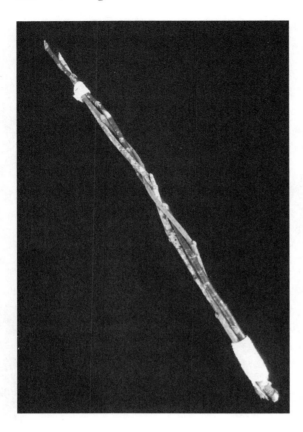

Figure 9.2. An entwined compound wand with three different woods.

and amplify their power by an amount equal to the number of individual wands employed.

The crafted wand is now ready to be added to the working tools for divination, where it will undergo the same additional cleansing and empowerment as the rest of the diviner's tools at the beginning of the divination working.

In crafting a **rod** the first step is to carefully trim away any twigs or unwanted blemishes from the length of the branch. The base end (handle end) is then cut square at a point where the branch is stable and solid. The rod length is measured from this base to a length of approximately thirty-six inches (ninety centimeters), marked, and cut to length. A cut is then made through the bark (only) around the circumference of the rod at a point three inches (seven centimeters) from both ends, and the bark striped from each end to expose the bare wood. The rod is now ready to join the other tools in the Druid's cache. If it is the intention of the Druid to use the rod as a Druid's brew rod in the fermentation process, it is important not to wash the rod between usages so that the natural yeasts will continue to live on the working end of the rod. To this end, make sure the working end is not allowed to contact the ground, and when storing the brew rod, place it on its side, raised off the ground and away from any contaminating contacts. Rods may also be crafted as embraced rods in the same way as embraced wands, with additional botanicals being wound around its shaft to add to its attributes and amplifying its power. Rods are never crafted as entwined.

Most Druids are rarely separated from their staves, and they are undoubtedly their most personal and cherished tool. Because of this, particular care is taken in their selection, harvesting, and crafting. It is not unusual for a number of staves to be prepared and tried before the perfect match of stave and Druid is found. To craft the **stave,** first the base end or heel is cut square at a solid point at the end of the branch. The length of the stave is then measured and cut to the same length as the user's height. A cut through the bark around the circumference of the stave is made two inches (five centimeters) from each end, and the bark is stripped away to expose the bare wood at both ends. This is all that is required to craft the basic stave, but as I have mentioned previously, some individuals choose to carve symbols and sigils along the length of their staves to strengthen their bond with the tool and imprint their personality and personal energies onto the stave. These carvings may represent ancient Pagan symbols, as we have seen earlier in the crafting of the Sevens, or images of personal significance. Occasionally individuals carve their personal mark or touch onto their stave; this is often the case with Craft Druids, who also use their touch on the many tools they regularly craft. Individuals may also choose to attach thongs, ribbons, or even pouches to their staves, symbolizing memorable ceremonies, convocations, friends, or workings they may wish to mark.

These pouches frequently contain cherished personal items and tools of the Druid who owns them. Tumbling stones, Sevens, and other small tools often find their way into the pouches tied to the Druid's stave. It is often the case that a stave be used or worn in for weeks, months, or even years before the owners commit to dedicating themselves to permanent ownership. During this trial period, it becomes determined through familiarity which end of the stave becomes the top (head) and the bottom (heel). Once this becomes apparent it is then maintained for the lifetime of the stave, which frequently extends beyond the lifetime of the Druid to whom the stave belongs.

Each of the tools described above should be carefully maintained. They must be cleaned and oiled using natural wood or nut oils to keep them in good order. They need to be stored with consideration and cherished as a donation and valued gift, not only from the donor tree but from nature herself.

THE CRAFTING OF A SLATE SPECULUM

The crafting of a speculum from a harvested slate shard is traditionally a long and painstaking process, requiring patience, dedication, and a degree of applied skill. The crafting procedure imbues a sense of achievement, bonding, and harmony between the Druid and the Druid's speculum that grows as the portal is used, and their joint experiences strengthen their connection.

It is important that diviners craft their own speculum from start to finish; this is the only way the physical, mental, and spiritual bond is achieved.

The provenance of the slate shard diviners choose to craft into their speculum is rarely questioned. The fact that the slate was formed some four hundred million years ago and has spent most of that period buried underground testifies to its maturity, wisdom, and integrity. Unless there is serious suspicion that the shard may have been contaminated by exposure to any malevolent influences at some point during its existence, it may be assumed that most specimens are suitable to be polished and used as a speculum portal.

The shard should be a minimum of twelve inches (thirty centimeters) in height and a similar size in width, though it will most likely not be symmetrical or even-edged. Slate has a layered, leaved structure, with the grain lying across the width and height of the specimen. The shard should be between ¼ inch and ½ inch thick. Any thicker and its weight and balance may cause problems.

Most slate shards are of random shape and size, with only the thickness being anywhere near even and flat. It is these flat surfaces that we intend to further flatten and eventually polish into a specular finish to form our slate speculum portal or black mirror.

Figure 9.3. A harvested slate shard with the base cut flat,
ready for grinding and polishing.

The flat surfaces of the slate shard may come in varying degrees of flatness and evenness. Some may be flat but undulating and bumpy, others may be uneven, showing layers of slate leaves as they were laid down during their formation. We need to select the flattest, most evenly surfaced examples for our crafting. Avoiding samples showing layering, blemishes, or any other malformations; this will make polishing a much more difficult task. Ideally we look for a shard of convenient size with a centrally placed flat area of around six to eight inches that can be polished into the speculum area. Remember, it is not the intention to polish the entire shard, only a central area. The rest will remain unpolished and still in its natural state to focus attention on the black mirror at the center. It is not acceptable to select a shard that has been machine-worked or cut to form a roofing tile or similar. The brutal forces involved in machine processing destroy the inherent energies of the slate and contaminate the subtle forces the slate has slowly developed over its lifetime, the very energies we plan to utilize.

Having selected the slate shard, we need to determine the orientation of the speculum. Placing the smoothest, flattest side uppermost, we rotate the shard to find the most harmonious orientation. Which edge will be the top of the speculum? Often a pointed edge or one with an arched peak will show itself to be the best choice. Where within the surface will we choose to polish the speculum area? If the smoothest surface has been placed uppermost, then the smoothest area of that surface is where we choose to polish. It need not necessarily be at the center of the shard, but it should not be against the edge either. It should be placed in a position where the surrounding raw, unpolished slate will help focus the concentration on the polished speculum, not where the edges or remaining features of the surface distract the diviner's focus.

Once the orientation of the shard has been determined and the top and bottom defined, the bottom edge is cut straight to create a flat base upon which the speculum may stand or so that the flat end will form a secure and stable base if the speculum is placed on a tabletop easel to enable the divination working. The slate may be cut with a reasonably fine-toothed wood saw or a hacksaw with a metal cutting blade. Either way, it may be best to consider the saw blade to be sacrificial, as it will be probably ruined by the slate-cutting operation.

The next step is to plan the polishing of the speculum area. This begins by defining the area to be polished with a chalk mark showing the area's perimeter. This will not be a well-defined edge, but as we go through the progressive polishing process the defined periphery will be a blended edge between the highly polished speculum area and the unworked, raw surface of the surrounding slate.

I was taught to polish my first speculum using the traditional method. Having said that, my introduction was over fifty years ago and, while these traditions remain alive, there are modern alternatives available that may take some of the hard work away. For my part, when I now craft a new speculum I still use the traditional method because I believe it creates a stronger bond between the diviner and the speculum, and I enjoy the slow, meditative experience. First we will look at the traditional method and then follow this with the more modern alternatives, at which point readers may make their choice.

In crafting the speculum, we are simply grinding and polishing an area at the center of the slate speculum to become a highly reflective surface. In engineering terms, this highly polished surface will have what is called a specular finish, a term borrowed from the fact that the surface will be finished to a standard that allows it to function as a speculum. In the Druidic tradition this is achieved by first grinding the slate to a flat, even surface and then polishing this surface using finer and finer grades of abrasive materials until the desired finish is achieved.

For our ancestors, who were crafting perfect speculums long before the influence of the Celtic peoples arrived on our shores, their choice of tools was very limited, and if we consider that the period of time we are visiting is the Stone Age, then the choice of tools becomes self-explanatory.

This then means that the first step in our crafting is to forage for suitable stone types, to be used as the tools for first grinding the flat, even surface and then other stones suitable for the fine polishing. The most prolific sites for all these stones are the nearest rivers or seashores. There are two main reasons for this. The first is that water-eroded stones tend to have smoother, rounder surfaces, which lend themselves more readily to being used as abrasive tools than those with sharp, jagged edges that may score the surfaced being worked on. The second is that most rivers and rocky shores have a wide range of stone types, ranging from hard to soft, and most of these are available in a variety of sizes suitable for the task ahead.

We are looking initially for water-eroded stones of a hard consistency, with at least one relatively flat surface (which we will subsequently use as the abrasive contact surface for grinding) that is comfortably held within the hand. This latter feature is important, as the crafter will be gripping the stone for a considerable length of time. These hard, abrasive stones are often porous in appearance and may be tested for hardness by simply rubbing them against the nearest large rock. If they are suitable, the result will be that the rock shows signs of abrasion, while the selected stone does not. You may wish to collect more than one of these grinding stones, and the grinding process is not a quick one.

Next we need to forage for softer abrasive stones to begin the polishing process. Select stones that again have a flat surface and an appropriate hand grip. The idea is to gather at least four grades of stone with varying degrees of softness to hardness. This can be tested by rubbing them against one another; the ones showing evidence of abrasion are of course softer than the ones that do not. In this way it is possible, though not always easy, to collect a range of abrasive stones that vary in their grade of abrasiveness. Bear in mind that this is a daylong task and patience always prevails.

Before leaving the foraging site, we also need to collect a good bucketful of sand, which will enable the intermediate process of the polishing before the final finishing. It is important to understand that river sand is very different from seashore sand. The first consists mainly of river-eroded stones, ground smaller and smaller over the eons. The individual grains are harder than sea sand and often smoother, as the edges are rounded by the constant water flow. Sea sand differs in as much as it is composed mainly of ground sea shells (as well as rock) that have been ground down by the motion of the waves, currents, and tides. It also contains an amount of sea salt, which in itself is also an abrasive. Ideally we will use both types of sand to achieve our desired finish.

Now that we have our slate shard, marked and ready for grinding, our collection of stones of varying grades of hardness and abrasion potential, and our two types of sand, we may begin our work.

Placing the shard on a flat, firm surface, we dip our first (hardest) grinding stone into water and begin rubbing it in slow circular movements on the area designated for the reflective surface. The objective here is to acquire a smooth, flat surface that we will subsequently polish. In this process there is no substitute for long, hard work. As the grinding continues, the grinding stone is repeatedly dipped in water; this provides a degree of lubrication and washes away the abraded slate, preventing it from building up on the surface. It also eliminates dust and avoids the crafter breathing in the harmful slate dust that has damaged the health of so many slate workers, though I don't think this was a consideration for our ancestors. It is also a good idea to have a damp cloth available to occasionally wipe the accruing slate slurry from the surface of the shard.

Eventually, the varying circular grinding movements will produce a flat, even surface, though this surface may still appear scratched and unpolished. This will be remedied by the subsequent workings. All we are looking to achieve at this first grinding stage is a flat, even surface as a base for the next stage. Once we have achieved the desired finish, the shard is carefully washed to remove any grit and dust that may spoil the later polishing. Once washed, the shard is wiped clean and lightly polished to ensure the finish is consistent and no blemishes remain.

Now we begin exactly the same process of grinding, only this time we use the other grades of stones we collected, working from the most abrasive to the least as the finish of the slate improves with each change of grindstone. Make no mistake, this is a slow, time-consuming process that requires dedication and careful focus if the desired finish is to be achieved. The result of this stage of the work is a dull, flat, and even surface that now looks as if it is ready to be polished. All the minor scratches and blemishes *must* be removed before polishing begins. Remember, polishing only heightens the reflective surface, it will not remove scratches or marks. It is too subtle a process to do that.

Next we must turn our attention to the two types of sand that we collected earlier. We are going to craft three grades of abrasive material for the next stage of our work. The first, and most abrasive, will be the raw sea sand, the next the raw river sand, and the last will be a fine-ground portion of the sea sand we used first.

Today, if we intend to produce an attractive smooth finish, we use proprietary sandpapers or other abrasive papers, pads, or compounds. Unfortunately for our ancestors in the Stone Age, there were no such tools available to them, but they were clever enough to use what they had at hand. Sand and other abrasive grits were mixed with animal fats to create an abrasive paste, which they used in making all sorts of jewelry, household equipment, and decorative artifacts. This is exactly what we are going to do here.

First mix an amount of sea sand with any chosen fat or oil to create a grinding paste or cutting compound, as engineers prefer to call it. Then, using a piece of rag, spread a convenient amount of the paste onto the cloth and begin rubbing the area to be polished in random circular movements with the abrasive paste. You will see improvement in the surface as you continue to polish; when no further improvement is observed it is time to move on to the next stage.

The second stage of polishing is exactly the same as the first, only

Figure 9.4. Polished slate speculum.

this time we use the raw river sand instead of the sea sand. Again, improvement in the surface will be seen as the polishing progresses. When no further improvement is seen, no matter how much more you polish, then it is once again time to move on to the next stage.

The final cutting compound is made from the ground sea sand we collected. The sand is ground in a mortar and pestle until it reaches the consistency of a very fine dust. When this is achieved, the fine abrasive dust is mixed with your chosen fat or oil and used in exactly the same way as the previous two cutting compounds. As polishing progresses, a reflective finish will start appearing, but keep polishing until no further improvement can be obtained. Wipe the surface regularly with a damp cloth, and polish lightly with a clean dry cloth to assess the finish as you progress. Finally, wash the surface with running water and polish with a dry cloth. At this point you should have obtained a good reflective surface that will only be improved by waxing to a highly reflective finish, which is the next and final stage in the process. But do not proceed to waxing if you are not satisfied with the reflective quality of your speculum. No amount of waxing will remove any flaws still remaining at this stage. This may only be done by returning to whichever stage of the polishing or grinding you think is abrasive enough to remove the flaw and then progressing from that point through the polishing as described above. Once you are content with the existing finish, it is time to move on to the final waxing and polishing.

The final waxing polish is achieved using natural beeswax, ideally obtained from a known, reliable source where the provenance can be guaranteed. Normally beeswax is in its natural, quite hard state. It may be applied by rubbing a block of wax on the surface of the slate, depositing a thin layer of wax that then needs to be polished to a high shine using a clean, soft cloth before further layers and polishing eventually produces the highly reflective finish required. It may also be applied by heating the wax into a more liquid deposit, which is similarly polished and reapplied until the desired result is achieved. Either way, the final waxing and polishing produces the final finish to the speculum, and it is then ready to be used.

The alternative, more up-to-date method of arriving at the same result is to use proprietary abrasive papers of ever reducing grades to grind and polish the speculum. These come in many varieties, and it may be useful to discuss the options with your local hardware supplier. However, make sure you explain the material you are using, the condition and quality of the slate when you start, and what you intend to achieve as a result. It is almost inevitable that every hardware supplier will recommend you use power tools and attachments, so make sure you tell them from the start that this is not an option, for the reasons I have explained at the beginning of this section.

Whichever abrasive materials you select, the process of progressively refining the slate surface will be similar, if not the same as what I have described above, and the wax polishing stage will remain unchanged.

It is important to remember that at each stage of this process you can only polish the surface finish that you began with. In other words, each stage needs to be worked to its fullest extent before you progress to the next. If you leave scratches when you are doing your initial grinding, all that the subsequent polishing will do, no matter how hard you try, is polish the scratches you previously left. It will not remove them. If you get to the polishing stages and you discover previously unseen scratches, you must return to the start and regrind the slate until the scratches are eliminated. Poor speculums are usually the result of a hurried processing and a failure to eliminate all the apparent blemishes before progressing to the next stage. This is just one of the reasons that perfect speculums are cherished and carefully maintained.

Once you have crafted your speculum, it needs to be wrapped carefully in a soft cloth to protect its surface finish and stored with care to avoid any possible damage. If you are ever tempted to carelessly place it aside without its protective covering, just remember the time and effort you invested in its crafting. Now that you understand the crafting process in detail, you will also understand why the tradition maintains that every speculum is imbued with the spirit and personal energies of its crafter and why it is so important that Druidic diviners craft their own.

Divination as Art

Druidic divination is, without doubt, a complex, sophisticated, and deeply philosophical practice that has been one of the most important responsibilities of the Druid since the earliest times of the tradition. Its importance is reflected in the many methods and techniques that have developed over its history and the respect that it has attracted from many of the most powerful figures of our ancient past, be they Druids, chieftains, or high kings. It employs a complex range of cosmic energies and requires dedication, perseverance, and commitment to achieve powerful and meaningful results.

Divination brings with it a responsibility to be honest, accurate, insightful, and open-minded. There is no room for compromise in any of these areas, so do not begin this journey of discovery if you do not intend to ensure the integrity of your beliefs and insights or clearly explain and implement your revelations with sincerity and consideration for yourself and others.

The first half of my career was spent working in the arts, and during this period, in which I travelled extensively, I came to know a Zen painter living (unsurprisingly) in Japan. I became fascinated by his uncomplicated ink-and-water paintings and even more captivated by his technique, which he described as "Simply Zen." As I developed my divination practices and expanded on my early learning of the methods maintained within the Welsh Druidic tradition, I recognized the close similarity between the techniques of Druidic divination and those of the Simply Zen methods of my painter friend. I discovered the greatest compatibility to be in the very core philosophy of both practices, and this subsequently allowed me to gain a greater understanding of the ancient Druidic divination process. At the time, and still today, I remain amazed at how two so divergent and disparate cultures could share common philosophies and develop such similar ways of interpreting them.

My Zen artist friend was kind enough to explain to me the philosophy he employs to create his artwork, and here I will attempt to explain it, together with how it corresponds to the Druidic tradition and informs a deeper understanding of the Druidic divination methodology.

The artist begins his work with a conceptual vision—an idea of what is intended to be portrayed—just as the diviner begins the working with a precisely defined quest. This vision is contemplated and explored from every direction until a clear mental picture is arrived at. This is the same process that the Druid undertakes to obtain a clear and precise intention for the divination quest.

The first practical element of the artist is to lay out the tools and canvas (in most cases bleached rice paper) on the chosen work surface, just as the diviner lays out the tools and portal (whether captured water, Sevens, or slate speculum) on the working stone. In both cases, the tools and canvas/portal undergo a spiritual cleansing using incense smoke and salt together with a spoken invocation.

The next stage is undoubtedly the most significant. Zen artists meditate on the intention and representation of the work they seek to create. They consider not only the placement of each element within the overall composition but every brushstroke required to create every individual element, every change of brush, every dip into the ink, and every application of water-wash, visualizing the results each action will achieve.

Nothing is done physically until each and every aspect and movement is established within the mental image. Once this clear insight is achieved, it is contemplated again, in every detail, and then again and again until the artist has an indelible image of both the finished work and the infinite detail of every movement needed to arrive at the desired result. So far, other than the preparation and cleansing of the tools and work space, the work has been entirely mental and spiritual; nothing physical has been done, the brushes remain dry, the inks are untouched, and the rice paper is still an undisturbed pure white. The artist, however, has a complete, finished painting fixed in mind, together with a detailed sequence of tasks that need to be completed to achieve that image. This is exactly the same process Druidic diviners undergo to visualize their quest—a meditative process that must be completed before any practical work can begin. Just as the Zen artist has a vision of the complete painting in mind, together with the actions necessary to create it, so too do diviners have a complete mental picture of the quest they wish to complete and the details of the spiritual journey they must go through to arrive at their insights.

At this point in the process, the Zen artist considers the painting as complete, even though the brushes have not yet touched the inks or rice paper. This may seem extraordinary to the uninitiated, but the actual, physical painting of the picture is a simple manifestation of the mental/ spiritual creation, which by now is complete. The result is that the artist completes the painting in an astonishingly short time, using precise, predetermined movements in what could mistakenly be interpreted as a mechanical process. I watched this happen a number of times and never ceased to be astounded by the resultant dexterity and precision of the artist, who gives the impression that he could easily create the painting with his eyes closed. This process is echoed in the divination succession of interpretation, where diviners use all the information they possess, together with their divination insights and intuition, to arrive at the interpretation and the conclusion of the quest.

Once the Zen artists' painting is physically completed, transferred from their mental visualization to a physical representation in the mundane world, the artists then meditate on the process and result. Have they achieved a true representation of their mental creation? Does the painting speak of the intended meaning(s) of the composition? Did the artist accurately comply with the defined movements and brushstrokes to create the work? Even more simply, does the artist like the work? These and other questions are meditated on until a full evaluation of every aspect has been considered and corrective actions planned. This corresponds to the Druidic divination succession of reflection.

I hope this comparative analogy helps in understanding the mental and spiritual elements involved in Druidic divination, a practice that has flourished for millennia and, if the tradition is maintained, will survive for millennia to come.

Index